TE PAPA TO BERLIN

TE PAPA TO BERLIN

THE MAKING OF TWO MUSEUMS

KEN GORBEY

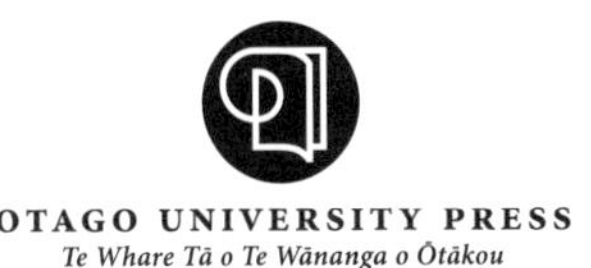

OTAGO UNIVERSITY PRESS
Te Whare Tā o Te Wānanga o Ōtākou

For Susan

Published by Otago University Press
Te Whare Tā o Te Wānanga o Ōtākou
533 Castle Street
Dunedin, New Zealand
university.press@otago.ac.nz
www.otago.ac.nz/press

First published 2020

ISBN 978-1-98-859237-4

A catalogue record for this book is available from the National Library of New Zealand.

Editor: Anna Rogers
Index: Lee Slater
Cover: Main staircase, Jewish Museum Berlin. Photo Jens Ziehe, Jewish Museum Berlin.

Printed in China through Asia Pacific Offset

CONTENTS

FOREWORD

WHEN, IN 1997, I accepted the German government's invitation to become the chief executive of a planned Jewish museum in Berlin, I had only a hazy idea of what awaited me. I understood that the project was deeply enmeshed in national politics, and for that I came with a certain amount of experience from my days in Washington. I had also just written a book on German-Jewish history. However, I was not fitted for the task of defining a viable concept and actually translating it into the creation of a living museum suitable for viewing by a broad national and international audience.

From the beginning, therefore, I was aware of the critical need to find a partner who would help guide the effort, someone with real museum experience and a proven record of accomplishment in the field. Finding the right one would be the key to the success or failure of the entire project.

To create a Jewish museum in the capital city of the recently reunited Federal Republic of Germany would surely be no ordinary undertaking. Given the terrible twentieth-century history of German-speaking Jewry, there were deep emotions and sensitivities on all sides. So what sort of museum would be appropriate and do justice to the ups and downs of Jewish history in Germany and its disastrous end under German Nazism? Should it deal primarily with the Holocaust? Should it focus on the longer history, on art or on the contributions of prior generations of German-Jewish citizens to national life? The Nazis had destroyed not only Jewish life in Germany, but also its symbols and artefacts, so what was there to exhibit? And how would any of it fit into the dramatic architecture of the building which the government had commissioned Daniel Libeskind to design for the purpose?

To get some clarity about these and related questions, I sought the opinion of a broad cross-section of scholars, historians and museum executives, whose advice proved to be highly diverse and, more often than not, maddeningly contradictory. Some even suggested that the whole idea of a Jewish museum in the land of the Holocaust perpetrators was a profoundly bad idea and should be abandoned.

Eventually one idea evolved that appealed to me. Jews had lived continuously on German soil since the Roman period. There had been good times for them when they lived in relative peace and harmony with their neighbours, and others when they were isolated, persecuted and harassed. Over the centuries, they had become deeply enmeshed in, and made major contributions to, every aspect of German life, eventually as full citizens with equal rights. All this had come to a bloody end under the Nazis. Hence, the idea was to create a storytelling museum – and this 2000-year history of the Jewish presence in Germany with all its ups and downs would be the story that the Jewish Museum Berlin (JMB) would tell.

But who could help me do it? Ideally it would have to be someone with deep knowledge of German-Jewish history and culture, and probably a Jew. He or she would have broad experience as a proven museum leader and manager able to function effectively in a German environment, preferably a German speaker. (The JMB was to be bilingual in German and English.) Furthermore, it would have to be someone with the imagination and skill to fit all this storytelling into the brilliant, evocative, but complex and intricate architecture Libeskind had designed.

This was a formidable combination of qualifications indeed, and very hard to find. Initially I had despaired of coming up with a suitable candidate. But then, in a near miracle, I got lucky.

When Shaike Weinberg, a brilliant museum expert, creator of the famous Tel Aviv storytelling museum of the Jewish diaspora and a leader of Washington's Holocaust Memorial Museum, agreed to join me, it seemed that my prayers had been answered. Shaike had virtually all of the qualifications needed and as he set about guiding the complicated task of translating our concept into reality, I thought I saw the light at the end of the tunnel. We were on our way, and I could not have been happier. But disaster struck less than a year later when Shaike fell seriously ill and died soon thereafter. We had become good friends and I mourned and missed him greatly. And once again I was confronted with the problem of finding someone with the right qualifications to continue the work he had begun.

Museum-makers experienced in strong storytelling museums are exceedingly rare because very few museums of this type exist. One of the best, I was told, was a wildly successful one in, of all places, faraway New Zealand. Te Papa, the country's national museum in Wellington, was said to be an extraordinary place that had attracted an unheard-of throng of visitors far beyond anyone's expectation. Its creator, a fellow named Ken Gorbey, was the kind of imaginative museum leader with deeply relevant experience I should be looking for.

I can no longer remember what possessed me to seriously consider actually reaching out to this fabled Kiwi as a possible answer to my increasingly serious dilemma. The Jewish Museum Berlin was under pressure to open within the impossibly short time of two years and I had no one to help make it happen. I therefore decided – in desperation, to be honest – to consider him more closely.

Yet to give serious consideration to someone who did not know Germany, or German-Jewish history, was not Jewish, spoke not a word of German and, as far as anyone knew, had never worked far away from his 'down-under' home seemed more than a little preposterous. And yet he was the creator of a highly successful museum of the type I wanted for Berlin. So without an alternative or a better idea, I decided to give this impossible idea a try.

I had my doubts, but when Ken agreed to come to Berlin for a talk, we clicked almost immediately. Offering him the job was, I realised, one of the riskiest gambles in a lifetime of management assignments with the responsibility to attract top-notch executive personnel. And when Ken actually agreed, I spent more than one sleepless night worrying about what I had done and how it would all work out. In Berlin, the scepticism, if not dismay, among my as yet small cadre of colleagues was also enormous. How could it possibly work, they argued, to bring in this man from faraway New Zealand, and expect that he could successfully work his magic in Germany with a Jewish museum, on a subject matter with which he was totally unfamiliar?

Only in hindsight have I come to understand that the personal and professional risk of coming to Berlin for this assignment was as great for Ken as it was for us. His fascinating, charmingly honest account of what it meant for him and Susan to make the move from Wellington to Berlin, and how he tackled the enormous challenges to create what became Europe's largest and most important Jewish museum, is the central theme of this book. It is, in fact, a unique story of late twentieth-century museum-making which makes compelling reading for museologists and the wider public alike.

Ken's account of his Berlin experience is many-faceted. There are the challenges he and Susan faced in adjusting to the radical change of environment from the modestly sized, culturally familiar environment of their home town, Wellington, to the large and mostly unfamiliar world of a major European metropolis, culturally and ethnically highly diverse, weighed down by a special history, and politically complex. There is the struggle to gain the confidence and win the hearts and minds of a conservative, cautious and sceptical German staff unfamiliar and at times uncomfortable with the idea of his kind of museum: visitor-friendly, state of the art, and with novel exhibition techniques he taught them to understand and apply. There is the process of creating a great museum when, given German history, so few artefacts were available to show the visitors, and the need to find ingenious alternative ways of making history come to life. Last, but not least, readers will be amused by his description of what it took to handle an unreasonable boss with little museum experience, always in a hurry, frequently impatient, and occasionally ornery and unreasonable. Ken made it all happen. *Te Papa to Berlin* is a story of learning, adaptation, great accomplishment and personal growth. It is, too, a story of leadership, relevant and instructive for anyone called on to help manage an important enterprise in unfamiliar surroundings.

What Ken accomplished speaks for itself. The Jewish Museum Berlin will soon be 20 years old. It has grown and evolved enormously over those years. From the beginning, however, it proved an enormous success. With 750,000 visitors annually, it has exceeded all expectations and it is widely acknowledged as one of Germany's premier cultural institutions. As a national museum telling an important, difficult story, it is the pride of the German government and enjoys the enthusiastic support of business, cultural leaders and the public. Visitors come from all over the world to see it. At a political level, it plays a significant role in Germany's determination to confront a sometimes glorious but ultimately tragic and painful history in an honest and open way. For a country that needs to integrate large numbers of refugees and asylum seekers into its national life, the Jewish Museum Berlin plays an important role in tackling the question of minorities becoming citizens, with all the many problems this raises, in emphasising the need for tolerance and understanding, and in battling prejudice and discrimination.

None of this could have happened without the foundation Ken Gorbey helped to lay, and the enormous contribution he made to the creation of this great museum. In the process, he won the hearts of his colleagues and of all Berliners. He is a Kiwi who also became an enthusiastic Berliner.

Ken and I were an odd couple. Our respective backgrounds and experiences could not have been more different. We had much to learn from each other in building our partnership in what, without a doubt, was the adventure of our lives. We became not only successful professional partners, but also good friends. Ken, and Susan, made that easy. Berlin owes him much, and so do I.

W. MICHAEL BLUMENTHAL
Founding Director of the Jewish Museum Berlin,
former United States Secretary of the Treasury,
retired businessman and CEO of Unisys Corp

PREFACE

THE TWO MUSEUMS COULD NOT BE FURTHER APART. One, Te Papa, is of the Pacific; the other, the Jewish Museum Berlin, is defined by its place in Europe. But search into their reasons for being and they are very similar. Each confronts the dangerous territory that is a nation's dark history while celebrating generations of life lived. They are magical theatres that illuminate and strengthen the fundamental morality which makes us human.

As it comes into being, New Zealand's new national museum, Te Papa, reaches for understandings of a changing society. A team of Māori, Pasifika and European people work together, though sometimes in dispute, to create a joyful celebration and sombre reflection of nationhood. On the opposite side of the world, another diverse community seeks to build a new and inclusive Germany, despite a harsh history that encompasses the Holocaust and a record of chauvinistic militarism. The Jewish Museum Berlin will carry this story.

In 1998 Te Papa opens. The crowds pour in, two million visitors in the first year. They find a place that is anything but a narrow narrative of officially prescribed nationalism. Rather, the museum's marketing slogan, 'Our Place', enters everyday language as a representation of the many cultural streams, here woven together, there diverging, that make up our country. I am well pleased, for at opening I can look back on 13 years of my life engaged in planning and achieving Te Papa.

Meanwhile the Jewish Museum Berlin is not in good heart. Its subject matter, the history of the German Jews, and Daniel Libeskind's lightning bolt of a building focus international attention on the project, but it is going nowhere. National reputation is at stake. In 1997 the German government turns for leadership of the project to former German-Jewish child refugee, now senior American statesman and successful businessman Mike Blumenthal. Not one to countenance failure, he calls for a high-powered review. I have been invited to take part.

The review team confirms everyone's worst fears. Blumenthal acts: at morning coffee on the second day he approaches me. 'Come to Berlin and see this museum through to opening.'

He makes it clear that my mandate will be revolution. I must not only dig this museum out of the quagmire but create a place that does justice to Libeskind's building and that captures the imagination of visitors by provoking profound emotion. It is a daunting prospect and the risks are huge.

I say yes and my life becomes an endless grind of achieving impossible targets. I have done it in New Zealand. But this is Berlin, cultural capital and centre of world history. The work is so very hard but there are moments of elation and deep emotion seared into my consciousness.

Finally, on 11 September 2001, the Jewish Museum Berlin is done. A few hours before the doors will be opened to the general public we meet to assure ourselves that everything is as it should be. Instead, in despair, we see planes slam into two towers a continent away. The army runs razor wire around the building. We know this to be a turning point, but towards what?

*

The liberal democracy is a fragile construct. It requires hard work, constant negotiation and accommodation, to maintain the openness and order that allow people of different cultures and origins to live and thrive together. Over the decades and centuries Enlightenment-based belief systems had grown, supported by functioning political and state institutions. These made sure that each generation would be aware of its obligations, while also doing its best to incarcerate the crooks, curtail the activities of the rapacious autocrats, laugh the petty tyrant off his soapbox, restrain and treat the psychopaths, and pity the sad fools. In their own ways Te Papa and the Jewish Museum Berlin were part of the machinery of two such moral nations.

In the aftermath of 9/11 some of the fragile tenets of that moral order came under pressure. Manipulative leaders rushed to claim the heroic high ground. Scapegoats were required and, as with the Jews in Nazi Germany, were named via a toxic mix of half-truth and lies. A new anti-Semitism was evident. This time, though, not only Jews were under suspicion, but also those defined by their Muslim faith. In so many countries nationalism was narrowed by official decree. Hate was in the air and the principles on which Te Papa and the Jewish Museum Berlin were based, that we might define our nation as a society of moral human individuals living together via complex yet civil negotiation, seemed under threat.

CHAPTER 1

GROWING UP AT THE BOTTOM OF THE WORLD

JUST US was a book of poems for young New Zealand kids. I treasured my copy. Though it is now long lost, lines, here and there, come to me still.

> 'Don't give me cake Mum and don't give me scone;
> I only want a piece of bread with Marmite on.'

I liked Marmite, the ultimate acquired taste. It was not for everyone; in later years a visiting American academic sitting at our breakfast table would describe it as 'unrefined crude oil'.

The cover featured children on a beach. Above, ships, trains and aircraft drove through the clouds, inviting dreams of travel to a world so remote that I sometimes wondered at the reality of countries beyond our coastline. My prized Arthur Mee encyclopaedias told me otherwise, describing exotic places filled with strange peoples and beasts. But the *Just Us* cover was wrong in one important respect. The children playing on the beach wore shoes and that was absurd. Even in midwinter, with snow on Maungatautari, it was a matter of pride to hobble to school down the gravel road, crunching underfoot the chips of stone held aloft by small ice pinnacles.

Dad knew the author, John Brent. I remember a conversation – at least I think I do.

'Shoes! The publisher commissioned an English artist to do the cover and I got shoes – on a New Zealand beach!' said John.

This mattered little to me. *Just Us* talked of and to Kiwi kids, used our language and was rooted in our land. There was not a thatched cottage in sight. To read those poems was to confirm that we were of New Zealand and our future rested here. I could become a boat-builder like Uncle Frank. For a time I crafted half-hull models of the ships of my imagination and sanded them to a smooth finish. Dad was inspired to build a model yacht and I followed all the steps closely, including pouring molten lead into a sand mould – the finished item would attach to the keel as ballast to keep the yacht from capsizing. Our first pour was a disaster. The sand was wet and the lead erupted in a spectacular fountain of dangerously hot material that could have done serious harm.

It was the most beautiful thing I had ever possessed, shinily painted and gaff-rigged, complete with a sail between mainsail and topmast. I could not wait to get to our summer cottage. Disappointment. Excessive sail area was but one of its problems; there was too much buoyancy and not enough weight on the keel. Once in the sea, all it could do was to flop on its side. More weight was applied, ugly slabs of lead. But my beautiful boat had lost its charm. It would never skip across the waves as I had hoped. My boat became an early lesson in the misery of failure.

But the dams we made never failed. As another *Just Us* poem implied, every stream awaited a grand construction: 'I must go down to Hukawai to dam the little stream.' And we did. With family or friends we set about stemming the course of every available flow of water. Those at the seaside would be washed away by the tide or the next rain. But one, a major effort over some days, brought together purpose (halt the stream), workforce (I was joined by the farmer's son) and materials (dam-building quality clay) with a flow of just the right capacity and sturdy bank configuration. The completed barrier flooded part of the paddock and the farmer insisted it had to be breached. Perhaps I was destined to be an engineer.

Another early career option was archaeology. Aged nine, I excavated in the back garden of the schoolhouse. My first dig was in the rough area outside the vegetable garden. I had enough knowledge to lay out a measured square, rather than just sink a pit. My parents' benevolent smiles turned to disbelief when I uncovered the first artefact, an old sewing machine. There followed a whole kitchen of pots and pans, and pieces of an old stove. Father asked around. The house had burnt down in the 1930s and I had struck a rubbish pit of charred remains. I reported each find to my class. More was to come of that hole in the peaty soil, for underlying it was a deep layer of most brilliant white, part of a huge valley-choking fan of pumice granules from several cataclysmic eruptions spanning many thousands of years. Dad and I now set to quarrying to create pumice paths and a driveway to the house. Although geology, geomorphology and volcanology remained interests that I would pursue into university, they would never be part of a career. Archaeology was different. It stuck, at least for a while.

After enduring the dreadful embarrassments of delayed maturation, the boy who had built dams and excavated kitchen rubble worked at a degree in

Pacific archaeology, then moved on to a career creating cultural institutions. Place imprinted itself upon me, a mixture of peoples in a unique, isolated landscape at the bottom of the world.

*

But to what extent can I trust my memory? I run a small test. The National Library has *Just Us* and sitting in a quiet room of serious scholarship I reread the poems of my younger days. I have a few words misplaced but the lines I have drawn forth are fundamentally correct. Dams are built at 'Hukuwai', and undoubtedly John Masefield, in another poem studied at my primary school desk, has given me part of what comes to mind 70 years on. All good so far, but there are a couple of slips. No train drives across the sky, only ships and an aircraft, and I have the illustrator incorrectly placed. It seems Stopford G. Wrathall was a Kiwi or at least lived in New Zealand. I was certain, and right, about the shoes, so inappropriate upon a New Zealand beach, but wrong in my assumption that only an Englishman could have fashioned a child's view of our coastline after the North Sea.

The lesson is that while some snippets at the front of my mind are clear and mostly accurate, others are equally clear but incorrect. Sometimes I can draw on papers and files, but memory is malleable, subject to fading, renewal, overlay and even embellishment.

I take comfort and instruction from that masterly exploration of memory, *Peeling the Onion* by Günter Grass. Throughout he pauses to ask: Did this actually happen in those early war-defined years? Was the wheel of the upended bicycle actually turning, turning as the fleeing German boy soldiers lay dying, or was this an after-the-fact piece of theatre overlaid on reality to lend additional drama? Such honesty is hard to replicate but I will try my best.

*

At 26 years of age I had my first real job: I was to traverse the 700 kilometres of a planned gas line checking for archaeological sites.

In some respects, this is my first journey of exploration, the step-by-step trudge of the no-longer-student among people who toil beyond the big smoke. My way is marked by yellow stakes across paddocks and cleared scars through forests. The abandoned village emerges out of the dense fog. But this dead kitten lying in the grass before me, where has it come from? Life in a small caravan parked in an orchard or deserted camping site, waking on frosty mornings to a star pattern of ice crystals across the metal ceiling. I stand on a narrow spit of land projecting into the sea; each time a wave hits the base of the cliff 30 metres below there is the marked quiver of a piece of ground destined soon to fall. I retreat. This is my Route 66, the precursor of other journeys to come.

The archaeology was easy, application of a training that veered from American to English theory and practice. But I was also able to venture into a society being redefined by assertive Māori leaders. Among them were my teachers: Hirini (Sid) Mead, Ranginui Walker, Pat Hohepa. I knew Sid Mead from his book, *The Art of Maori Carving.* As a high school lad, I had bought a set of chisels and, following Sid's detailed instructions, carved my own tributes to Māori culture, colouring each with shoe polish. Now we rubbed up against each other, and a growing Māori student body, in the clapped-out, weatherboard Victorian villas that housed our department. Despite reactionary voices of complaint, heard to this day, Māori demanded an accounting of rights abrogated and a strong voice in the decision-making that attends nationhood. There was no going back.

Part of my task was to consult with Māori groups in far-flung rural communities to check the proposed gas-line route for places that held spiritual value. Such contact with rural Māori was not entirely new to me. Maungatautari School, part of my early education, had a very large proportion of pupils from Pohara Pā (village) along Oreipunga Road. I mixed with these kids naturally in the classroom, at play and through sport. Māori society was part of my family's life, perhaps in a small way but more than for most Pākehā New Zealanders.

Pākehā is a term that has travelled far in my lifetime. We are the New Zealanders of European origins, the white-faced ones. For many it was, perhaps still is, a pejorative term, a dismissal. But this was not so in my family. I know this because of the political discussions around the dinner table. There was little about art and literature, but those free flows of opinion were so often about our identity as New Zealanders, and that included being Pākehā. The local farmers would talk of their planned trip back to the old country, Britain, as 'going home' but my mother and father dismissed any such idea.

To be Pākehā at that time seemed to include being ambitious for your kids' future. We should aspire to careers. In support the parents would quote a cautionary tale: how unthinking Uncle Bill had shocked his mother and father by announcing that he wanted to be a rubbish collector and further reinforced his desire by acting out the role around the house. He had grown up to do other adventurous things throughout the world as a marine engineer. On his return he had become a good friend of the people of Tūrangawaewae, a place that would figure in my later history. Apparently, he introduced us to Māori leader Princess Te Puea as she dug potatoes in the communal garden. Margaret, my older sister, was disappointed, expecting gown and glitter, but I have no memory of this meeting. I admired handsome and athletic Uncle Bill greatly; although having none of his physical prowess, I was determined to grow up to be something like him.

That gas-line winter of 1968 is known still for the king of all storms. In April a violent cyclone had blown the inter-island ferry *Wahine* onto a reef at the mouth of Wellington Harbour. Fifty-one people had drowned on the day; two more would die later. As I trundled along the route in my sturdy Land Rover, and walked the inaccessible sections, I negotiated fallen forest and slips. The coast was a tight mat of trees brought down flooded rivers. Dead cows, bloated and with legs askance, protruded from this vast funeral pyre without dignity or grace.

At each marae I met the kaumātua, the elders. They would peruse the plans, and occasionally point to a place where the gas line was uncomfortably close to a sacred site, once where it crossed an ancient fortification.

On the killing floor of the local abattoir, the old chief wiped his hands and took hold of the large bound wodge of strip aerial photos that showed the pipeline route. 'Clever Pākehā.'

There was quiet admiration in his voice at this heavy statement of his land overviewed and captured on paper. This annoyed me for I read his response as acquiescence, almost submission. But who was I to judge a man raised in another world? A few years later I would return to his marae for a commemoration of war 100 years before. The tribe's meeting house was a statement of defiance built over the top of the still visible earthworks of a British redoubt. One of the speakers was a Pākehā historian who persisted in describing each army campaign in terms of 'enemy killed'. We few whities attending were dreadfully embarrassed and knew not what to do. The matter was taken in hand when a man, perhaps sent forth by his elders, wandered up to the podium and laid his considerable bulk down, back to the speaker, looking out at the gathering. It was an act of stern and rightful challenge, also of dismissal.

For so much of my wintry journey the looming symmetrical volcanic cone of still dangerous Taranaki was a solitary companion to thoughts about the future. Soon I fell into a job with the local regional museum. Naively I read this landscape only for its boundless archaeological promise, but it was not a good choice. The director proved intensely suspicious of book learning; the board met as regional crematorium committee in the morning and museum committee in the afternoon. For both subjects they showed equal enthusiasm. A few months later another job came up, essentially a start-up. The current director would be standing down and I was his designated replacement. It seemed like a good place to secure a career as an archaeologist.

CHAPTER 2

WAIKATO AND TAINUI

HAMILTON HAD OTHER PLANS. It was a fast-growing inland town bent on casting off its reputation as an agricultural village and doing everything it could to become a true city. 'Opportunity aplenty,' explained my new city manager, Stuart Lenz. In his administration I would no longer be focused inward on a museum but would have a wider commission as head of a city department. I would sit on city planning committees and have charge of developing city policy that reached beyond the museums into the boundless world of culture. Furthermore, I must lead an efficient operation.

A degree in anthropology would not suffice; management training was required. After seven years of confinement within a narrow academic frame, my reading exploded with frequently serendipitous samplings of fresh approaches and ways of thinking. Futurologist Peter Drucker was certainly about management, but equally this escapee from Nazi persecution wrote fundamental morality. I was led toward broader considerations of the very structure of knowledge, perhaps articulated best by philosopher Frederick Turner, who talked of new understandings created and communicated at the messy intersections of different ways of thinking. He spoke, too, of the potential that comes with admitting new views of the world. All this resonated with a young museum director struggling to place two culturally determined knowledge structures, European and Māori, alongside each other. It was heady and liberating stuff – there was a sense of being able to infringe boundaries and flout rules.

I threw all my energy into the job: running an enterprise, merging the old art gallery and museum into a single unit, liaising with architects who were designing a new museum. Above all there was the particular joy of building a like-minded staff group.

I owe a lot to Hamilton but, decades later, it still holds an uncertain place in my heart. It was there I had to cope with a marriage that had failed – I was still too immature – though I was the proud father and carer of two self-reliant young children. There was little time for anything except work and domestic duties.

*

The early 1970s was an interesting time to be working in museums. We tried to practise what came to be known as the 'new museology', born of a dissatisfaction with the old static array of acceptable professional methods, and a desire to involve, reflect and influence society. It was us youngsters in the smaller museums, fresh from university, who led this drive for new perspectives on our country as a place of diversity. The more established, larger places felt threatened, particularly our national museum and gallery. Like naughty schoolkids, we delighted in conference behaviour that bordered on taunting. John Maynard at the new Govett-Brewster Art Gallery in New Plymouth, Luit Bieringa and Mina MacKenzie (and her students David Butts and Greg McManus) at the Manawatu Art Gallery and Manawatu Museum in Palmerston North, Jim Mack at Lower Hutt's Dowse Art Museum, John Perry at the Rotorua Museum, and Campbell Smith and I in Hamilton, experimented with fresh approaches, sometimes did outrageous things, made and learnt from mistakes. Campbell, for years my deputy and art man in the now combined Waikato Museum, doubled as a playwright, and at each new exhibition of note would craft an accompanying play. For some time we had a resident theatre company attached to the museum, care of a government skills programme. Campbell would never say if I was the hero of his children's Christmas offering, *Kenny Kiwi Learns to Fly*. I liked to think it was so.

We did a series of exhibitions about changing and emerging identity: that shift from New Zealand as an outpost of empire towards a home of people of many origins negotiating their future in an Asia–Pacific world. The place of Māori loomed large. Contemporary Māori artists were beginning to seek space and to organise. We sent a truck around their studios, garages, classrooms and spare bedrooms; what came back formed the exhibition. Locally, Rangimarie Hetet and her daughter Diggeress Te Kanawa were keeping alive the art of weaving fine flax cloaks, korowai. Their exhibition was one of our most successful. Curator Rose Young researched the life and art of soldier of fortune Gustavus Ferdinand von Tempsky, and his role in the campaigns of the colonial period. We brought works from all over the world. I pursued an interest in ceramics, with exhibitions including one on the Japanese and English potters and friends Shoji Hamada and Bernard Leach. An exhibition of photos of the civil unrest that accompanied the 1981 Springbok tour by a racially selected South African rugby team got me in deep political schtuck. I should have known better.

But perhaps the most challenging exhibitions were the two portrayals of the lives of Māori prophets Te Whiti-o-Rongomai, most associated with Parihaka, and Te Kooti Arikirangi Te Turuki. 'Rebels!' said one prominent citizen. No, we said – they were Māori leaders of their age. These events could be achieved only with the full involvement of the prophets' descendants, who descended upon us in large numbers to open the exhibitions with lengthy church services. We would organise everything, including the food – vast quantities of bread and sides of beef cooked overnight in a local bread oven – and plenty to drink. Otherwise we, the museum staff, stood back.

Waikato Museum was within the territory of Tainui. Because they were tangata whenua, the people of the land, who had sovereignty over this part of Aotearoa (New Zealand), it fell to them to invite and welcome the prophets' people from other tribal domains. It was during the first of these welcomes that I had the good fortune to meet the gentle, yet strong, woman who was Te Arikinui (supreme leader) of Tainui, Dame Te Atairangikaahu, and her people. Te Ata was also the Māori Queen (Kuini), leader of the Kīngitanga, an association of tribes which, though normally fiercely independent, in the 1850s had found common cause in the face of increasingly aggressive European pressure on people and land. These Europeans, reasoned the tribes of the central North Island, had their Queen Victoria; they could assert their sovereignty in similar manner and form a political alliance under a single leader.

*

Tainui were part of Waikato Museum's vision for the future. At first it was a bookish commitment arising out of university learning. Of course, we would seek to develop further understanding between all people of Waikato, Māori and Pākehā, but there was so much for me to learn. My limited understanding of mātauranga, Māori cultural knowledge, was all too obvious.

I began to visit Te Ata and her husband, Whatu Paki, journeying a few kilometres out of Hamilton to Ngāruawāhia and Tūrangawaewae Marae, the central place and ceremonial focus of Tainui and the Kīngitanga. Here we would sit in the carved house Māhinārangi, surrounded by tribal treasures, and talk of coming events, a bit of history, museums, family. Once one of her senior advisers said, 'Ata really enjoys your visits.'

Te Ata gave responsibility for my further tuition to two of her trusted people. Much-loved Sister Heeni Wharemaru became the museum's front-of-house presence, a role to which she brought grace and calm. The other was one of Ata's elders, the Reverend Dave Manihera, who took me in hand, guiding me about the territory that was Tainui.

On one occasion as we stood on the banks of the Waikato River, Dave pointed at the water mid-stream.

'The canoe *Tāheretikitiki* rests out there.'

How could this be? As far as I was concerned *Tāheretikitiki* was very much alive and in use, at that moment safe in a canoe house upriver. But this was a lesson in another vision of cultural property.

'That is the new *Tāheretikitiki*. The mana now resides in the newly crafted canoe and the old has been given a dignified burial.'

For Dave, schooled in ancient traditions, the concept of an artefact as a single inanimate physical object was quite foreign. Of primary importance was the living essence, which transcended the current physical husk and could be reborn in new form.

On a huge black sand dune at Taharoa, overlooking the Tasman Ocean, Dave told of how as a young boy he came with his whānau, his extended family, to the stream below us to trap the first fresh of eels, the tastiest. Then he had sung a famous waiata, a lament composed by the chief who stood on that hill – Dave pointed it out – then turned back and looked towards the land from which he was being expelled before heading south.

Slowly I came to understand, just a little better, ways of conceiving and giving a life force to ceremony, song, oration, sense of community, history and valued object. This included the dignified transfer of mana (power) and wairua (spiritual presence) from one deteriorating physical object to another.

Back at Tūrangawaewae Marae I stood with Dave Manihera and the aged Rawiri Tumokai Katipa. He had been husband to Princess Te Puea, who had disappointed my sister with her lack of regalia. We were looking down at a small engine. Tumokai told a story.

'The 1918 flu epidemic hit our people hard. My job was to take our little launch – it was powered by this engine – to the isolated settlements up the Waipā River and pick up the bodies. We would wrap them in blankets and old clothing and lay them on the deck. Once I was drowsing in the heat when a body suddenly sat up and began to dance about. I was frightened out of my wits – almost jumped over the side. What had happened was that a loose piece of material had caught in this fly-wheel and tugged away at the body. I've never been so scared in my life!'

Māori children orphaned by the epidemic were also gathered up to become part of the kibbutz-like settlement that Te Puea was developing at Ngāruawāhia, Tūrangawaewae. It was a centre of revival and pride. Clearing the land, building shelter, teaching, performing. A carving school was established.

Shortly after we met, Dame Te Ata made a decision. As a gesture of goodwill, testimony to the growing relationship between Hamilton City and Tūrangawaewae Marae, she would place the ancient canoe *Te Winika* in Waikato Museum. This beautifully carved waka had reached the end of its useful life, but retirement to a museum was not a decision universally approved among her people. Many of the elders, I would learn, had other thoughts. *Te Winika* had the mana and wairua of a great personage. Traditional belief decreed that the canoe should be laid to rest in the river, not become an object on display.

Te Winika had been one of the carving school's projects. The hulk of the old river canoe lay on the sandbanks at the mouth of the Waikato River. In the 1930s Te Puea had decreed that it be recovered and fully restored, the beginnings of a revival of canoe building in our country. *Te Winika* plied the river on ceremonial occasions but was deteriorating.

On a clear winter's day I stood with Te Ata and Whatu at Days Park. It was here that *Te Winika* would be landed, accompanied by the new canoe *Tāheretikitiki*, each powered along by paddling warriors. They pulled in to the river edge. The crews stood along both sides and, chanting, began to heave *Te Winika* up the steep bank. The bow of the canoe rose higher and higher and then suddenly tilted forward to rest before us. A dramatic gesture of farewell, or was it greeting?

I turned to Te Ata. 'That is how we should display *Te Winika* – looming up from the river toward the visitor.' She agreed. That gesture, *Te Winika's* farewell to the Waikato River, would become a large part of the design of the new museum building.

*

I travelled, a lot. All Kiwis do this. It even has a name. Our OE, overseas experience, is a reaction to our isolation. In our late teens and twenties we are driven to get out and find our place in the bigger world. My quest was narrower. I went to see museums, seeking out the innovations of the time. Often I found tightly woven cocoons of authoritarian museological dogma in which the primacy of the original physical object was all important and where community and visitor stood for little.

But there were like-minded spirits out there and I sought them out. Doreen Nteta from Botswana told of a nation's success under leader Seretse Khama and his much-loved English wife, Ruth. Neil Cossons introduced me to Ironbridge Gorge Museum in the depths of Shropshire, a sequence of historic sites in the valley where the Industrial Revolution began. The many children's museums scattered across the United States demonstrated what it meant to make an honest commitment to the needs of an audience, in this case family groups. A bunch of museums as activists, such as Vancouver's Museum of Anthropology, promoted new views of society and involved people who had until then been excluded. I was impressed by the shift achieved at the Imperial War Museum in London, from a place glorifying conflict to one exploring its causes and social consequences.

As I explored I came to realise that the leisure industry, frequently scorned by my colleagues, had much to offer, as did the wonderful community facilities that were libraries. Those places raised questions about how museums served their communities. Did our concern with holding, and retaining at all costs, significant original objects place us on a par with that pitiful figure, the hoarder? I can think of one particular case when the invasive conservation procedures being applied to an object seemed totally inappropriate to the Māori staff, who saw the taonga (treasure) as a revered ancestor. Their pleas, that this representation should be allowed to slip away, had not been heard. Equally there was little acceptance of the view expressed by Dave Manihera, that the mana of the old might be reborn in a similar or another form.

Two cultures clashed. For many of my Western colleagues there could only be one true original object, which could not be modified or replaced. Thanks to an almost religious zeal, the object was frozen within a controlled environment, hedged about with uncompromising standards. But, in New Zealand, others had a more fluid and inclusive vision of an object as part of a broadly defined cultural continuum, to be created and replaced as circumstances might dictate.

I was in the middle of this debate, drawn this way by my Māori tutors, that way by the standards of my chosen profession. Increasingly I was finding traditional museums austere. Surely the creative cultural process allowed for greater flexibility, more acceptance of normal human behaviour. I found what I was looking for in Japan.

It started with a major exhibition of contemporary Japanese ceramics that we had stolen from under the nose of the big smoke to the north, Auckland. That led to a correspondence with one of the artists, Yasuo Hayashi. Japan had been a reviled and defeated enemy, but now, as an ally, was a place of growing interest. Following my normal practice, I began a course of reading, which inspired a first visit. My focus was the crafts but I became fascinated by the juxtaposition of the ancient and modern. I visited gardens and ancient temples. The narrow snow-covered valley leading to Onda, a village of 14 families, was full of the heavy thud of the *kara-usu*, traditional water-driven mortars, not unlike long-necked dinosaurs, that pounded clay. Yasuo Hayashi showed me his work and through an interpreter I learnt how, as a very young teenager, he had trained as a kamikaze pilot. 'I was saved by a lack of aircraft and 500-pound bombs!'

Inspired to learn more, I began serious negotiations to take up a Japan Foundation fellowship. The plan was to investigate in some depth the workings of the agency responsible for Japan's system of national treasures. On the day I was expecting the confirming letter, I was home with a heavy cold. The telephone rang; the letter had arrived. I dressed and raced into the museum. The staff clustered about as I tore the envelope open. I couldn't believe what I was reading. Fiscal problems … all fellowships to be reviewed … letters of the alphabet into a hat … sorry, Mr Gorbey, 'G' was among those rejected. Many apologies; please feel free to come back to us next year. At the end of the work table was a large cardboard box for scrap paper and card. I laid about it, kicking and cursing. But the staff could only grin. Then it came to me. This was my birthday and it fell on April Fool's Day. Over the years many pranks had been played, to the point where I believed almost nothing that happened on that date. In retrospect, the letter was not that good a forgery, but I had been caught. I duly left for Japan.

This time, with greater knowledge and the expert guidance that accompanied a fellowship, I burrowed into the formal systems that the Japanese had had in place for well over a century to protect their traditional heritage. It was a time of intense learning. Some of it I knew – such as the best systems being focused and tightly defined – but the surprise was that the whole National Treasures system covered little more than 12,000 objects, ranging from vast temples to small pots. Further, not everything had to be state-owned; most of the items were in the hands of private individuals or agencies. Economic realities were important. Although it is easy to feel good about 'protecting' multitudes of objects, the number of items designated must be limited by the availability of resources. And perhaps most importantly, the skills behind creating and nurturing these traditional crafts, the intangibles, were as important as the objects themselves, the tangibles. Craftspeople, from thatchers of old roofs through temple restorers to potters, sword makers and weavers, were appointed as Living National Treasures and supported in their work.

One other thing became apparent as I met people who aspired to this honour: the whole system was highly politicised. In their eyes I was aligned to the designating agency back in Tokyo and so might influence the next set of choices. This was not so, but as I travelled about Japan I was wined and dined in the best establishments.

Running through the Japanese system was the cultural acceptance that the original object was a matter of essence, and not necessarily original substance. I was taken to an important temple, itself a National Treasure. It looked to be in very good condition.

'Look, see that beam up there.' My guide pointed to a warped and wizened piece of timber no more than a metre in length.

'We believe that to be part of the original temple – perhaps 1400 years old.' The rest of this vast wooden structure had been replaced in rebuilds over the centuries. I thought back to *Tāheretikitiki*, the personage maintained and given new life force in recreated physical form.

I also sought to explore the other end of the cultural scale, the youth culture of Tokyo, and purchased the commercial rip-offs of their doll-like costumes and manga images for my kids.

*

I could not have had a better training ground than Tainui, Waikato Museum and Hamilton. There I lived, rather than just studied, museums as cultural facilities owned by their communities. They could be places of diversity and differing cultural visions working together to strengthen the moral foundations of society. The traditional and restrictive collection-based definition of museum, born long ago in lands far distant, just did not fit where we Kiwis were at.

There is a magic about a working moral society – the special charge we feel, the inexplicable qualities that arise, when the exercise of the ordinary virtues animates our sense of humanity, brings understanding and the satisfaction that results from people's lives being somehow made better. That magic is intangible; it may be supported by the physical object, but mainly it lies within storytelling as practised by ordinary people in everyday life, as well as by the deep thinkers, great novelists and historians.

However, tangible objects have a place in museums. They carry cultural significance that can trigger memory and emotional response. Despite my administrative duties and those endless committee meetings, I acquired objects for the museum. I chose crafts for a number of reasons. For one thing, it seemed to me that they appealed to those who might feel distanced from high-end painting or sculpture. Craftspeople, too, were interested in identity. There was little evidence of the stiff rules of engagement that seemed to be part of the fine arts community, the sense of hierarchy and constant critical review by self-appointed colonels.

A particular friend was Barry Brickell, an eccentric character who used ceramics to channel and control his natural pyromaniac tendencies. He loved trains and had established the Driving Creek Railway as his own personal line. It had started small but had progressively climbed into the steep hills above Coromandel township. To many, his surges in production would be read as the surfacing of some creative impulse, but to those who knew him, it was a sign that Barry was planning an extension to the railway that, likely as not, would include a long and expensive viaduct. When I was present at a firing or viewing a commission, or plying a pick and shovel on a new length of track, I would think about the nature of the life Barry, and other craftspeople, were creating for themselves. Utopia was too strong a thought, yet they created works, and almost invariably living environments, that reeked of New Zealand identity. In my mind I formed an exhibition, never to be realised, which I called *Visions of an Imperfect Utopia*. In it, craftspeople would introduce us to the places they had created in their inner-city gentrified bay villas or rural environments that were much more than a place to live; they were their particular expressions of self. Barry Brickell would be central – not just his large steam pots, but the special value he brought to his life, and to ours. This was magic.

CHAPTER 3

TE PAPA

SOME THREE DECADES ON and midway through my tenure at the Jewish Museum Berlin I attended a museum conference in Texas. A small New Zealand company had a stall, touting their computerised cataloguing system. I wandered over.

'I'm …'

The young Kiwi woman interrupted, grinning. 'I know. You escaped Te Papa.'

It is true that I had been pleased to leave Te Papa. It was time and I had other things to do. I had not realised that others in the profession would read this career move as a get-out-of-jail card.

*

Te Papa was 15 years of my life. A time of wonderful colleagues, new views of the world, something achieved for my nation, joy. Also, some desperation and hurt.

It sounds like a long gestation period but it was actually quite short for a national museum to be conceived and built. Others have taken longer. Typically, they start out as a glossy promotion of fine words and dream-world illustrations. Michelle Tayler, a senior Te Papa project manager, termed these Mormon pictures. 'You know, flat, colourful rendering of middle-aged American couples, women just out of the local hair salon, taking an escalator through the clouds straight to heaven.'

But the process of detailed creative thinking that is museum development does not necessarily align with the rise and fall of political parties' hold on power. The backers become history and a new force stops work or calls for another glossy book that better expresses their view of the world. Another launch of an improved nation-building idea, another stutter and failure. The cycle goes on, keeping hope alive and the living standard of consultants at an appropriately elevated level. In one notable case, the National Museum of Australia in Canberra, this went on for close to 25 years until, after a series of accidents, the museum was built and opened – to a storm of political abuse.

Te Papa was different, largely because it was conceived out of changing times and the blaze of glory that was *Te Māori*. Perhaps this was something just too hot to cool down.

For some years there had been talk of a major international exhibition of Māori art. At first the concept was boring, little more than an ethnological exploration of an interesting topic for study. The idea did not fit modern New Zealand and faded from view. But many of us continued to hold it in our minds. In 1975 I had discussed the idea with Douglas Newton, who headed the Arts of Africa and Oceania department at the Metropolitan Museum in New York. He confirmed their interest but I did not have the clout to take it further. Then Hamish Keith, chair of the New Zealand Arts Council, chose to champion the exhibition and to begin negotiations with New York. He telephoned. Would I come with him?

'Am I the right person, Hamish? Shouldn't it be the president of the Art Galleries and Museums Association of New Zealand?'

He was way ahead of me. The current president was director of one of the bigger metropolitan museums and was not displaying great enthusiasm for the project. Hamish wanted the support in the museum world, which I was offering in full.

'You will come with me as AGMANZ president-designate.'

New York, New York! Noise. Buildings. Also an air of decay. Fire trucks, old and battered. Steam venting from jerry-built stacks in the middle of the roadway. One of my case studies in management, more mismanagement, would ask why streets once paved with gold were now so very decrepit. Despite this, New York was hyper-excitement. I kept an eye out for Woody Allen. A no-show, but in the downstairs bar the aged pianist sang gravelly pieces that reeked of sophistication. We were assured he was locally famous. This was impressive, for was not New York the centre of the known world? We met New Zealand artists Len Lye and Max Gimblett in their studios and set the Met staff to work identifying the best hot pastrami on rye in the city, a task they took very seriously. My role as a parent carried demands that could only be answered at F.A.O. Schwarz toy store. Roller skates and the first electronic game I had ever seen – one function only, noughts and crosses, with robot voice and flashing lights.

The negotiation with the American Federation of the Arts and the Met spanned a week. Trying to cover all the bases, I took extensive notes and each evening went over them, picking out the areas that required further clarification. Certainty was the aim; an agreement emerged. The return trip home was a long loop of visits through the southern states to see museums in their city settings.

Chattanooga. The taxi driver hears that the guy with the strange accent comes from a land far away. She leans across and switches off the meter.

'I'm gunna show you a dark place.'

We pull off the main route and climb to graves on a craggy clifftop overlooking town and river. A Civil War story unfolds, about brave southern warriors 'martyred' by dastardly Yankees. There is passion in her voice. I hear no reconciliation. Only then am I delivered to my hotel. The following morning I take breakfast in a side-street establishment. My accent marks me out.

'You're the first person ever we've had from Noo Zealand. You set down over there an' I'll fetch you a real southern breakfast.' Hers is a breakfast bar voice that capitalises Real and Southern.

The food marks the gulf between South and North: it is the first time I have tasted grits. I am disappointed that Granny Clampett's possum gizzards are not on the menu.

In the few days that followed I was charmed by Chattanooga. This place had been paired forever in my mind with the song about the choochoo; now exchanges with the citizens added an undercurrent of secessionist history and a damaged psyche that comes with defeat.

Yet who am I to discount these people's experience and their need to persuade me of the legitimacy of their story? The mode of presentation was the theatre of charm, carefully crafted and delivered to explain the shame and bubbling anger that emerge from a way of life reduced. Back in New Zealand I played a small role in drawing all museums, including the hold-outs, into the exhibition. I then stepped aside: planning *Te Māori* could rest only with Māori. However, the accelerated cultural effort that followed was to dominate my life for some decades to come.

After the United States, *Te Māori* came home, as *Te Hokinga Mai*, to tour the country. Wherever it was shown it touched emotions, and not just among Māori; it proved to be a statement of national pride for a much broader range of people. Calls followed for museums to encompass the spirit of the exhibition. This was happening at the right time, as Pākehā, too, were searching in literature, arts and academic studies for an identity less of Europe and more of the Pacific. Wellington, as the capital, was a focus of this identity search; at various times plans for a new national art gallery and national museum had been floated. Moves were afoot that would eventually lead to a new manifestation of New Zealand, Te Papa. My Waikato days were numbered.

*

I am very fond of the 1980s. Mind, the 1960s and 1970s hadn't been bad. While my daughter and I were watching a programme on the Beatles, she said, 'You were so lucky to grow up in that era.' Yes, but Susi missed the fact that for much of that time I was a rather lonely single parent. No, the 1980s were a cut above what had gone before.

For it was in that decade that I met Susan Foster and suddenly my life was transformed by this intelligent, vivacious and witty woman. She lived in Wellington. It was time to move, a decision that was embraced by Conan and Susi, who were ready for the stimulus and opportunities available in a larger, very lively city. I turned my back on a steady salary and became an independent consultant. One of the first jobs was with Susan. She ran a very successful exhibition-touring service and had been contracted to mount a large craft exhibition to be toured by the Smithsonian museums throughout the United States. I could offer practical experience, about crates and shipping requirements, and it was a delight to work so closely with carvers, weavers and potters, many of whom I regarded as friends.

However, most of my consultancy would be based on the dramatic sense of change that was in the New Zealand air. In a few short years the tightly controlled country of old would become a poster child for the frequently disruptive forces of deregulation. Wellington became restructure central and, early on the scene, I grabbed a role.

New Zealand's capital, Wellington, is not large – about 400,000 people. But it has a character all of its own. Steep hills force it onto harbour and coastal fringes where buildings push upward. Extrusions up valleys and onto surrounding slopes are served by narrow, winding roads that require a special set of protocols to navigate safely. It feels larger, more cosmopolitan, than it is. This is reinforced by its climate which decrees, in blustery interventions, that for much of the year social life is conducted indoors around dinner tables or in restaurants.

With time I came to see the landscape as Libeskind-esque – a shaken, fractured, shattered construction from the mind of the architect I would come to know so well in Berlin. Every Wellingtonian is aware that the topography they claim as their own is a surface manifestation of deep geological forces. From the east an immense ocean-wide slab of rock moves beneath the Pacific. Moving at roughly the rate our fingernails grow, it drives into and slips beneath another resisting slab, the Australian plate. The clash pushes up the islands that are New Zealand. Wellington stands at the centre of this activity. Over millions of years, the sudden movements of its many earthquake faults have formed serried lines of jagged hills. The last really huge shake was in 1855 when the Wairarapa fault, 25 kilometres over the hill from us, ruptured, thrusting the land upward more than six metres and sideways more than 18.

Some of the earthquake-formed hills of Wellington are so steep that even the most imaginative feat of engineering cannot place a dwelling there, perhaps only a crazily projecting platform for a car or two. More moderate slopes are building sites, but in our city 'moderate', when attached to slope, is a relative term. Commonly, writers and poets would have houses 'cling' above the harbour. Tourists see it as 'cute', at least on a good day, dangerous when the weather is foul.

My first house was on a cliff, fault-formed and immediately above a rocky bay. Waking in the morning to the sounds of the sea was comforting, but with time the realisation dawned that those cracks in the brick walls indicated that the building was on the move. It was time to embrace change. My maturing and increasingly independent kids suggested I should move in with Susan. The subtext was 'allow us sole occupancy of the house'. Because Susan's flat was cosy for one, cramped for two, in time we bought a house on the hill overlooking harbour and city. Stretching to the north, we see steep ranges meeting harbour in a line that is the best natural processes can make of straight. This is marked by a motorway, a stream of red and gold light in the early morning and the evening. But to us this line is something else; it is the Wellington fault, active and waiting its moment. It passes down our street, just 160 metres away. We are safe, we tell each other. We sit on rock, the best possible foundation, and our house is resilient. It is 1920s weatherboard, in the case of an earthquake 20,000 nails all clinging on for dear life.

A few years ago we felt the 2011 earthquake that devastated Christchurch; we were about to have lunch, on a beach 300 kilometres away from the epicentre. Subsequently we have experienced a 6.6-magnitude quake and not so long ago a nasty thump, 7.8 at its origin in the South Island. Just a minor crack in our office wall gives us an Earthquake Commission file. The best current information is that our personal earthquake fault has only a 10 percent chance of moving in the next 100 years. We make light of it, all part of the defence mechanisms that go into living on a shaky isle.

Despite its location on such unstable ground, strangely there is a vitality that attends living here. Some of the great civilisations of this world had their origins along fault boundaries. Perhaps the threat and periodic disruption of massive earthquakes has caused people, including the citizens of Wellington, to embrace radical forms of reinvention in the face of the transient nature of existence, to be better attuned to thinking of change as a constant in life.

*

My first big project as a consultant had little to do with change. Perhaps that is why it did not survive. There was to be a sesquicentennial. Few knew the word – we learnt it was 150 years, in this case since the signing of the Treaty of Waitangi. There was to be a celebration and the prime minister, Robert Muldoon, needed a ribbon to cut. He had no particular interest in the arts but a new national art gallery would suffice. The PM waved his hand at a site deeply embedded in the dead administrative landscape of the government centre. 'There.'

The old gallery occupied the upper floor of a reddish, stone 1930s pile across town on the edge of a CBD twilight zone. Few visited. As I was leaving one evening a guard mumbled out of the side of his mouth, 'Nine through today, Ken.' I began work with the director, Luit Bieringa. A knowledgeable man, Luit had brave ideas about art as contemporary life, contested ground, something all the better for being wrangled over. Our biggest societal debate at that time was the sovereign place of Māori within the nation. Feelings were running high about the Treaty of Waitangi between Māori and government, signed in 1840 and largely abrogated over the century and a half that followed. Regional museums and galleries close to their local tribes, Waikato Museum among them, had been particularly courageous in addressing these dramatic changes. They had sought ways for Māori to be part of redefining the purpose and responsibilities of tax-funded cultural institutions. The sesquicentennial, however, was only a few years away and there was no time to make real change before then. We knew this to be a missed opportunity but our planning could only fall back on the cultural traditions and standards of North America and Europe.

Muldoon was voted out in 1984 and the incoming Labour government brought revolutionary ideas that were broader than just regulatory reform. The gallery project was abandoned after an investigation decided that the site was promised elsewhere. The idea might have died there but a short annex appended to the decision opened up a wondrous opportunity. The new government, full of gifted and enthusiastic newcomers and pushed by a group of local members of Parliament, described the need for a Pacific cultural centre to replace the old national museum and art gallery. This was to be built on a new waterfront site. The odds on completing such a costly endeavour? My best guess was about a thousand to one. But it would be an interesting piece of work and I needed it: as the liberated and ill-disciplined economy reeled, the interest rates on my house mortgage had rocketed.

*

It fell to Dr Peter Tapsell, incoming minister of internal affairs, to investigate the new centre and then to promote the emerging concept to the people of New Zealand. An orthopaedic surgeon, and Māori, Tapsell was wise and politically astute. Later he would become Speaker of the New Zealand House of Representatives and be knighted for services to the country. He was an old-school traditionalist. His view of womanhood came out of a former age when the sexes understood and conformed to established roles. But in other areas, particularly his vision for Māori in New Zealand society, he was closely aligned to the radicalism of his colleagues.

An advisory committee was established; I was to be the museum consultant. At its first meeting, Tapsell went around the table asking each person to explain their vision for the new centre. His own was based on a New Zealand that properly juxtaposed Māori, the first-nation inhabitants of New Zealand, with the later settlers, and acknowledged the unique right of Māori to stand as tangata whenua. He gave the example of Waikato Museum and was surprised when I pointed out that I had built and directed it over the previous 12 years. The report covered the necessities, including a shot at price – not so much what this new vision might cost, but what the politicians would buy. The newspapers had just announced that the government had committed $179 million for a couple of new aircraft. If they could spend that on planes, the reasoning went, surely they would be in the mood to spend the same on a new national museum.

No government would commit that sum to culture without some display of public support. Peter Tapsell took up the task, but what was he to sell? The minister had four other projects that were the subject of media debate. For each he had summary points that he would trot out with unerring consistency. The museum needed such a set. He offered a few broad guidelines.

'I don't like the current museum and gallery. They're so dull. It's not to be anything like those places.' Also: 'I admire the way Australians celebrate their culture and country. They're so exuberant. Can't we be more like that?'

Ministry man Geoff Knox and I started on a text. Geoff had been with UNESCO and was well versed in those United Nations statements crafted more to satisfy delegates rather than to convey meaning. But our endeavour was important for our nation. Our description had to be more than wordy gymnastics.

We would take the current effort into Tapsell's office. Too dense; try again. Our turgid little booklet was stripped to one page of essentials. Even this was not good enough. Finally we had a quarter-page of succinct aspirations and commitments that pictured a quite new concept of museum.

These 'stakes in the ground', as I came to call them, were: be for all New Zealanders, tell all our stories and be bicultural. The museum would be inclusive, welcoming all peoples of a multicultural nation, no matter what their ethnicity and education. By exchanging their stories people would feel that the museum was about them, their origins, beliefs, values and hopes. Finally, it would experiment with the formal relationship between Māori and the later settlers, European and peoples of other origins. Governance would be shared, though just how we did not know.

Biculturalism was a problem, the subject of much misunderstanding. Successive boards would speak of partnership. It was a comfortable word with its connotations of happy workers pulling together, setting aside differences, toiling to one end. It was also part of the political patter imposed from on high to smooth the path of treaty-based legal proceedings. Partnership was happily embraced and promoted by a predominantly Pākehā board; sometimes the language was embarrassingly condescending. For me, biculturalism was a negotiation of sovereignty within a nation among people who might have quite different views of the world.

For all our fuzzy understandings, these stakes in the ground would give a simple clarity to a huge cultural undertaking. More than jargon, they became an essential part of the philosophical horizon to which we would lift our eyes from mundane desk-level work to remind ourselves of the prize we sought.

Tapsell wove his magic. Cabinet approved the new museum as an expression of our identity. (This was unsaid, but it also met the need for a good news story and antidote to the bitter economic hardships of that time.) Former prime minister Sir Wallace (Bill) Rowling was appointed to chair the project.

'I distrust consultants. All care, no responsibility. Here's a job. Take it or go.'

It was one of my first conversations with Bill who, like Mike Blumenthal, proved to be a great boss. I was not about to give this opportunity away.

*

We established a project office in a nondescript downtown building. Graeme Shadwell led a growing team. We both had vague memories of having met before and one day the lightbulb clicked on – Graeme was the man in the Ministry of Works to whom I had reported my gas-line findings years before. Te Papa would never have succeeded without Graeme's steadying leadership. He was sanity, a person of level judgement and great experience who was always available to offer advice. On many occasions Graeme would take me aside and suggest that a particular course of action might be appropriate. Even when I had moved into my own directorship, Graeme was there, quietly interceding when unfortunate behaviour embittered Te Papa's management. I am proud to say that, together, Graeme and I saw this project to a successful end.

In many areas I was a novice. With size comes complexity and I had no experience in initiating really large projects. In the very early days I admitted as much to Peter Boag, the head of the lead government department, Internal Affairs. He wanted a solution. I knew of a group, E. Verner Johnson, who were experts in doing everything necessary to establish new museums. I interviewed them when in the States for another client. We met in a fish restaurant overlooking Boston Common. Shortly thereafter EVJ, the first of many acronyms, joined the project.

The company sent Joanne Horgan. A woman of vast knowledge born of worldwide experience, she would help us to build a museum concept based on the Tapsell pronouncements and translate this into an architectural competition brief. A New Zealand-centric concept started to emerge. 'You don't have snakes!' exclaimed Joanne after she had proposed a secure snake room.

After some months' work the brief was done, and Verner Johnson, the CEO of EVJ, arrived to guide it through Bill Rowling's Project Development Board. No problems there. Verner was a suave operator and his quiet demeanour, backed by weighty international experience, wowed them. The new Museum of New Zealand would be a triumph. That was all they wanted to hear. But there was a rider.

'You need to police this big idea, testing every development and refinement against the purity of the founding concept. Otherwise it will be diluted and fade back into the comfort of traditional belief. Someone must act as concept owner.'

He stood at the head of the table talking to the board, but I doubted they and others in the room heeded his warning. I did. As the only museum person there I understood the size of the shift away from the known towards an atmosphere of productive discomfort. It was as though Verner was talking directly to me. Indeed, we had already discussed the matter. He had, as an aside, talked of the danger of the concept becoming stale. 'It needs to be reviewed every 10 years to test relevance.'

I understood the idea and its fit within New Zealand society and had the museum background necessary to maintain 'storytelling', 'all New Zealanders' and even 'bicultural' as the central principles that formed our new place. There was no formal recognition, no appointment to a position with a terms of reference. Instead I quietly claimed this role and did my best, as head of the institutional planning team, to push the concept of a museum as statement of national identity.

The first big test followed shortly after Verner's performance before the board. For the museum to encompass the values of Māori society it must incorporate a marae, a central place of discussion, decision-making, learning and hosting. Certain protocols, functions and tradition-based forms dictated the type of place this should be. In its standard form in a rural setting, a marae had a beautifully carved wharenui, or meeting house, facing the new dawn. This was a statement of tribal pride and cohesion, also of constant rebirth with each rising sun. A traditional marae was a place where visiting parties, who in some circumstances might be deadly combatants, could, in culturally prescribed ways, signal peaceful intent; it provided a range of welcoming and discussion opportunities; it could accommodate and feed visitors who might stay for some days. As consultant Elaine Gurian once famously summarised these hosting functions, 'We go to a service at Notre Dame but we would never have a sleepover in it!'

The newly appointed Māori officer described such a traditional marae, but the resulting concept was a sort of fenced off and culturally exclusive lager. And it was huge – many thousands of square metres, bedecked with traditional carvings, and requiring a large dedicated support staff. This was space and money we just did not have. I took the problem to Bill Rowling. He called for submissions from the project's Māori officer, the directors of the National Art Gallery and National Museum, and me. Mine was a page and a quarter. It drew on everything I had learnt in my Tainui days, about adaptation to changing societal needs, and my understanding of the emerging museum concept. I stressed seamless integration, multifunctional usages, the need to create a central forum space for the whole museum. I had my own vision for the Te Papa marae, based in large part on a huge chapel-like integration of multidimensional artwork and architecture by David Alfaro Siqueiros, which I had seen in Mexico City. My final paragraph took the form of a set of principles and an indication of an achievable form.

The board's decision came surprisingly quickly. The paragraph was adopted as policy. The revolution was alive. The decision caused bad feelings in the project office – 'How come Māori protocol is ignored and a Pākehā's position is adopted?' – but the board's decision was the right one, and the result is the wonderful marae at Te Papa, Rongomaraeroa. The Māori officer did not last that long. He made a number of fundamental errors of judgement. Until he departed the fuming and anger had to be endured. But as Blossom Dearie's attorney Bernie says, 'You keep on hanging tough.'

*

Although an administration quite distinct from the project office, the National Museum up on the hill in Buckle Street took hold of the new concept and determined to test it out. We in our downtown office observed with interest. The exhibition *Voices* was an integrated span of our country's natural and human history, with an interactive resource centre devoted to the natural wonders and animals of our land. At the opening, in October 1992, a small plaque was unveiled that mentioned the Museum of New Zealand, as the new museum was then known. The powers-that-be used the acronym MONZ. In a flash, with much quiet sniggering, naughty staffers called our concept 'mons Veneris'. Perhaps it was this that led me to check all acronyms and once discover that a proposed title for a project with a large Māori component spelt out COON.

In grappling with the museum concept, *Voices* had identified those who could see the worth and relevance of the new, and remove themselves conceptually from the old. The old gave voice to their deepest fears as scientists lined up against me for destroying a critical biosystematics institution. But some wanted to be part of the new. They were the people I needed.

Raewyn Smith-Kapa was one. As the key manager, she had pulled off *Voices* in the face of crisis upon crisis – for example, the complaint from curators that the cleaning woman, who was Māori, should have such a strong voice in an exhibition team. These were testing times demanding fresh thinking, but Raewyn understood how exhibitions were developed and the common language that everyone would come to use. More than anyone she saw the need for expertise beyond that normally admitted into museological halls, such as writers, concept developers, interpreters and audience researchers. As our lead museum professional project manager, Raewyn would be critical to our success. Another National Museum star performer was senior scientist Geoff Hicks, who, unbeknown to his director, walked down off the hill to become, after a little negotiation, the first of our conceptual leaders, in his case for natural history.

Other people joined the institutional planning team, adventurous souls all bursting to apply what they knew and be part of a project that explored and expressed the state of their nation. The words of a job advertisement could never capture what was required. The process was more spontaneous; word of mouth and personal initiative loomed large. Steadily the office became a place of expansive thinking, deep reflection, even nurture, and not a little noisy fun. Then suddenly one morning we awoke to the shocking news that Geoff Knox had died the previous evening.

Graeme Shadwell looked in on my expanding team and decreed that I would need project management assistance. The downtown office, now overlooking the waterfront site, was crowded with all our people plus a growing numbers of engineers and technical managers.

'We have just the person for you,' said Graeme. He took me across town to a construction site in Thorndon, a refurbishment that would house the National Archives. In the centre of all the noise and seeming chaos was Sean Sweeney, impossibly young and energetic. He joined the team, applying rigour and the common sense that took us to opening. He also brought with him a way of yawning with exaggerated enthusiasm when I was considered to be rambling on too long.

*

A group of senior Māori elders from different tribes blessed the site of the future museum. On a chilly morning, I proudly walked with them. We needed all the blessing we could muster, for this was land reclaimed out of Wellington Harbour. The location was magnificent, touching the water close to the city's CBD, but the land was also soft and spongy, anything but a firm foundation for a major museum in an earthquake-prone area.

So, the engineers decreed, the first phase would be dynamic consolidation. Those two words held such assurance; they were heavy with technical perfection, even certainty. Yet the reality was a group of jerry-built praying-mantis-like machines that dropped crude 25-tonne concrete blocks from a great height to pound the site, producing a small earthquake every minute or so over a large area. Once I stood at the office window watching, mesmerised, as each weight was craned up to be released and – thud, shiver – hit the ground. But this time the block of concrete came down on a particularly soft spot, and disappeared. A bulldozer had to be called to dig it out. Some residents found the continuous hammering exceedingly distressing. Graeme arranged for one to spend her day in a hotel out of the shock zone. Soon concrete footings appeared out of the consolidated ground. The building was on its way.

I never liked it. Graeme did. I think I am in the majority. For so many people it is a building marked by a bulk that sits heavy on the ground, a throwback to an authoritarian Victorian civic structure. We had tried to write into the brief an approach to the building that would be an interesting adventure, something with a bit of joy, but this was never achieved. Why?

I had no part to play in the selection of the architect. This was not a staff role and Bill Rowling even separated the board from the process. Geoff Knox and I had recommended that the competition be for an architect and not a design, pointing to the danger that a spectacular edifice – think Mormon pictures – might well be a functional disaster. So we sat back to watch as a panel under Californian architect Joe Esherick assessed entries, produced a shortlist and then, after a further limited design stage, selected the winner. One of the panel was Ngāti Porou leader Apirana (Api) Mahiuika. He later confided in me that the first thing that he and fellow panel member Kara Puketapu did was to 'weed out' all the literal expressions of Māori as symbol – the fish-hook shapes, overblown wharenui and feathers. As a result some interesting designs ended up on the committee cutting-room floor.

The winning design, by Auckland practice Jasmax, was light and airy. However, as the design process proceeded it became an introverted building of heavy façade that reinforced a museological ethos about control and exclusion. The building won no awards; a critic described it as 'a washing machine factory'. Te Papa's fame and popularity would instead come from the way in which it welcomed and embraced its audience.

*

Peter Tapsell had stressed the 'Be bicultural' principle. I knew that this was going to be one of those ground-breaking ideas that would mark our new museum off from all others. For me, biculturalism had little to do with two cultures, and everything to do with negotiated sovereignty at all levels. There was no clash with that other principle, 'All New Zealanders'. We were all in this together and had to talk our way through every issue, exercising the utmost good faith.

The board established a Māori advisory committee, though I suspect for some this was an exercise in window-dressing, an arm's-length gesture to Māori input, the expected thing at this time in our nation's history. But it was a fortunate move that had far-reaching consequences. Chairman Bill Rowling was an exceptional leader but his Project Development Board was not an impressive group. There were a couple of people of great talent but most of these political appointees were aged, heavy on tradition and committed to the importance of tightly defined fiefdoms. One member would last through the morning agenda to invariably fall asleep after lunch. Revolution was not central to their thinking. Ngā Kaiwawao, and their chair, would change that.

Api Mahuika was a man of substance and a leader who had the necessary mana to cross tribal boundaries. Because he had a terrible fear of flying, we got to know each other through negotiating how he would travel to Wellington and about the country. Easy – by car. Api insisted that I should be secretary to Ngā Kaiwawao, as the group named themselves at their first meeting.

So began four years, 1988 to 1992, of further learning at least as intense as my time in Waikato. For it was soon apparent that so much that would make this museum unique would come from Ngā Kaiwawao. They would be worthy successors to Peter Tapsell.

Api was an achiever with ambition for Te Papa. No cultural organisation with which he was associated would make just some slight sideways nod to Māori culture; no, at his insistence every idea would be tested against Māori understandings and perspectives. We talked of this incessantly, often in serious business sessions at the hotel bar. Drinking was not one of my strengths and I had to employ complex manoeuvres – serious note-taking, lengthy oration on some discussion point, consulting documents – to avoid at least every second round.

Api phoned his contacts and soon a group of Māori leaders, people strong not only in their Māoritanga but also in Enlightenment and universal values, were gathering to talk about this new creation. They had the cultural confidence and political position to provide the vision that was beyond a lacklustre board. Balancing far-sighted dreams with pragmatic good sense, they helped to redefine what a museum in New Zealand might be. Their fledgling aspirations became the subject of consultations throughout New Zealand: the place of a marae within a museum and the fact that it would be a covered forum space; the ceremonials for our unique cultural mix; new ideas on the nature and nurture of collections. They struggled with how all kinds of people might be drawn into Te Papa and stand as equals. They contributed to and reviewed architectural concepts. They brought deep cultural understanding to the messages carried within 10,000 square metres of exhibitions and how this new place would welcome and nurture its visitors. Ngā Kaiwawao was also responsible for 'Te Papa'. One meeting sought to capture their expanding set of ideas in a name. At times names had been suggested, mainly attempts at literal translation. But then Professor Tīmoti Kāretu sang a haunting waiata that contained the phrase 'Te Papa Tongarewa'. The hidden meanings were drawn forth: the reference to our earth mother, Papatūānuku, southernness, treasures, along with the multiple poetic references that delved deep into a knowledge that I, and so many others, were not privy to.

This became part of our thinking and then the official name.

CHAPTER 4

THE GENIUS OF CLIFF WHITING

CLIFF WHITING, a gentle man of quiet strength and a leader of great mana and knowledge, was an early member of Ngā Kaiwawao. His involvement was critical to the success of Te Papa.

I first met Cliff in 1973. His reputation as an artist was growing and we wanted his works for Waikato Museum's art and historical commentary exhibitions. His huge mural, *Te Wehenga o Rangi rāua ko Papa*, was the feature of our 1976 *Contemporary Māori Art* show. It formed the cover of the catalogue. I talked long and hard with him: 'I'll have the new Waikato Museum designed around your work – just sell it to us.' Cliff held back. He had other thoughts. The work is now in the National Library.

I was drawn to this man of dignity. His approach to art reached beyond the individual artists whose status is measured by position within sanctified gallery walls. Part of his genius lay in creating a marae as the very heart of a hapū's cultural and artistic knowledge and pride. Cliff relished reinforcing this sense of ownership by giving each person a role in the process. Under his tutelage they became artisans who, by investing something of themselves in the project, moved closer to a culture that many of them were on the edge of losing. From his place on Ngā Kaiwawao it was natural that Cliff should soon become director Māori and shortly thereafter kaihautū, the Māori CEO.

*

As our guide in mātauranga, the Māori knowledge system, and as leader of the Māori exhibitions, Cliff was a constant presence in the project office, plying the teams with ideas and requirements via esoteric language that was frequently mysterious to us all. Sometimes, in an aside, he would announce that the primary reason for his visit to the project office was relief from the fractious managerial scene, which he abhorred.

An easy and respectful relationship enabled us to tackle our first big issue. Some strongly voiced opinion within the office considered that the bicultural principle demanded two separate project structures, one Māori and one for the settler cultures. But Cliff and I soon determined that such a dual management system would be confusing, potentially messy and expensive. Our application of the same principle, plus a bit of managerial reality, led us to develop a partnership of defined complementary roles. Two bosses in one area can be problematic; we agreed to strike an accord. Cliff was happy with a verbal agreement but I wanted something more concrete. 'Bloody Pākehās, always having to write things down!'

I insisted. The accord quickly established who 'owned' an area, and which of the partners' positions would prevail in what circumstances. Cliff would be responsible for initiating and developing Māori exhibitions at the idea and content level. He would be guardian of the Māori spiritual dimensions within the exhibitions and would have cultural oversight of members of the Māori team. As director museum projects, I stood alongside Cliff, making sure that all Māori exhibitions were valid and achievable, and integrated with other exhibitions. Also, at the planning and process level, I oversaw the Māori team but only 'performance against planning schedule targets and budget'. The Māori exhibits went through all the same project management processes and disciplines as those of the other areas, although Cliff had other cultural imperatives that would structure his exhibitions. Part of our partnership meant that I must try to understand and encompass his approach, modifying our systems accordingly.

But of greater importance was to understand at least something of the cultural position he brought to Te Papa. It was as though I was back in Tainui days with Dave Manihera, being tutored on ways of life to which I had not been born.

*

We were in our shared office area. The conversation was about a small theatre that would stand between two exhibitions, bastions of Western scholarship. To one side, *Awesome Forces* covered geophysics, geomorphology and meteorology; on the other side, *Mountains to Sea* was about New Zealand's fauna and flora. The theatre would carry the Māori world view of nature and a pantheon of demigods would be the players. One was Rūaumoko, he of earthquakes. When Rūaumoko stirred in the underworld the ground shuddered and split.

But the godly realm Cliff was talking of seemed to be a reality in the contemporary world. 'You can't believe in Rūaumoko!' I exclaimed.

It was an ill-considered intervention but perhaps a necessary part of my evolving understanding. Had I been a little more reflective, I might have accepted that I could encompass Cliff's heavenly, albeit in the case of Rūaumoko subterranean, realm. There would be moments when I would allow Zeus to cast his thunderbolts or Noah to set out across the global flood to save all living things. Fine, atmospheric electricity does not work like that. The flood could not be as expansive as the book said, nor could it be sailed by such a shonky piece of marine engineering as the ark, and with a cargo that constituted the most dangerous assembly of beasts ever brought together in one spot. That did not mean to say these poetic tales of long pedigree should not be maintained as cultural markers that enriched our storytelling. No – Zeus, Noah and Rūaumoko were all right.

But that was cultural equivalence, not differences. What was evident, and the cause of my impulsive objection, was Rūaumoko being part of the world, now, in the midst of modernity. Cliff paused. He had a way of drawing still time into a discussion, so it resumed, but several phases back. Yes, with his Māori identity to the fore he could believe. He explained again.

'Past, present, future.' With each word came a small graceful flick of the arm, time given a place in the cosmos.

'Past.' His arm was held naturally, without strain, just behind his left shoulder.

'Present.' Hand now hovered above his shoulder.

'Future.' A small ballet-like movement and the future hung before us. The whole progression was minimal, no more than a brush. There was his point. The three states to which I would ascribe years, centuries, epochs, were to Cliff part of a continuum of knowledge and being.

'It's all bound together with whakapapa. Every Māori has whakapapa.'

Whakapapa (lineage) fused tangata (people) with whenua (land) and gave to all the certainty of belonging to a Māori place in the world, physical and spiritual, where they could stand – their tūrangawaewae. Rūaumoko was in the family tree, back beyond founding ancestor, but there nevertheless with all the other demigods. He was part of the knowledge, cultivated generation upon generation, that made sense of a rich, if shaky, world. The restless old fellow could not be set aside, even as science could now talk of the massive geological forces that were plate tectonics.

Māori, the tangata whenua, arrived from tropical Polynesia some 750 years ago. They lived upon, observed and made sense of their new land, building, in isolation, a society attuned to these large temperate islands in a huge ocean. Then little more than 200 years ago came brash newcomers, part of a huge international diaspora of anglophone people. Initially Māori saw their arrival as opportunity, bringing an array of new, useful innovations: education, guns, the trappings of commerce. For many years the new settlers were dependent on Māori trade for their survival. In my archaeology days, I had seen the huge Waikato agricultural enterprises: dams, mills, soils remade to produce the food necessary to keep Auckland alive in its first years.

The newcomers imposed themselves. Their culture was of the Industrial Revolution. Individualism was on the rise. With little thought, or prospect, of returning to their country of origin, they invaded and possessed and disrupted. Māori were an obstacle to achieving their purpose of advancement beyond anything possible back home. It was held that, in the face of the inexorable advance of civilised nationhood, the native race would assimilate or die out. Denigration on the basis of race – pure racism – was practised in a most vile manner and is part of our Pākehā inheritance. Māori did not die out but they did suffer terrible loss, of land and culture. As Te Papa was being developed, that injustice was being tackled politically.

Cliff improved the knowledge of so many of the young Māori in our office, teaching them of what had vanished from their lives while talking to us all of historical time as part of living today. He insisted that Māori had a view of the world as a seamless entity. Their sense of emotional well-being was bonded to iwi and hapū, and land, through whakapapa or genealogical lineage. Deep-seated cultural traditions of seeing the world as two forms, tapu and noa, would be manifest within Te Papa. Tapu was the sacred realm that established what might be prohibited; noa was the profane, the ordinary and expected. The museum would have zones and behaviour accepted as either tapu or noa. All would be carried and nurtured by language and ritual.

For me, the most critical element of contemporary Māori identity was the struggle to reclaim at least some part of what had been lost. This brought a personal sense of shame, that part of my identity was a collective form of guilt at a people dispossessed and wounded by my ancestors' greed and sense of racial superiority. I struggled to keep up. But despite those years playing with the kids from Pohara Pā; despite my university training and largely failed attempts to learn the Māori language; despite what I had discovered among Tainui, I knew I could not fully understand what I was hearing from Cliff.

Emerging, however, was acceptance that in this museum we could encompass many cultural systems that enriched the way we thought about the world. The human mind could hold, even make sense of, swirling clouds of heroic beliefs, the stuff of myths and legends, while at the same time understanding the scientific foundations of the modern world.

These belief systems occupied their own universe. Sometimes they could be brought together into a single discourse. Frequently they could not and, indeed, if attempted, the result could be ludicrous. One staffer, keen to reclaim his culture, exclaimed with confidence that the Māori myths encompassed, and pre-dated, understandings of the Big Bang origins of the universe. This was quietly dismissed as cultural overreach and we moved on.

*

When it came to the Māori permanent exhibitions I sometimes found Cliff's language difficult to translate into concrete buildable terms. Then he produced a series of drawings, rich in detail. We had it. A set of paths wound through the exhibition *Mana Whenua*, with the beautiful carved meeting house Te Hau ki Tūranga looming high above.

Cliff spent much of his time on the road, consulting with individual tribes, identifying those that wished to join Te Papa. A number signed on to feed in their specialist cultural knowledge – house-building, weaving, navigation and so on – to their exhibition segment. This meant that he was frequently away as the design progressed. As a result the exhibition team was forced to cope with complex streams of new knowledge that had to be retrofitted into the designs. I well remember the distress caused when Cliff insisted that an expensive piece of artwork be redone. I supported him in the face of vociferous complaint from one of his teams.

Our partnership was further tested by the frustrations that accompanied the Treaty of Waitangi exhibition. It had to be a statement worthy of our core principle, 'Be bicultural'. The first team failed, producing a divisive statement full of staunch, strident voices of rage rather than dialogue. Cliff was unimpressed by the inability of some of his people to negotiate. I closed the team down. A second team, of more mature stature, headed by our senior designer Robin Parkinson, produced a flag-based idea and, at Robin's instigation, brought to the concept the idea of size emphasising significance. It filled the tall space but was problematic – among other things, which flags should be included? Enter the third team.

Here I encounter a Günter Grass moment. I have an image of four treaty team members standing in the Lincoln Memorial in Washington, DC. They are Robin Parkinson, architect Pete Bossley (the exhibition was to occupy the most architectural of the exhibition spaces), Paul Thompson and Haniko Te Kurapa. The scale is massive, as befits Lincoln's importance to a nation struggling to unify. Walls to either side of the huge seated figure are chiselled with the great man's words. The team agrees that this is the model for our exhibition, a huge treaty replica in glass with equally sized wording standing either side in Māori and English.

The memory is flawed. The core moment of decision is right but I have the personnel all wrong – no Robin, no Pete, but yes Paul and Haniko, plus history concept leader Jock Phillips.

*

My accord with Cliff was about exhibitions, but his role in Te Papa was much wider. He led all iwi liaison, and as artist and cultural leader he formed and sculpted the new marae, Rongomaraeroa. His decorated house within a house would be Te Papa's Māori cultural centrepiece, carrying the origin story of Tāne separating earth and sky and bringing light to the world. As we passed each other in a corridor, or in the quiet of our office, Cliff would mumble a new thought.

'There's not going to be one primary colour anywhere,' he once told me, and proceeded thereafter to deliver an exercise in pastel. The end wall became Cliff's tribute to all his fellow citizens, several tiers of Kiwi characters ordinary, yet noble, in their working pursuits.

'Perhaps even a jailbird.' There is.

*

Bill Rowling, dear man, died when large pōhutukawa trees at the old museum site were to be relocated and planted along the museum's harbour-facing wall. Cliff decided that the first of these should honour him. But this tree did not come willingly. First there was a negotiation to be concluded. The local high school firmly believed that we had no right to the trees we had identified. What is more, even if they did belong to us, generations of kids had passed the line of trees every morning. We listened to and respected the concerns expressed. One night I joined the tree shifters in the glare of floodlights. A digger cut a trench and a man with shovel followed behind. Suddenly, there was a shout and everything stopped. A large and dangerous-looking electrical cable had been exposed; it passed right through the tree's root system. The digger and the big truck went home. The cable was investigated. It was dead. Not plotted on any site plan, it had probably been laid in the haste of war to run power to an underground command bunker 50 metres away. On another night, the cable was cut and, with difficulty, the tree was loaded onto the huge flat-deck. I followed. It seemed to take the full width of the deserted early morning street, scattering leaves and twigs as it went, a sort of anointing of the path.

Cliff named the pōhutukawa the 'troublesome one', a sign that Rowling had not yet left us. His view was reinforced when Sir Wal, as the tree was also known, refused to take root and became a sorry sight, thin and too bare to be deemed healthy. Then an arborist found that Sir Wal was waterlogged, sitting in its own little lake. Once drained, the troublesome one flourished.

Cliff and I were the products of different cultural upbringings, respectful of each other's position. But believing? I'm not sure. Cliff's application of mātauranga Māori sought life-affirming myths, whereas I was always more drawn to the same affirmations but via rationalistic, testable Enlightenment values based on science.

Yet I know those myths to be so important to us all. There are stories that help make our lives full and profound. When the tethered cable on the first dynamic-consolidation drop broke, Cliff and his assembled elders read this as some form of forfeit and a sure sign of the beginning of a successful project. Equally the engineers could explain the forces that caused that tethered wire to whip, break and flail about, just as they had investigated and rendered safe that pesky electrical cable. Both approaches were valid within their own but parallel cultural spheres, mātauranga and science, and both could be rationalised according to situation and personal circumstance and woven into life.

CHAPTER 5

TELLING OUR STORIES

BUT TO REWIND. Back in 1988, beyond Peter Tapsell's critical 'stakes in the ground', we had only a few descriptive papers and a wish list of bright ideas. We required a conceptual blueprint for the exhibition planners and architects who were laying out the museum.

I remember only one meeting, attended by Jenny Harper, Bronwyn Simes, Rose Young, Geoff Hicks and Bill Tramposch, an American museologist who was in New Zealand on a Fulbright scholarship. In very short time we had what we needed, at least in outline. One frame for the natural environment, one for Māori, one for all other cultures. I drew a triangle – the pointy bits would carry each of these frames. But we also recognised that much of our society was a shared experience. I laid across the triangle a circle for the zones of cultural interaction.

The framework went to Ngā Kaiwawao. They agreed and refined the terms. Papatūānuku for our natural environment, enriched by the cultural layers that are part of the land we occupy. Tangata whenua for Māori, the people of the land. But a term for all other cultures evaded us. To begin we had described the later settler groups as non-Māori, but a board member quickly put us right. It was not acceptable to describe a key cultural group as a negative. Of course, he was correct. Some were of a mind to contain all later arrivals in the term Pākehā, commonly meaning New Zealanders of European descent. But we knew that Pasifika, Indians, Chinese and others of the smaller-percentage cultures would not accept being included in an amorphous mass. Another term suggested was tauiwi, but this won no support because it carried connotations of foreigner, and none of us were prepared to be foreigners in our own land. The matter rested until, in a speech, Māori leader Judge Eddie Durie referred to the later settler peoples being party to, and given place within the nation by, the Treaty of Waitangi. The settlers would be 'Tangata Tiriti: those who belong to the land by right of the Treaty of Waitangi'.

Then came the backsliding. A board member, expressing the view of many of his colleagues, said that despite anything indicated by the conceptual framework, to which he had just agreed, 'All I need to know is where the door to the National Art Gallery is!' I have always been disappointed that the creative spirits of the art world were territorialised; I would have preferred art to be given a roving brief so as to explore, in yet-to-be-thought-of ways, new understandings of our land, our society and our future. As natural historian E.O. Wilson has asked, "Would the humanities care to colonize the sciences? Might poets and visual artists consider searching in the real world outside the range of ordinary dreams for unexplored dimensions, depth, and meaning?' That idea could have been tested at Te Papa, but exceptionalism carried the day, placing art behind its own fence, unsullied, over there.

I got myself into a spot of bother with the board by arguing too determinedly for the purity of the conceptual framework. Bill Rowling wagged his finger at me and made threatening noises; I had sailed too close to the wind and needed to draw back to survive.

*

Three-tiered concept in hand, it was time to move on to the actual exhibitions. Knowing that we had never confronted such a large-scale project, EVJ recommended appointing an exhibition development consultant. I favoured a group called Jean Jacques André, which had been responsible for inventive and theatrical British Columbia and Canadian cultural developments, but the job went to RAA, Ralph Appelbaum Associates, of New York. I found them too traditional, in a modern sort of way, and overly architectural, but I kept my head down.

I suppose I was always destined to be disappointed with the interpretive plan that finally emerged in 1992. RAA man Scott Simeral, working with a team including a number from our old National Art Gallery and Museum, produced a document to please any traditional board. There was an automatic assumption that the museum would have 'an organisational structure based on four curatorial departments: Natural Environment, Māori Art and History, History and Art'. Grey-shaded narrow strips between these solid academic floor spaces, 'areas of interaction', seemed to be the sole concession to the reality that we lived most of our lives together in work, social and recreational groupings. Even then, these zones were to be thickly lined with barriers of furniture. In the rush to bring collections to the fore there was nothing about those visiting the museum, no sign of the principle of telling all our stories. And Tapsell's desire for exuberance had no place. However, the plan did capture good stuff that would flow through into future experience planning, for which I was thankful.

Part of the RAA brief was to work within the Jasmax design process to make sure exhibitions and architecture were aligned. Here Scott's traditional view of the museum world and his architectural training was obvious. Consider the case of the Core/Ihonui. Scott had a thing about punching holes through museum floors to form visual links. It was a dubious concept at best, explored in designs for the Museum of Melbourne, but not realised. A large hole would run up from Level 2 to the ceiling above Level 6. More than just linkage, the Core was to be a vertical temporary exhibition gallery bedecked with changing exhibitions of artefacts. The architects immediately identified this as the ideal place to run their main vertical circulation, which was totally logical since it was close to the lifts. But Scott was adamant. For a few tens of thousands of dollars we would have a unique, ever-changing exhibition experience at the centre of the museum. Finally, I had an engineer review the floating exhibition idea. He concluded that earthquake requirements would add a crippling cost. 'That,' he indicated one of the concepts, 'looks like a quarter of a million dollars of supports and restraints.' I went straight into an exhibition team meeting and closed the whole idea down. Yet, to this day, the Core/Ihonui remains a vestige of planning gone wrong, a waste of valuable space and an obstruction to expansive circulation on all levels.

*

In 1992 Cheryll Sotheran was appointed CEO of Te Papa. By then the dreams had been dreamt; the revolutionary idea of the new museum carrying the narrative of a nation was in place. It took time and a number of slides across the organisational chart but finally everything was official. Cheryll decreed that I would head all exhibition planning and realisation. Other titles, every one of which fudged what I actually did, were abandoned and I was now director museum projects.

First, we needed intellectual grunt if powerful narratives were to be a part of the Te Papa experience. We already had Cliff Whiting for Māori and Geoff Hicks at work on the natural environment. They were followed by Jock Phillips for history, Janet Davidson for Pasifika efforts and Ian Wedde for art. Each had a strong vision for their area and in short order a range of exhibitions was established. I worried that the zones of cultural overlap were being overlooked, but this was a time of moving quickly.

With the exhibitions decided, a team was assembled for each and set to work under a project manager. At defined stages along the way they would report to my review group. Check concept, audience, storylines, interpretation, language, collections, props, design and budget. No messing about. Approval granted and on to the next stage. Later I would tell Mike Blumenthal of the 'grind' involved in producing exhibitions.

The exhibitions juggernaut was steered by the Day 1 Management Team. It was a big but disciplined group of key personnel, not just managers, around a large table, where each team's progress was tested and retested against the schedule. I chaired and wrote the minutes. Raewyn Smith-Kapa and Sean Sweeney rode shotgun.

In all honesty, once they were running, the detailed exhibitions process rarely needed me, other than as the figurehead whose signature of approval went on the bottom of an exhibition document at a particular stage in its development. But as the now official guardian of the museum that visitors would encounter, I kept track of and was constantly refining the approach that on opening day and beyond would mark us off from all others. Neil Anderson, who came out of museum and gallery education to head all efforts about the programme, championed the much-expanded audience that was part of the Te Papa idea. No longer would we just open the doors to be surprised (or not surprised, more likely) at the limited group with courage and confidence enough to cross our threshold. Rather, our approach would be to determine the audience we sought to involve and find new ways of attracting them. Te Papa, we told ourselves, was to be a place well loved by all New Zealanders, an extension of their selves. Neil, with a new star in the project office, Christine Fitzgerald, had begun defining the characteristics of different audiences – their database was on our computers and we could test our thoughts about what might connect with people. We learnt much: our fondly held beliefs about who would flock to what were often well wide of the mark.

*

The leisure industry interested me. Whatever it did, it tended to do well. I had visited examples in the States and England. A very open bunch of people pleased to share knowledge, they talked of the age of experience. I took from one place the idea of the visitor stream, a structured approach to establishing an attraction in people's minds as a place to visit, even if some years into the future. They reinforced that idea through focused marketing, then planning the visit from journey to entry, welcome, catering for all needs (signs, parking, food, toilets – particularly toilets), moving through the experience, pace, safety and finally, leaving happy. The aim was affirmation. Commonly, visitors found museums to be dead places and advised their friends against visiting. We had to buck that trend. We wanted our visitors to broadcast the worth of the place to everyone they met, to tell them, 'You must visit!'

This goal was a challenge to some in the museum. We broadcast an early concept for the outdoor Harbour Park, only to find it tarred with the dreaded Disneyland jibe. In my response in the museum newsletter I decried Disney's 'sanitised, mid-50s view of USA history … that had its origins in tinsel-town myths', but rejected the 'dismissive and disparaging comparisons' my colleagues had made. I went on to list the positive developments we could take from an industry that was 'arguably the single most important influence [since] the Great Exhibition of 1851'.

Then, early in 1995, a senior executive of the Disney Corporation arrived to join some of our exhibition workshops. He talked of Mickey's Ten Commandments. There was much lip curling among us all that the famous mouse should invade these halls of serious scholarship, but on reflection there was sense in every one of those pronouncements. They were honest in their commitments to the audience and paralleled our endeavours to communicate with 'all New Zealanders'. Soon, Mickey was pinned up at our desks and being mentioned in development meetings.

Shortly thereafter I met theme-park developers at Disney Imagineering, in Glendale, California. I was shown the holy of holies – the archive of early illustrative material presided over by an ancient, obviously illustrious, early imagineer. In the cavernous but unexceptional industrial buildings that made up the complex, large models sat on elevated tables, sketches covered the walls. No photos were allowed. Market research had found that their visitors were firmly of the opinion that their theme-park visit was an educational experience, and the educational market is a lucrative one. Our approach had resonated with chief executive Michael Eisner, whose current pet project was Disney's America, an exploration of United States history. They, too, had a three-tiered conceptual framework: those who were here (Native Americans), those who came here (the 'founders' and the huddled masses) and those who were brought here (African American slaves).

'Amerindians? Slaves? Was Disney really going to explore dark history?' I asked George Washington University historian Professor James O. Horton, who had advised the Disney team. We were in the National Museum of American History staffroom in Washington.

'Yes,' he replied. 'The commitment there seems to be to do more than a museum would. But then, I'm a resolute critic of American museums. So often they avoid what is inhuman in our nation's history, including the States' own holocausts, the destruction of American Indian peoples and slavery. At best they treat it with lamentable accuracy and honesty. Our museums are playing with history as comforting nostalgia. They avoid contentious subjects.'

It was a damning critique from an academic whose field was slavery.

In the end, Disney's America did not happen. It ran into strong opposition from the super-rich landowners surrounding the favoured site outside the nation's capital. But equally, although a saccharine vision of mid-America as a pastiche of a historical memory was marketable, slavery and the slaughter of the Indigenous peoples of the Americas may have proved just too big an obstacle to ticket sales.

A few days after returning from that visit I gave a couple of lectures to staff. My theme was the challenge of getting 'All New Zealanders' across our threshold and how the leisure industry did it. I drew diagrams on the board showing the pulses of energy and emotion expended by visitors that mark an exciting experience. Museums did not emerge well. They were flat. I broached the idea of introducing more high-adrenalin experiences that might lure the notoriously hard-to-attract teenage and young-adult visitors.

It was an enthusiastic performance. My vigorous emphasis of a particular point caused my can of beer to spray across the front row. The ideas struck a chord and within a very short time a couple of creatives came to me with proposals for our own leisure industry spectacular. The search was on for ideas. We even had a new term that I had brought back with me – high energy attractors or HEAs. Geoff Hicks' exhibition on the geological processes that had shaped our land was to be called *Awesome Forces*. Volcanologist Alan Hull stood with Cliff, Geoff and me on the crumbly edge of the Whakaari White Island crater. We agreed, however, that we could not achieve any of the earth-shaking power, the heat, the roar, the hellish feeling of mortality in the air that day. There would be no volcano HEA.

Instead we would stay with ideas we could achieve: Hillary and Tensing conquer Everest, the beautiful John Britten motorcycle streaks across the sky, the time-capsule operator presses the wrong button and we are plunged back to dinosaur times. It was all fun and finally achieved as *Time Warp*, a spirited, activity-demanding exploration of our past, present and future. It was one of the first things the visitor saw. It was also expensive and only partially successful. But *Time Warp* gave Te Papa a clear marketing advantage with the young, one that differentiated us from other world museums.

In creating *Time Warp*, many great ideas would be promoted and argued about, then shelved and forgotten. Some, though, were almost immediately dusted off and used. The media, hunting for bad-news stories, found a catchphrase with which to belabour the yet-to-be-opened Te Papa: it was, they warned, nothing more than a 'Māori museum'.

Cheryll Sotheran called me in. 'How can we respond?'

'We have 90 square metres of spare space and can dip into the contingency. Let's do an object theatre.'

'What's that?'

I saw my first object theatre in New York in 1975 and returned two years later to get a personal tour by the creator, Joe Noble. Joe was one of those highly ethical and socially conscious museum leaders to whom our younger generation was drawn. He went public about an illegally acquired Mesoamerican temple held quietly in the basement of the Metropolitan Museum.

Joe was also a cinematographer and had created an animated theatre about his museum's city, New York. In a darkened gallery a voice guided the visitor through a history of the Big Apple; an aria accompanied the illumination of a box recovered from the Metropolitan Opera; other objects were drawn into view; Central Park was planned; New York was on show. But most important to Joe was the room housing a clanking old punch-card machine that turned lights on and off and brought in the sound. There was also the Disneyland production, *It's a Small World*, a hall of audio-animatronic (sound/movement) puppets that built an environment of feel-good joy, or total boredom, depending on one's point of view.

Cheryll supported the idea. She had just seen the work of a new design group, Story Inc. They could do it. We pulled together the rejected *Time Warp* ideas and several of the team wrote briefs, about emotional highs, achievements and disappointments. From these, and their own in-depth knowledge of New Zealand imagery, the Story Inc boys – Steve La Hood, James McLean and Dean Cato – created a 12-minute show set in a junk shop that came alive after hours. Unlike the rest of the exhibitions, it was designed to have emotional appeal. *Golden Days* was incredibly successful. Despite its limited seating and scheduled performance regime, 25 percent of all visitors decreed it to be one of the highlights of a Te Papa visit.

*

Our isolation, in two downtown buildings cut off from the old museum and art gallery, helped us to plan for the new, which included building an experience that attracted people who would not normally be drawn to a museum. This did challenge some. Part way through a presentation on audience segments to a board member I was interrupted by a booming voice: 'You're not bringing in the riff-raff, are you, Ken?' Taken aback, I did not know what to say because, yes, part of the drive was to make this a place for even the riff-raff, however they were defined. Then there was the constant pressure from the board to protect art from any form of change.

But at the same time I was borne along by an in-house bunch of trusted achievers. It was generally acknowledged that I had my uses, but when necessary should be saved from myself. Raewyn Smith-Kapa and Sean Sweeney would corral me as required, using dry wit and direct language.

'Ken, you will not be part of the workshop that allocates money across the different exhibitions!'

'Aw, that's my job,' I whined.

'Ken! You'll be too partisan!'

They were right, of course. As a matter of philosophy, I held that Te Papa would be something special if the high-adrenalin and emotion-rich experiences were properly funded, and would have stripped the budgets of the lower-energy exhibitions, thereby causing great angst among those teams.

'We are very aware of what you want and we'll take that into the workshop.'

And how I valued Elaine Heumann Gurian, who joined the team as our fresh pair of eyes on everything. We had first met in 1975 at the Boston Children's Museum and she came to mind when we needed a knowledgeable person to review our work. Elaine and I had similar views on what a great cultural institution should be and enjoyed working together. We tramped through Abel Tasman National Park, Susan and I, Elaine and her husband Dean. I accused Elaine of being the museum profession's archetypal Jewish grandmother. She laughed at my jokes.

On numerous occasions I would pick her up at Wellington airport and, no matter how long and arduous her flight, we would start work immediately. She was tough but always civil when reviewing, checking, suggesting, ordering, inspiring. Late in the piece she would smooth disturbed managerial waters.

*

One evening in 1996 we had a party celebrating the closing of the project office. We acted up, had photos taken, ate, drank. Elaine sent a taped message. So why did it feel like a wake? The next day we would all move to posh quarters in the completed, but yet to be opened, waterfront building. We mourned our characterless warehouse, the ideal place to hatch revolution. The protection of isolation would soon be no more, although even in our new quarters my division would still be a long hike, over 100 metres and one building level, from the senior management enclave.

As we settled to our partying I suspected that few believed I would survive the shift. Perhaps this final farewell served a dual function. Goodbye to the old place, and to me. These sombre thoughts were based on my relationship with the Te Papa CEO.

In 1992 a new act of Parliament formally established Te Papa, and Cheryll Sotheran was appointed CEO. It fell to her to create the organisation. To do this she would have to take a new governance group along on an adventurous ride, and that would prove difficult. The Te Papa Board had some bright stars but also included a number who carried very traditional views of what a museum could be and, in their heart of hearts, denied the demand to explore the nature of negotiated sovereignty in our nation. Our new leader showed great courage as she battled domineering characters who, in their own minds at least, were born to command and who had great difficulty with any discussion that seemed to be about surrender of power. In what I regard as her greatest achievement, Cheryll won out.

She, and Cliff Whiting, formulated an important step towards the idea of biculturalism in action: she would be the CEO in the formal administrative sense of relationships with government and broad public, while Cliff would be the kaihautū, the CEO before Māori and iwi. Another of her achievements was ridding Te Papa of the idea that the museum would be a loose federation of subject-area fiefdoms, each with its own director. That would have been most debilitating, a structure good only for encouraging dispute. No, we would be a single integrated organisation, an expression of a cohesive nation.

Cheryll appointed me to be in charge of the visitor experience. In the first couple of years of her regime, my work circumstances changed little. To start with, it was a matter of geography. Whereas chairman Bill Rowling had worked out of the downtown project office, under Cheryll the administrative centre shifted to the old museum on the hill. I would go this short distance to attend meetings and report on progress. She would listen but so often her mind was elsewhere, preoccupied with myriad governance issues. Her response was always the same: 'Just keep going with those exhibitions. I have other things concerning me at present.'

We heard about these concerns at gatherings of the management team. To begin with this was to be expected. Cheryll's relationship with the Te Papa board was obviously close to dysfunctional and we felt for her. But progress was being made. Take the issue of raising money. The government challenged Te Papa to raise much of its own budget and they set a limit on their subsidy. Cheryll's response was to bring in a strong commercial leader, John Field. We would earn at least some part of our keep through shops, food outlets, parking, provision for conferences and other events. Money would be required to invest in new facilities. I am deeply ashamed at my first response in a meeting when I protected my budgetary patch like a kid lying across his corner of the sandpit. Soon I was thinking otherwise as John demonstrated how commercial activity was a necessary part of delivering services to visitors and further humanising the museum, demonstrating to a broad public that we were of their world, commercial interactions and all.

Perhaps I redeemed myself a little with the Espresso saga. There was a space on Level 4, narrow and hanging between cavernous Core and tall foyer, which was designated for an integrating exhibition between Māori and later settler zones. Cliff and I had struggled with this but it was not a comfortable place for an exhibition. Moreover, it was strategically placed for another public Te Papa service, food and drink. Taking matters into my own hands, I decreed that before cladding went on the critical pillar we should run all necessary plumbing for a future kitchen. Furthermore, the work would be paid for from the exhibitions budget. When John Field arrived at the museum he was overjoyed to find such a money spinner waiting to be fitted out. Every time I see Espresso buzzing with people amid the exhibits I think, again, that this is a great humanising space.

In one area a fundamental difference in thinking began to emerge between me and my management team colleagues. I saw no objection to charging entry to Te Papa, especially for international visitors. Through my exposure to the leisure industry, I knew that charging would greatly increase earnings and would not prove a barrier to entry. It was also the ultimate test of whether people considered the experience worthy of their hard-earned cash. We would learn very quickly indeed, I explained to my colleagues, whether we measured up. My position was just too radical. I got nowhere.

In the right environment any team of broad-ranging talents can have a discussion and reach an understanding without becoming disputatious. But it was becoming clear that this was not possible as the Monday morning meetings became lengthy and tiresome tirades.

My natural response was to try to lift the mood with a bit of humour. Cheryll announced a committee to organise the visit of Queen Elizabeth II to Te Papa. I was on it. Perhaps not a good move – a republican in such a position. Immediately, I suggested that an appropriate gift would be to continue the long Māori tradition of using dog skins to form very fine cloaks, symbols of chiefly status. We would make this gift particularly relevant to Her Majesty by sourcing the pelts from among the best and healthiest Corgis available to us. My membership of the committee was quietly discontinued and the Queen saw the still-under-construction Te Papa without me.

On another occasion, totally unexpected, Cheryll and I laughed together. I had a decision that needed Cheryll's approval. In the face of an uncertain reception I planned carefully. Scowling behind her desk, she agreed. Still agitated, I swept up my jacket and tried, repeatedly, to put on her similar dark coat. It was too good a moment not to acknowledge the absurdity.

But these moments of levity were rare. Initially, her attention was focused on her relationship with the board, but then it became apparent that Cheryll had set her sights on one of our colleagues. Apparently she required enemies, created if they did not exist, to do battle with. Good people bursting to contribute became sacrificial victims, scared, their spirits cowed by focused ridicule and abusive language. In some cases they were subjected to messy and painful dismissal. An intelligent woman was first to go, then that guy, followed by him, then another poor chap was looking ill at management meetings. Some of the current targets dragged their way to my work area. I could only express sympathy, offer condolences and advise getting a lawyer pronto. They would go away, head bent forward, shoulders down. I knew that it was only a matter of time before I would become the focus of Cheryll's rage.

Much of my life became protecting my staff and the progress we were making, which was threatened by Cheryll's niggling and shouted demands. We were deep into the exhibition development, with its complex set of concepts and designs and text and contracts. To break the interdependence and continuity of any of these was to imperil a successful opening.

Cliff resisted. He had position, mana and deep knowledge and could deny Cheryll her ultimatums. 'I will do this my way,' he once stated quietly, with a stony face.

After one unpleasant session I marched into the human resources office. It was almost as if they were expecting me. Staff turnover was alarming, with some losing appetite for fractious encounters and others forced out. HR seemed to have a full-time job dealing with such situations.

'I've had enough. It's time to go.'

'You can't do that,' Mark Fell, an HR manager, told me. 'You're the glue that holds this place together.' I doubt he was right but it was nice of him to say so.

Finally, Cheryll had to acknowledge that a dysfunctional relationship with the key driver of the visitor experience project was dangerous at such a critical time. She agreed to the HR recommendation that I report through the highly experienced and unflappable Graeme Shadwell. This allowed me to get on with the job, although her interference was never far away.

Part of the problem, perhaps, was that I carried with me too much early Te Papa project history, having been involved for at least eight years before my colleagues. A paper came before the management team, a first shot at a bicultural policy for an operating institution. It accepted the founding status of the Treaty of Waitangi but beyond that was seriously flawed because its whole premise relied on 'two distinct cultures': biculturalism was equated to the relationship between Māori and Pākehā. To be part of Te Papa you had to join one or the other. The treaty as a founding negotiation between Māori and government about sovereignty, was lost. I responded with my own paper, which suggested, first, that biculturalism was a 'constitutional' negotiation that involved the museum as a Crown agency at many levels – 'definition of relationships, establishment of rights, and redress of rights violated'. But I then went on to talk of New Zealand as a pluralistic society. It was just too authoritarian to demand that New Zealanders from India or the Pacific Islands or anywhere else must become Pākehā just to be part of Our Place. By right all people were part of Te Papa; this was something at which Ngā Kaiwawao had worked so hard. 'Let us,' I said, 'parallel the bicultural policy with a broad but operational cultural policy that is inclusive and finds a place for all cultures and visitors'.

My intervention was greeted with a very long silence. Some time later, after Te Papa had opened, I was summoned to a meeting with Cheryll and a couple of others and accused of being insufficiently bicultural, and too multicultural. I defended myself vigorously, drawing on my knowledge of the Treaty of Waitangi debate and the museum's founding principles. Finally, one of the participants made the mistake of claiming that Māori were incapable of making racist comments. I could instance a notable comment from a Māori redolent with insult and rejection and based on nothing more than race. I offered to show my prosecutors the record in the minutes. The meeting folded and we retired to our respective corners. It was becoming clear to me that I must find a future elsewhere.

Cheryll Sotheran was a highly intelligent and courageous woman, who must be honoured for those things she did achieve. But she was a complex character, with her own demons, and she bred a sour and even cruel human environment. After the opening this became evident in the film *Getting to Te Papa*, which positioned her as the leader fighting malignant and incompetent bureaucracy. I saw it another way. The film, which included the board chairman, was very like those films from my management training days where John Cleese would cause endless problems for the organisation, consuming time and resources by stupid, disruptive behaviour. The people cast as obstructive in *Getting to Te Papa* were our political leaders and support organisations. Certainly, they had to be guided, and at times told a thing or two, all in the name of being part of the winning team and sharing the successes. But, for heaven's sake, negotiate, never malign.

Like others, I saw and experienced the almost daily meltdowns, the uncontrolled, senseless anger. Cheryll was dubbed 'Chernobyl' for good reason. When I survived until the opening and beyond, I could thank the gods, whom I deemed not to exist, for offering me a fortuitous 'escape' to the far side of the world.

CHAPTER 6

OPENING DAY

'IT TOUCHES MY EXPERIENCE,' said one of the first visitors to camera. I wanted to hug her. Crowds had gathered early that morning, 14 February 1998, first to watch the ocean-going canoe *Te Aurere* approach the museum and then to join a long snaking queue defined by hay bales. There were thousands of them, visitors and bales. It was a time of informal pomp, with our America's Cup yachtsman hero Sir Peter Blake, accompanied by Cliff's grandson Tama, and Sean Sweeney's daughter Grace, leading the way. The crowds kept coming. Around 40 exhibition project people patrolled the floors, ready to pounce should something go wrong. As the day wore on and it became apparent that all was well, I told my team they could go, but none did. They just joined the crowds. Finally, around midnight, I went home and slept.

In the first year over two million people came to Te Papa. We were stunned. The numbers exceeded even our most outrageous imaginings, for we had firmly in our minds a research company's commissioned assessment that projected a best-case scenario of 723,000 visitors in that period.

Among those visitors were some pleasant surprises. Māori people came to Te Papa in large numbers as whānau, hapū and iwi groups, or, like the rest, as couples and with friends. They owned and made demands of Te Papa. Cliff had delivered for his people. Surprise became disbelief when we observed bikies clustered in worship before the speed goddess that was the motorcycle John Britten had built in his garage. It was a rare gathering. Jeans and leathers were joined by a fair sprinkling of suits to have serious conversations with much intelligent pointing and chin-scratching. They were of a similar age, their mid-life crises averted by their love affair with Harley Davidson. But this bike was not out of the United States. It was our own, a beauteous, sculptural object. Project manager Bronwyn Simes wrote a poem about boys 'wound so tightly around the bike; they were almost licking the tires'. People who were not committed museum goers crossed the threshold, kids ran, young adults queued for *Time Warp*, the place buzzed, people had fun. We were well pleased.

*

We came to realise that Te Papa was one of the world's great identity museums. It was a term we had used within the project office, but tentatively. Typically, an ethnic or origin group, such as Irish Americans or a part of the Jewish tribe, might present in their museum a coherent, yet inward-looking, way that drew them together in the face of their sometimes threatening neighbours; most likely the approach would be commemorative. But with Te Papa, identity was defined not just by shared behaviour and collective memory but also by conversations among ordinary people with differing personal and family histories. Yet somehow we could work our way through disagreement.

For example, in my Waikato Museum days, Campbell Smith had brought playwright Mervyn Thompson and musician William Dart to Hamilton. A small group of us watched as their new musical, *Songs to the Judges*, was workshopped. Mervyn, the judge, sat high and mighty on one of our collection items, the old mayoral chair. William played away on an old upright piano. The company acted out a sorry history of injustices, violent suppression, confiscation, peaceful and not-so-peaceful protest. At each step along the way they would talk and make refinements. Then came the final number, a song of redemption.

This is bigger than both of us
I think you'll agree.
This is bigger than both of us
Pākehā and Māori.

In the face of civil unrest, when treaty negotiations were marked by dispute and newspaper headlines shouted forth demands made and rebuffed, this was a message of hope.

The players hesitated and stopped.

'Too soon,' said one.

All, including Mervyn, seemed to agree and eventually the song was dropped. That discussion was a negotiation; two groups of many ancestries and aspirations said this message of hope was not wrong, but also not right. We had work to do yet. Perhaps later but not now.

Similarly, at Te Papa exchanges across tables, new research, the process of forming stories, selecting this and discarding that, saw the birth of measured exhibition concepts. As the treaty negotiation process moved forward, the exhibition zones would be formed as cultural poles: *Mana Whenua* on one side, *Passports*/Pasifika/arts on the other side and *Treaty of Waitangi* as separation. Yet the visitors could handle this, for at the same time ours was a bubbling, even optimistic, vision of New Zealand as Our Place.

*

Christine Fitzgerald and Neil Anderson probed away, asking questions of our visitors. What came back was not just attendance figures. The other indicators that gauge the performance of a museum were also very high: duration of stay, satisfaction, affirmation, visitor profile, specialist and new audiences achieved, return visits, involvement of young people (who may have come with school groups but returned of their own volition), social interactions, spend per head, name and brand recognition, and so forth.

It was soon evident that the stand-outs were Geoff Hicks's two natural environment shows and Cliff's *Mana Whenua*. These were followed by Ian Wedde's review of art broadly defined in a New Zealand context, the animated object theatre *Golden Days*, Jock Phillips' history/culture exhibitions, the marae and the outdoor *Bush City*.

There were criticisms. It is a sign of a healthy cultural institution that it generates and can respond to critical analysis. Also, size matters. By the time we were finished the cost of buildings and the exhibitions was over NZ$300 million. The New Zealand public had taken Te Papa to their hearts. But the surprise was the lack of in-depth criticism that I felt was thoughtful. Beyond news reports, there was little of the deep observation that Te Papa deserved. This was a national cultural statement at an important point in our nation's history, yet there was little penetrating criticism.

Except from those self-appointed spokespeople at the threshold of art. 'It's so successful – I hate it!' an ex-National Art Gallery board member admitted as the noisy crowds milled about that opening day. She and others found Te Papa wanting, despite the fact that there was actually more space devoted to art, many more works on display than there had ever been, and crowds unheard of at the old National Art Gallery. So, what was their complaint? I suspect that a significant number of the arts audience mourned the loss of the *idea* of a national art gallery. It was not that the old gallery had been of much worth. It was badly positioned and underutilised to the point of being a national cultural embarrassment. But any thoughts of a replacement had now disappeared with the huge investment that was Te Papa.

Then came the problem of juxtaposition. Te Papa offered an 'art' space but within 10,000 square metres of diverse offerings. In this place art did not reign supreme; it was one of a number of choices visitors could make. Despite the increased area available to the arts, the perception was that the gallery had been downsized. For some it seemed to be an afterthought.

Then there was the saga of the painting and the refrigerator. Art concept leader Ian Wedde had placed a canvas by New Zealand artist Colin McCahon near a refrigerator. He was making a valid point about creative sensibility at a particular point in time. But for some this association was an act of cultural vandalism that sullied the sacred object, the painting. Even Prime Minister Helen Clark willingly joined the criticism. Although her stance was welcomed in art circles, it was an ill-judged intervention.

But perhaps more than anything, Te Papa challenged the norm. The 'riff-raff' was welcome. Market research had indicated what might make Te Papa available to 'All New Zealanders' and we had worked hard to achieve that. It was a place of engagement, even fun. There were indications that it would become a place of pilgrimage, not of the quiet and reverent kind but more akin to the bawdiness of the Canterbury Tales. I could not help but conclude that the offence was the democracy of Our Place and the fact that there was no significant art portal, beyond which language, behaviour and even dress would allow at least some in the arts community to feel assured and comfortable in their artistic authority.

I stored away all this experience and the overwhelmingly positive response of visitors. I knew that I would soon leave Te Papa, probably moving back into a consultancy role, perhaps a job in Australia. But my next challenge was in fact a Jewish museum in Berlin.

CHAPTER 7

WHAT'S THE BOY FROM MAUNGATAUTARI DOING HERE?

THIS IS MY SECOND TRIP TO BERLIN IN FOUR WEEKS. The car awaits me at Tegel Airport. For the short ride to Gendarmenmarkt I choose to sit in front. Obviously I am not a frequent user of limousines.

The hotel had been the best the old communist East Germany, the Deutsche Demokratische Republik, the DDR, could offer. But now its socialist paradise modernism sits awkwardly in the city's most elegant square. By 4am I am awake and, despite the cold, venture out. The light of shopfronts, floodlit historic façades and street lamps spills into the damp air. I am humming 'Lili Marlene'. Half a century ago my teacher father ran evening film showings for parents and I saw the movies during after-school previews. Some were leftover war propaganda, about plucky Cockney firemen, toiling workers and happy Londoners – about the story of this song. These memories give comfort, a distraction from thoughts of the next day.

A few hours later I wait in the lobby for Mike, Werner Michael Blumenthal. Three cars drive aggressively into the covered entry. The huge door, which could accommodate small crowds, rotates. The first person through is not Mike but a wiry character who immediately brings to mind the feisty little detective from *Hill Street Blues.* He is stubble-faced and wears a beanie, but his sharp movement marks him out as a person trained to search for threats and act decisively if necessary. He moves straight to the centre of the floor, eyes scanning the far reaches of the lobby. Hotel guests pull back. Two further characters from the same TV series push through and fan out.

Only then does Mike stride forward, in long black cashmere coat and black homburg. He shakes my hand and welcomes me back. Now, from the back seat of a large black Mercedes, I observe a choreography of cars. One pulls into the centre of the road, bringing traffic to a halt. The second manoeuvres to the front with the Mercedes behind. The other car releases the traffic and falls in behind, tail-end Charlie. There are sirens as we pull away but now they are switched off to leave just flashing lights. Our motorcade weaves through the traffic at dangerous speed.

Settled into the car's plush leather seats, we talk. At least Mike talks, a great deal. He moves through his agenda for the week. Distracted, I take on board only that he wants me to decide where to locate the project office. Perhaps it sticks because that seems so minor. The project will succeed because the vision and culture are right but he is talking about space for the workers.

The cars speed through the Berlin streets. John le Carré would never be guilty of such a cliché but it is mental pictures of Cold War spy novels that play in my mind. I am in Berlin, place of mythologies learnt from childhood, and next to me sits a man in a black homburg who is under diplomatic protection.

'We'll need to close that contract.'

I surface again. Half of me believes we are still at an early discussion stage. Then again, I have a draft contract in my pocket, carefully worked out with the involvement of one of those firms that research economic and legal conditions in other countries. Later this week Mike will see it. 'That's not chickenshit, Ken!' he will observe.

Then, on the edge of a huge decision that will have me throw in my lot with this man, this city and the Jewish Museum Berlin, I ask myself, 'What's the boy from Maungatautari doing here?'

Despite my unease, there was good reason for my presence: I had achieved significant success in the museum world. But this new challenge was in Berlin, not New Zealand. I did not speak German. This was a Jewish museum and I was not a Jew. The culture and history were different. The project's timeframe seemed impossibly short. The existing staff was small and inexperienced. The budget was shaky. Beyond some worthy platitudes, the museum's identity had not been thought through. Those technical challenges I could face. But my biggest problem was in the mind. I was a Kiwi, far from home, planning to command a national project in one of the world's great centres of intellectual power and cultural tradition. Was I up to it?

*

It had all started six weeks earlier, in the New Zealand spring, with two phone calls that followed each other in quick succession. I was at my Te Papa desk when Elaine Heumann Gurian rang; such a delightful surprise to hear that familiar crackly drawl.

'He's a big guy.' She mentioned his name. I had never heard of him. Elaine listed the big guy's achievements. 'He'll phone you shortly. He wants you as part of a review I'll be chairing. The Germans have asked him to run the Jewish

Museum in Berlin. Shaike was doing the exhibition concept but he's collapsed and is in hospital.'

Shaike Weinberg was known throughout the museum world for the United States Holocaust Memorial Museum in Washington and for the pioneering Museum of the Diaspora in Tel Aviv. This was the first I had heard of him being associated with this new Jewish museum.

As Elaine talked my mind went to a conference a few months before. I was sitting with Nigel Cox, the head writer at Te Papa. An architectural academic was taking us through her visit to the newly completed building for the Jewish Museum Berlin. It was annoying, not because of the material but because she had no sense of time. I was on next and could see my presentation being reduced to a few minutes of hurried summary. It was also confusing, since Daniel Libeskind's building was like nothing we had seen before. It was a sculptural statement so strongly symbolic that it could surely never function as a museum.

Nigel leant across. 'Pity the poor bugger who has to put exhibitions into that space!' he muttered.

So I had some prior knowledge when, a few minutes after talking with Elaine, I answered the big guy's call.

'You don't know me. My name's Mike Blumenthal.'

The voice had that authoritative quality perfected by those who have honed their skills in the diplomatic arena. Unmistakably American, it was a pleasure to listen to. He briefly outlined his background and current task.

'The German government has asked me to sort out this museum and I need a review of where we're at. Elaine Gurian was deputy to Shaike Weinberg at the Holocaust Museum and she's the obvious person to run it. Shaike's in a bad way. You know that?'

Yes, I assured Mike. I did not say I had known for 10 minutes.

'I'd like you to join us. I'll have my assistant in Berlin, Margarete Sabeck, get in touch to make arrangements. She speaks English.'

Indeed, Margarete spoke excellent English, but Mike was one who guarded his adjectives.

I immediately telephoned Susan. 'I'm going to Berlin. I've just been talking to the former secretary to the treasury under Jimmy Carter.'

I had caught Susan at her desk in the Alexander Turnbull Library, where she worked for a trust set up to establish an archive of political cartoons. Because the trust received limited financial support, a large part of her work involved generating revenue through touring exhibitions, sponsorship and other activities. At this she was extraordinarily successful. I admired Susan's entrepreneurial spirit and perseverance, given that the commercial demands to keep the organisation afloat were out of kilter with the civil service culture that surrounded her.

Over the next few weeks I learnt more about the task and more about Michael Blumenthal. Among the review materials that arrived on my desk was his recently published book, *The Invisible Wall*, a family history that managed to both affirm his relationship with Germany and describe the schism that existed between him and his country of birth. He was the young refugee whose family was forced from Germany by the Nazis but who had become highly successful in business and politics in the States. His native country had now turned to him to grapple with the problem of what sort of museum should occupy Daniel Libeskind's newly completed and highly acclaimed building. The debate mirrored the state of modern Germany but finally it was agreed that this would be a museum of the history of the German Jews. Shaike Weinberg was to create the exhibitions but on his last visit he had been found unconscious in his hotel room. It was a heart condition that would prove fatal.

*

In October 1999 the review team met in Berlin. We came with different cultural perspectives but were united by the belief that museums could achieve fundamental improvements in the attitudes and behaviour of individuals and communities. I had worked with Jim Volkert before. A designer and project director of rare talent, he was currently leading the new National Museum of the American Indian project in Washington. At one time I tried to convince him to come to New Zealand to join the Te Papa project office, but he had challenges enough to fill his life, after which he went back to being an artist.

This was the first time I met Dr Martin Roth, an anthropologist who had made a name for himself transforming the old East German Deutsches Hygiene-Museum, devoted to medical history, with a series of controversial exhibitions, one of which confronted the Nazi doctrine of racial purity. By now he was in charge of the exhibitions for Expo 2000 in Hanover, and after the review would become director of the state art collections in Dresden. As I took over the Jewish Museum Berlin, I sought his help as my contact with the German museum profession. Martin has a habit of making news in the cultural world. One evening, years later, Susan was reading a commentary by contemporary East German writer Christa Wolf that referred to a conversation with a person identified only by his initials. 'That just has to be Martin,' she exclaimed. After five years as director of the Victoria and Albert Museum in London, and disillusioned at Britain's ill-considered decision to leave the European Union, he quit the V&A and England. Not long after, he died of cancer.

Our meeting did not go as any of us had expected.

*

I have three photos, perhaps the only visual record of that week of intensive assessment. Certainly, they were in demand some years later to illustrate Mike's eightieth birthday Festschrift. Each shutter click captured an important theme.

In the first photo, five of the staff cluster around a section of a large gallery model and entreat Elaine to consider the quality of their exhibition proposal. She is less than convinced. She leans away from them, head tilted down and eyebrows raised as if to say, 'I can't believe you.'

With some hesitation, and body language that spoke of fear and embarrassment, the staff had announced that only one exhibition had been developed to show the panel, not the number promised. We then moved out into the galleries to stand around the prize exhibit, a large zigzagging model that mirrored the shape of Daniel Libeskind's building. It was raised high for better viewing, but small people like Elaine and me had to peer over the top in comical fashion. The one exhibit on show covered the era-defining year of revolution, 1848, and sat lonely in little more than a metre of the model's considerable length.

'This exhibition is pretty flat.' I held back. It was a clutter of cases containing minor objects and text, a throwback to a former exhibition era: static, serried, didactic and joyless. There were many other words waiting to be used – traditional, uninspiring, boring – but this was not yet the time to be totally honest. Instead I asked, 'How do you plan to enliven it?'

'We will throw a light through a slowly turning wheel and this will cast a moving shadow on the wall. To denote industrialisation.'

The rest of the model was blank. Had we really been brought to Berlin from all corners of the world to review one exhibition? A genuine demonstration of progress would have been eight or 10 exhibitions, perhaps more.

In many ways the model said it all. An empty model in an empty gallery. Instead of emphatic confidence and future potential, it spoke only of a lack of achievement and vision. In what soon became a recurring motif throughout the review, failure was signalled as the most likely result. That first morning we suspected that most energy had gone not into exhibitions but into building the model.

We were in for a further surprise when it emerged that the Holocaust would not be covered. Although there is a danger in seeing the Holocaust as the culmination of all German and European Jewish history, it is the most potent marker of what can happen when hate rhetoric becomes action and when indifferent former neighbours allow a people to be denigrated as lesser beings and then murdered. To the reviewers, it seemed inconceivable that the Holocaust should not to be part of the Jewish Museum Berlin story.

We had some warning of all this the evening before. Elaine, Jim and I, and a few of the staff, met informally over drinks at our hotel. The conversation was disquieting. With pervading panic, the museum project was described as a trap, a floundering monster, almost an impossibility. Shaike would visit Berlin and progress seemed to be made but then everything would regress. There was no continuity; catastrophe seemed certain. Mired in inaction and the shame that makes all things Jewish difficult to confront in Germany, the Jewish Museum Berlin was failing. I still have a note that records 'a fatal malaise'.

Part way through the first morning of the review Elaine called a halt. 'Enough! I think we should talk about this.'

The panel gathered in the boardroom. I was drawn to a window. Not just any window; this was a Libeskind statement of eccentric shape, although, unlike so many others, this one was positioned to be looked through. Immediately outside were the heroic figures that topped the neighbouring 1737 Kollegienhaus, and beyond, the traffic on Lindenstrasse. This ordinary Berlin view of survivor buildings, the gaps, the untidy infills, the ubiquitous graffiti and the skyline of the modern city beyond had yet to mature in my mind into a coherent landscape. Later I would go to that window with ever-increasing knowledge of how this urban cluster had been formed: by people's aspirations, the driving development of the city, the bombing, and then all-out assault. For the Russian army had ground through this very piece of territory in late April and early May 1945. People had died violently as artillery shells destroyed apartment blocks that inhibited the advance on the Reichstag at the heart of Berlin. The rubble was cleared to leave open space. Now, 55 years on, this section of emptied land found new life as the location for Libeskind's Jewish Museum Berlin.

But today other things were on the agenda. One by one we expressed our doubts. The museum was not going to achieve the planned opening date. Even if the staff could accomplish something partial, it was inconceivable that such an important cultural initiative should open as a series of stutters and with an incomplete visitor experience. We could not disappoint. The German-Jewish story, and the building, already an architectural masterwork, deserved better.

For the first time I took Mike through developing an organisation.

'A great museum is more than just academically sound exhibitions. Of course, they're critical, but our visitors need to be offered an engrossing, welcoming, safe and comfortable place. Mike, for your museum to work those exhibitions have to be part of an integrated whole, a marketable intellectual and emotional experience that operates perfectly and that exceeds expectations.'

I was speaking to a chief executive out of the commercial world and used managerial language.

'There seems to be no sense of overarching purpose. The one exhibition we've just seen fails as a visitor experience. There is no museum culture and no thought is being given to an operation that will make it a pleasure to visit, a place so good that visitors will have difficulty tearing themselves away. None of this comes automatically. It has to be planned. I see no evidence of such planning.'

Mike looked perplexed, then sulky. In his mind he had the building and now all he needed were exhibitions. What was the Kiwi talking about? One thing we could all agree on was that there was nothing to be gained from further review. Instead we would shift into project mode, offering the staff at least a glimpse of how they might achieve a successful opening.

*

The review has reconvened. I take the second photo. Jim Volkert has stepped forward and stands at the wall of the review venue, one of the galleries in the Libeskind building. An arrow-shaft window points at him. Another lunges towards the 20 or so participants. The architecture demands that everyone pay attention. Collegial empathy has become the order of the day. Elaine, Jim and I have built careers creating and fixing museums. We are no longer imported examiners; instead we are part of the staff.

Jim waves an arm toward sheets of paper full of drawings and text.

'Pull back,' he says. 'Look at the whole museum space. What does it suggest and allow us to do? The individual exhibitions can only be placed on the floor when we have a set of larger intellectual and planning structures in place. Think of how the story will be told and how this bizarre architectural environment will influence the telling.' Jim is a master in these matters.

The discussion became lively, talking of the physical track, a clearly differentiated pathway that visitors would feel confident about. I still have a plan of the Libeskind building through which, as Jim was talking, I had drawn a bold circulation route that responded to the jagged turns and edges of the building. My doodling also began to recognise places where the power of the building was visually strong and some form of special treatment seemed to be required; I marked these with swirls. We would come to call these Libeskind moments.

Every other museum I had dealt with had either traditional galleries of rectangular shape or, as in Te Papa, vast open volumes in which we could build what we wanted. But the long string of twisting spaces that made Libeskind's building was quite different. It was unrelentingly linear. Such a layout seems good, so logical. It gives direction to visitors as they move from the first experience to the second and then on to the third, and so on. But visitors also like to make their own decisions about what to see and where to go next. This creates a real quandary for the experience developer. If contained and herded, visitors can rebel; if the exhibitions are too unstructured they will lose their way. In both cases they might defect, the official term for giving up and leaving in bad humour. How to achieve that balance?

I kept on plugging away with that most important of all questions: 'How about the fundamental purpose?'

'Why should visitors come to the Jewish Museum Berlin? What will they take from their visit? Why should the government fund us? What is the sense of purpose that guides the stories you tell? Can you write it down? Have you ever tried?'

The answers were too drawn-out. The small Jewish Museum Berlin staff had the idea that visitors would read through a logical chronology of facts, supported by relevant objects. Somehow, they would learn and be better informed. The museum was to be little more than a textbook. A guiding statement did not exist, and without such a test of purpose staff could become bogged down in the minutiae of history and give no thought to the visitors.

'But,' we explained, 'quantities of data aren't the same as having people in the contemporary world – each with a personal background of concerns and relationships – make some sense of this monumental saga and its most terrible chapter.'

The young staff had been born into a Germany marked by a ubiquitous sense of always being blamed by history. Perhaps the focus on the minutiae was a form of avoidance. Then again, they always showed courage and honesty. But a purpose that would allow the museum to contribute to creating something better was not part of their thinking.

This was my area. To lighten the mood, very necessary after that morning's debacle, I talked about a bright future and the need for inspired thinking. We would start with small ideas and steadily build a picture of a museum that everyone, in their heart of hearts, knew to be good. But a persistent and worried intervention confirmed that the personal concerns of old would be hard to set aside. It was a small group that sat around the review table, yet power was a dominating issue. One person stated the case: 'We need to be certain of our position in the organisation. We can only work within staff groups that are ordered and managed according to the defined roles that recognise our special skills and career paths.'

It was best that I should lead on this. A new sheet of paper went up on the wall and I began to draft a fluid structure that would enable people to be moved quickly across the whole museum to make progress and resolve issues. Power was not a term we would use from now on. Our whole ethos would be about creative interactions. I used the buzzwords. We would all lead with our particular skills and the structure I was drafting would enable that to happen.

I sensed that this was important. Normally a scribbler, I drafted my diagram of a matrix approach with great care. It would probably have a life in the days following the workshop. I was not sure just how much was being absorbed or understood, though Mike got it. He was suddenly at my shoulder, examining my prize exhibit.

'My God! It's just like a business,' he muttered.

Did he mean, 'Yes, I know the business world so let's get on and do it!'

Or was he saying, 'I realise now that even a cultural enterprise needs to be run on a business-like basis using the systems and best management practice of the commercial world'?

My strong impression was the latter: surprise that the discipline of business should be applied to a museum. There was something unguarded and spontaneous in his voice, not the usual brusque insistence that we move forward.

This was not a long session but in some ways it was the most important hour of the whole October 1999 review. I had been forewarned that some of the staff were driven by personal power. Later Mike and I would discuss this at length. He liked to explain such attitudes as 'a German thing', but I thought of them in more universal terms: as the default condition of a rule-bound museum, resistant to change, slow to react and difficult to circumvent. Fortunately, in the coming months Mike proved to be an ally in helping to disassemble these internal obstructions. Also, I would come to value the freedom he gave me by using his knowledge and prestige to work through and around the convoluted bulk of the German civil service.

But, most importantly, Mike was now a potential partner, one who would not just accept but demand a systematic and well-organised approach.

*

The gathering in the third photograph looks small beneath one of the most dramatic of all the Libeskind moments, an array of windows incised, like wounds, across the gallery wall. The whole is Libeskind: walls, windows, ceilings, floors, the narrowness, the intersecting blackness of the Void, the light falling across ceiling, and even the sound of the space. This is the spatial wreathed in symbol.

There was an audible gasp from those of us new to the building as the steep ascent of the main stairway opened after the claustrophobia of the underground Axes. Overhung by skewed beams in the tall, narrow volume, it was relentless, one long climb out of a bunker to light. The galleries were unlike anything we had seen before, a weaving zigzag. Windows were like exploded shards in the act of falling to the ground after frenzied attack. The blackened line of the concrete Voids sliced straight across the building, their emptiness representing a culture evicted from European society.

We get it; we get it!

One of our most important tasks became to review how a 2000-year history might be accommodated in a building that spoke, and speaks still, the language of the few short years of the Holocaust.

At Elaine's insistence we did a tour of the building complex 'from the perspective of the visitor'. That meant that we should begin in the baroque Kollegienhaus. The Berlin City Museum had occupied this old government administrative building. Now the idea of a museum of Jewish history was taking over and steadily forcing this small city museum out. Part of Libeskind's concept was that his extension building should offer no obvious place of entry.

Search in vain, visitor! My building's anonymous façade repels any approach.

Rather, the main public entry was through the large wooden doors of the Kollegienhaus, grand and in the best traditions of the early eighteenth century. But beyond those doors the problems began and we scribbled pages of stern notes. The arrival and ticketing sequence was a confused jumble. There was no sense of welcome and direction. An imposing interior was reduced to just plain mean. This would never work; the whole area would have to be rebuilt. Little thought had gone into the upper level of galleries in the Kollegienhaus and how these could be public spaces. The offset of lift and stairs meant that the accessways to the main public galleries delivered visitors to different places. Those galleries: dramatic but also eccentric in shape, almost corridor-like. We listed problem upon problem of function and operation for future consideration.

'If only this building had been constructed with function in mind we wouldn't have all these issues to resolve.' That was the common response that we all stated at this first meeting of professional museologists. But I was to change my mind, and it did not take long. Everything about this place evoked shock, tension, even horror at the attempt to obliterate an entire people. Alongside such a strong and graphic statement of human failing, and yet at the same time of promise, the received tenets of the museum profession – white cubes (for paintings) and black boxes (for heightened dramatic context) – looked weak, very weak indeed. The Libeskind building was neither white cube nor black box. It denied easy definition. It was its own universe. I came to love that building dearly and relished my relationship with the creative genius who had conceived of something that few museum people would ever describe as a proper space for their endeavours.

*

At the end of that first intense day it might have been possible to give in to despair. Despair was not available to us. By the evening, Mike had made a decision and he moved quickly, testing out Elaine. 'Would Jim or Ken be available to drive the project?'

Her response was, 'Ask them.'

So it was that at coffee on the second morning of the review, Mike came over with an unconscious rhyming couplet. 'You'd better come to Berlin. Unless you've got a twin? I need the right person to see this museum through to opening.'

It was not really a request; that was not his style. I remembered his exclamation 'It's just like a business', and knew that I could work with this man. The timing was right: I was searching for a change. But this was a big decision and I would need time to think about it.

Word travelled quickly. That evening as we left the museum, tall handsome Stephanie Kluth and smaller Oliver Bätz bailed me up at the door. 'You *must* come to Berlin.'

A few hours later I rang Susan. It was morning in Wellington. We began to talk about a new phase in both our lives.

*

'Anyone for the opera?' We are several days into the review and Mike announces that an entertainment will be arranged for the coming evening. Berlin is home to three of the world's greatest opera companies.

Jim and I hesitate; we have found something that intrigues us and it is not opera. Our first wander from the hotel has taken us along Kurfürstendamm, that shopper's bulwark against the threat of the communist regime across the Berlin Wall. There we have discovered the Theater am Kudamm, tucked among the high-end brand shops, and on the bill is *Cabaret*.

This is awkward. Elaine is trying her best to bond the review group together, but the opportunity is too good to miss.

'Thanks Mike, but we'll give the opera a miss. Jim and I are intrigued at the prospect of seeing *Cabaret* staged in Berlin. German-style.'

I go on to explain that musicals have always been one of my great loves. I know *Cabaret* fairly well. It is in the tradition of those wonderful social commentaries that the American musical industry has done so well throughout its long history. At home I have the script and a rather tame CD. Everyone becomes enthusiastic. It is decided.

Cabaret opens with that wonderful blend of music and commentary as the Emcee, Cliff, Sally Bowles, the Kit Kat Klub girls and the other characters evoke the sexual, social and political chaos we tend to associate with Germany of the 1920s and early 1930s. I know the storyline well enough not to be troubled by my complete lack of the language, and anyway the songs are in English. But as the underlying threat of the age begins to emerge, the players bring to this particular production an intensity that we have failed to anticipate. This *Cabaret* is not only set, but played, in Germany. Night after night the actors, on a stage but just a few metres away, live out a shameful inheritance. It is of their very being: a nation lacerated by its past. This is theatre personal, raw and unequivocal. It is not some second-hand Broadway plaything.

In the final scene of the first act the players start to sing a pleasant folksy song. The first lines describe an idyll of meadow and forested landscape, complete with wandering stag. But then the song transmogrifies into a chilling vision of what tomorrow will be. The ensemble moves toward us and lines up across the stage. Faces harden. Swastika armbands appear and flash their menace. They lean out beyond the stage in the confined theatre space. The message is terribly clear. They seek a sign, a proper leader for the Fatherland. Captive in our seats, we are targets for their hurled abuse.

Sitting one row in front, and one seat along from me, is a man shrivelled with age. I judge him to be about 80 and cannot help but see him as a young adult in the war years. Line upon line hits him as a physical blow and he recoils.

There is a long, glowering pause. The lights go up, bringing relief. We retire to the foyer, leaving the old man hunched in his seat. We talk of the performance nervously, using terms like painful and courageous, perhaps as a cover for the shock of it all.

Back for the final act. I know it well. The Emcee will transition from cabaret to KZ – Konzentrationslager – uniform and face his fate as a concentration camp victim. But this German version is laden with additional symbols of terrible memory. For the Emcee there is to be no uniform. On the stage, close before us, he suffers the humiliation of being stripped naked. This reveals one of his legs encased in a metal leg brace. He is a defective Untermensch, sub-human, good only for euthanasia. Now the set is dominated by the gaping white-hot maw of an all-consuming crematorium oven. The Emcee limps into oblivion.

As we leave I glance again at the old man. He remains in his seat as others push past. Head down, he is grey and battered.

*

After a memorable week we said our farewells. There was much to ponder during the long flight home. The prospect of driving this museum project to opening was exciting, yet daunting. I had seen with my own eyes and sensed with all my being the angst that formed so much of Germany's cultural character. History so close it wounds. Memories like salt in those wounds. Was it really possible to do justice to the German-Jewish story in Berlin? Our museum would throw out a challenge to contemporary Germany. Not only would we have to open in a very short time, we would have to capture the essence of a story whose penultimate chapter was genocide. Yet that long story dealt with real people, most of whom were neither anti-Semites nor Jewish victims. Early on Mike and I would agree that we would honour where honour was due, as well as talking of the origins and pursuit of that genocide. In the German *Cabaret* there was little of the tonality that such a history demanded; it was black all through. Could this museum be something more than that?

CHAPTER 8

STORYTELLING

NOVEMBER 1999: our Mercedes, and its attendant police cars, slows and pulls into the Jewish Museum Berlin. We start work immediately with the first item on Mike's agenda. I soon surmise that a list of Things To Be Achieved on my second visit has been compiled by staff and at the top is a decision about a project office. I know that the staff will grow beyond the capability of the existing building, but hiring space is not what I would start with.

A hundred metres along Lindenstrasse is a grand old building, probably from the late nineteenth century, in which space is available. At its entrance Mike and I are joined in the gloom by a couple of staff. In its day the building would have conveyed the resilience and confidence of officialdom. But the façade of heavy, geometrically proportioned stone blocks has suffered misfortune. The arch over the main entryway has scarring that I have seen before. At the Imperial Palace in Tokyo giant wooden fortified gateways were built against the smooth-faced rock defensive walls. Under attack these burnt with intense fury, causing outsized flakes of super-heated rock to spall off. Here, too, flames have fountained from this doorway as the building behind was consumed. The arch stands but each stone has lost its geometry, as if a giant hammer has been deployed about its finished edges. For many this might be perceived as the stonemason's intent, but not so. I see the flames, feel the heat and smell burning.

The carriage-width entry through to the inner court is blackened and similarly ravaged. I point this out to Mike. He is not that interested. As a son of one of the victor nations, I have this city composed as theatre flats painted in shades of war. It is a place of bullet-marked buildings and gaps. Over the next few years this will change. Berlin is destined to become our home. The imagined soldiers and cowering civilians will fade to be largely replaced by new friends who defy the received mythologies of German character.

We enter the building and Mike picks the route, this way and that. It is almost as if he is testing his minders. They scurry ahead, only to find that our party has headed off in another direction. They check, turn and brush past, making sure that they are the first into the next room, where they search corners and alcoves.

I am not impressed with the building and say so. I require a light, open environment, and this old building with its poky rooms, thick walls and small windows will not do. Perhaps it once served well as a dispenser of decrees, policies and decisions, and a vault for the safe-keeping of files, but that era has long passed. The place has no democracy, is little more than a gloomy relic.

*

We retired to Mike's office, where I was introduced to the slow mesmerising lighting of the day's first cigar. I had missed this during the visit in October when time had been at a premium, and this ritual needed time. The leather pouch would come out of an upper pocket and a cigar would be selected, examined, clipped. The aroma would be savoured unlit, followed by the lengthy lighting process with a long, taper-like match. The best cigars are always reluctant to fire up: perhaps several tapers would be required.

Over the next few years, I would reflect upon the true nature of this smouldering log of cured leaf. For Mike, there was undoubtedly pleasure. For others, did the soporific qualities of the smoke encourage expansive thinking? It certainly had a calming effect on those reached by its fragrance. And to what extent was it an instrument of control? I noted that the cigar was lit for important gatherings, then used to conduct the pace of an interaction. As part of the right gesture it encouraged openness or closed a matter down, reducing or accelerating the flow of words.

Just once, some months and many cigars later, as the lit taper hung in the air, he paused and looked up.

'Mind if I smoke?' he asked.

That was one of the few occasions when our discussion took place in my office. To this day I associate the smoke and rich smell with Mike's office, with its windows looking out to the smooth concrete wall of the Holocaust Tower and beyond to the stark modernist apartment buildings of Mehringplatz.

The cigar lit, I started to hear this man's dreams and stories. I listened intently. Nigel Cox, the second-in-command I was to bring from New Zealand, would say, in his book *Phone Home Berlin*, that in his opinion 'Ken listens too hard when Mike Blumenthal speaks.' But listening was important. I needed to know this man's personal vision and to establish a strong relationship with someone to whom I would answer over the next few years. I also had to get up to speed on all that had gone into the idea behind the museum. And this man had been part of the history of the German Jews.

Robert Gordon, writing of that great Italian Jewish humanist Primo Levi, talks of people becoming friends by telling each other stories. Gordon sees stories as the raw material of Levi's ethical universe, fomenting his enquiry and never stalling at the merely anecdotal. If we define Levi's 'friends' as the people with whom the author makes contact through a book – or that the museum attracts as visitors – then storytelling is perhaps the most potent of all humanising forces. Museum visitor research reinforces Gordon's assertions; through storytelling, people around the world forge emotional links across the centuries and across national, ethnic and cultural boundaries.

As with Levi, Mike's stories were never mere anecdotes; in those urgent early days of planning they became an important means of gaining understanding that would allow me, as a recently imported Kiwi, to make instant calls on difficult questions.

As a young boy in Berlin, he had been Werner. In 1947, starting a new life in the States, he had decided that a name change should mark this shift and he became Michael. But the two personas were always there. Werner was the child who had seen the Nazis rise to power, as a young schoolboy made the best of disruptive and confusing changes and then escaped with his family to Shanghai. As Michael he became an American citizen, an actor in that nation's postwar rise of large corporations, taking on political and diplomatic jobs with the Kennedys during the Cold War and then with President Carter. Now the circle was joined with a return to Germany to save a floundering Jewish museum in his old home town.

Now that Mike had his project director, making progress towards opening became the primary focus, and that involved as much storytelling as decision-making. There was always the suspicion that Mike had had plenty of practice, and sometimes the same story was recycled.

'Have I ever told you this one?' Before I could answer I would hear it again. I didn't mind. Each time there was a bit more detail that brought more life to the incident than at the last telling. The stock was seemingly endless and he would haul out what best fitted the subject under discussion. On each of Mike's visits to Berlin I would take home to Susan fresh insights and anecdotes, along with the lingering smell of cigar smoke.

*

My second Berlin visit, in November 1999, was a chaotic time. I can place only a few specific happenings within those 10 days, and memories that contain food survive better than others. The minders were dismissed and Mike and I walked to a favoured restaurant, local in every sense of the word. We stepped over the owner's slumbering dog, stretched across the entry, into a warm and homely environment where most of the clientele probably came from within a kilometre circle. Perhaps it was here that I first learnt the word *gemütlich* – cosy, snug. The specialty was peasant Prussian cuisine: a large plate of boiled meat with horseradish sauce, dumplings, sauerkraut and a range of pickled vegetables. Afterwards, we walked the streets of Mike's childhood. He was the small boy going to school the day after Kristallnacht, wondering at the thickly scattered broken glass. His aunts, uncles, cousins and school friends lived here. He ran errands, put out the rubbish, did things that any small boy does for aging relatives. Many of Mike's family and others in the area were herded to the extermination camps from the streets Mike and I strolled through that night.

Yet in all this, not once had he used the words 'never again'. This declaration is often heard, as though the European Holocaust was to be the final atrocity and some grand change in human behaviour would mean there could never be another. Such a thought is part of the better side of our nature, an idealistic wish for a better world. It is also political, a pillar of Israel's nationhood. However, a propensity to eliminate the 'other' is clearly part of our raw human condition.

Mass slaughter has been visited by one group upon another, over and over again. The Bible documents a case or two. Surely the Holocaust was warning enough but, no, there have been genocides since then and the pressures of a global population growing beyond 10 billion make it likely there will be more. As a social democrat, Mike saw the museum as a force for good assisting our dream of a better future; as a realist, he knew that 'never again' was unlikely to be achieved.

Perhaps because of the strange disparity of setting, I remember other Mike stories from long phone conversations. Back in Wellington, in summer, I would be sitting on our deck high above the sparkling harbour in that particular Southern Hemisphere brand of sun, not necessarily hot, that is always capable of searing the skin. Mike would be talking from Princeton, heading into winter. The answers to my questions would almost invariably be illustrated by a memory. The delivery, usually measured and even restrained, would often become animated. Then I might hear Mike laugh. Not that the stories were necessarily funny. Most were not. The amusement was so often a response to the ironies within this dark history. Little Werner's fondest wish was to join the Hitler Youth. 'Why?' He chuckled. 'Because I wanted to have a knife to wear at my belt! The first thing I did when I got to Shanghai was to join the British Boy Scouts for that knife.'

The young boy who became Jewish by decree could no longer attend his state school but lost his friends and was sent to a Jewish school. One day he learnt that soon all Jews must celebrate Hanukkah. This new knowledge he took home to his mother. 'That's nice,' she replied. The product of a family long shorn of ritualistic knowledge, she then wondered aloud what Hanukkah might be. He told of his father enduring Bergen-Belsen immediately after Kristallnacht and a driven mother organising their escape. I felt the fear of the young boy sitting with his sister at a railway station in Italy, guarding the family's few suitcases while his worried parents went to the bank, hoping that the money from distant relatives in South America had arrived. It had, and they were on their way to Shanghai in an ancient freighter. Sometimes the stories triggered further reflection. After one discussion of the 'U-boats', as the Jews who went underground called themselves, he paused. 'What if we had not got out? Would I have gone underground or marched with the rest to the station?'

I encouraged this flow of stories. At one level, my motives were entirely selfish. I had learnt history at a considerable distance from the political arena of Europe and North America. Beyond natural disasters and some social experimentation, things of note did not happen in New Zealand. But for Mike contemporary history was not a subject area to be studied, it was his life. Insights into the Bay of Pigs and the Cuban missile crisis, the workings of Cabinet decision-making under Carter, trade negotiations, greeting and being greeted by world leaders and as CEO managing some commercial empire. He would have it that all this was accidental. Perhaps, but it mattered not.

At another level, my motives were not so self-centred. I had the task of fleshing out the character of the new Jewish Museum Berlin. The visitors would be ordinary folk, who would likely know little of the German Jews but who could relate to the individual and to the family. As the frequently quoted truism suggests, you can understand at least some small part of the plight and suffering of slaves if you can feel for them as people just like yourself. Then you might even be moved to seek their freedom.

*

From the moment of the first telephone call from Mike in September, I had done what I always do, read myself into the subject. As well as managing a complex operation, a project director has to be aware of current scholarly thinking, and consider how this might be drawn upon to achieve the museum's purpose. You cannot lead an organisation that becomes known for its shonky scholarship. A few decades earlier, I had read Raul Hilberg's monumental *The Destruction of the European Jews*. This had been part of a discussion I had had with a Waikato Museum curator on the experience of minority ethnic groups, as we were wanting to draw the local Māori tribe into our operation. I spoke of the plight and fate of the Native Americans. A practising Jew, the curator responded with *The Destruction of the European Jews*. Beyond that I knew little but the general information that most people accumulate about World War II and the Holocaust.

I had a great deal to learn, and within hours of Mike's September 1999 phone call I was standing before the relevant section at Unity, the best of our local bookstores. A book fell into my hands: a collection of essays, *Confronting the Nazi Past: New debates on modern German history*, edited by Michael Burleigh. This was a fortuitous find as it was written for those with my level of knowledge. At the local library I soon became aware that German history was dominated by the Holocaust and the War, shelf upon shelf of books, including a forlorn and soul-searching discourse by John Dippel called *Bound Upon a Wheel of Fire*, on the impossible position of Jews in German society under National Socialism, and the terrible ironies that were part of their history. My understanding had to encompass something much wider, the many centuries and generations of the Jews in Germany, including at least the beginnings of a golden age as they became a seemingly favoured people. Fortunately, Mike's *The Invisible Wall* arrived by courier and gave me the story of a family of Ashkenazim Jews whose memory encompassed 400 years in Germany. The pile of books grew.

Within it was Primo Levi: *If This is a Man* and *The Drowned and the Saved*, followed later by *The Truce*. I compared Michael Blumenthal and Primo Levi. One had escaped, to suffer the privation of wartime Shanghai; the other had not but, despite the 'useless violence' of Auschwitz, had survived. There were huge differences in their stories, but enough suffering for them both to study nothing but hatred, had they so chosen. Instead their storytelling brought life-defining affirmation. There is a sense of good, these men said to me, and a museum can aspire to, emphasise and even increase that good. Not that 'good' is a set, unitary thing. A moral position is negotiated through intelligent discussion, storytelling and the ability to acknowledge and respond to different attitudes and beliefs. In my view, no museum aspiring to cultural leadership could adopt the authoritarian voice of absolute certainty.

Mike and I would soon agree: the Jewish Museum Berlin would take great care that its scholastic authority should never allow abuse to be poured upon generations who were not perpetrators but who yet bore the sins of their grandparents and great-grandparents. In this we would have been supported by Primo Levi.

*

During the first review there had been no time to get to know Mike Blumenthal and my verdict on his museum had been harsh. But we had parted on the best of terms with promises of continuing contact. I began work straight away, plying Mike and staff with instructions, briefs, commentaries, demands and reality checks. I also started writing a defining description of the new museum, which would give direction and certainty to our planning.

Even then I came to Berlin that second time, needing to be sure about my relationship with Mike. The negativity, meddling and capricious, even cruel, behaviour at Te Papa had wounded me. I therefore carried to Berlin a checklist of needs: energy-boosting and predictable leadership; honesty and direct communication; challenging the traditional; respect for each other's expertise. If these qualities did not exist, Mike and I could not hope to achieve an extraordinary museum.

I had also done some preliminary research, which included a 1978 *Time* magazine article written when he parted ways with Jimmy Carter. Apparently the president's staff had seen him as a brilliant, brittle man with an enormous ego. The only comment he ever made on this was to once observe wryly that someone inside the Washington Beltway had said that he must have been doing a good job for Carter to move him on.

Sitting in his office, I saw that the grumpiness from a month before had been replaced by unbridled enthusiasm. His face lit up at the prospect of success. There was more humour in his eyes. His project was back on track. He had no doubts and uncertainties. The stories flowed, his face a changing landscape strengthening the words. With serious stories, not just the mouth but his whole lower face would droop to emphasise heart-rending desolation. Bursts of laughter were short but animated. The hands would sweep through the air, sometimes sending cigar ash flying. This was theatre even if nearly always theatre of the seated. He rarely rose from that chair.

He was a handsome old guy. He favoured darker suits and a tasteful, if limited array, of shirts with different – sometimes matching, sometimes discordant – body and collar combinations. His ties were chosen to match. Sometimes, I would observe, a tie became an interesting archaeological site of layered food remnants gathered in different eateries about town.

But what of that gossip, that egotistical man? I never really saw him. Mike had achieved in a cut-throat, even life-threatening world, and a well-developed sense of self-worth would be a natural part of his armoury. Yet I would later notice that even on the few occasions he joined a staff team, he would be encouraging, with little hint of domineering behaviour. People soon felt comfortable in his presence. He assumed leadership roles naturally, even eagerly, but was not to be feared.

Part of this condition was the place where the Blumenthal ego was grounded. 'I leave the States an American – I land in Germany and I am a Jew,' he once explained. His stories, though born of the European Jewish tragedy, were told from the perspective of the American dream. He was an outsider. This was something we shared.

My checklist was ticked off. As smoke rose and spread through the room we started planning the next 18 months.

*

Another food memory: a late dinner at Dressler's on Unter den Linden to discuss contracts and requirements.

I pressed for simplicity. 'I need all exhibition design and delivery to be wrapped up in a single one-signature contract with a major design firm.'

No problem. There was already an agreement with a design group, but they were not capable of achieving a large museum experience. There would have to be a clean break.

I also wanted a single board decision on an integrated museum concept. 'We can give the board just one opportunity to comment on and sign off a description of what the museum will be. I'll include a preliminary business case.'

Although I was asking Mike to trust me, he had no problems with my approach, and welcomed my sense of urgency. Then I broached the need for staff experienced in large project delivery. 'I want to bring four battle-hardened members of my team with me.'

Mike drew back, thought for a moment. 'I can't agree to four. You can bring one. I'm going to get enough flak bringing a Kiwi from the far side of the world.'

His worries did not prove well founded. Many in the media would praise the astute politician Blumenthal for hiring someone distant from Germany. Such a museum could only succeed in the hands of a person who came from the 'here be dragons' part of the global map.

As I walked the short distance to the hotel the old fears of failure returned. I had experienced this all before with every other project, no matter what the scale. Those anxieties were part of my being but, I told myself, had always attuned and sharpened my performance. Mike and I had made sound decisions and set manageable targets, even if the time frame was extremely tight and the eyes of the world were upon us. For the last four weeks I had felt very isolated, but now I could bring a trusted support person from Te Papa. I would make the best use of the staff group I had inherited. They would be added to with new appointments and I would work diligently to develop and expand their skills.

'Buck up!' I mumbled to myself. 'We've made real progress.'

*

Late one evening, at last on my own, I wandered up to Level 2, partly because I could. I had the security pass and the keys; I was starting to find my way about. But there was more to it than that. The Libeskind building was invading my mind.

I was drawn to the spot where I had photographed the October review group standing in front of a spectacular array of windows. Then, little more than a month before, I had read this building as recent history, the brutality of the Holocaust made manifest. Now I had come to see this sombre place as a character in its own right within a universal theatre. This was Daniel Libeskind's take on his family's history as Polish Jews in the Pale of Settlement, that swathe of territory across middle Europe in which so many Jews had lived over the centuries. He had drawn on his understanding of that history to create much more than a museum venue.

Less than a year since its completion, the building was already timeless, speaking as much of the Thirty Years' War as Daniel's take on the Holocaust, a set waiting for Bertolt Brecht to stage *Mother Courage and Her Children*. I saw a way ahead. We would treat the Libeskind building not as difficulty but as infinite opportunity; as though, I later explained to staff, we were putting a museum into a 300-year-old castle. It would receive the respect it was owed.

The doubts of the last month were set aside. I could not deny this chance, this history, in this city; in this building.

The contract was on the table: what I was to do, and at what price. Done. That evening I made my commitment. There was no turning back. I phoned Susan. Our future lay in this vibrant city. We shared our excitement and our fears at the enormity of the change we faced.

I left Berlin that second time fully committed to the job but with the usual travel angst. This had nothing to do with a fear of flying. I have no trouble with aeroplanes though I have a greater passion for trains. It was the ongoing problem of my sinuses. Each plane trip was a lottery. Would they freeze solid, or whatever they do, and subject me to the most excruciating pain across the forehead and deep into my skull, or not? I had developed techniques to get pressure equalised but sometimes it did not work and I would have my half-hour of 'extreme discomfort' (medical euphemism for hurts like hell) as the plane climbed or descended. This could not go on. As I boarded the plane at Tegel I resolved that back in New Zealand I would have that long-delayed nose job, no matter how inconvenient.

I would also have to face leaving Te Papa and abandoning, at least for some time, the cultural certainty of New Zealand. That might be as discombobulating as any surgery.

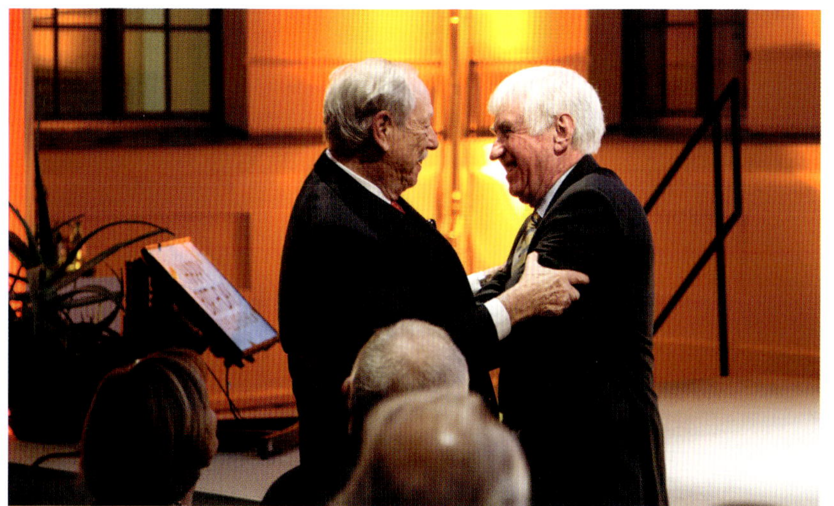

Ken (right) is the surprise guest at Mike Blumenthal's ninetieth birthday celebration in Berlin, January 2016. Despite being 16 years Blumenthal's junior, Ken is the white-haired one.

Photo Wolfgang Busch, Jewish Museum Berlin

BELOW: Dreams of an idyllic youth. This book of poems, *Just Us*, was much loved – but the shoes on Kiwi kids at the beach were just wrong!

Stopford G. Wrathall (illustrator), *Just Us* by John Brent (aka William Free Cresswell), Morning Post Printing House, Rotorua, 1944

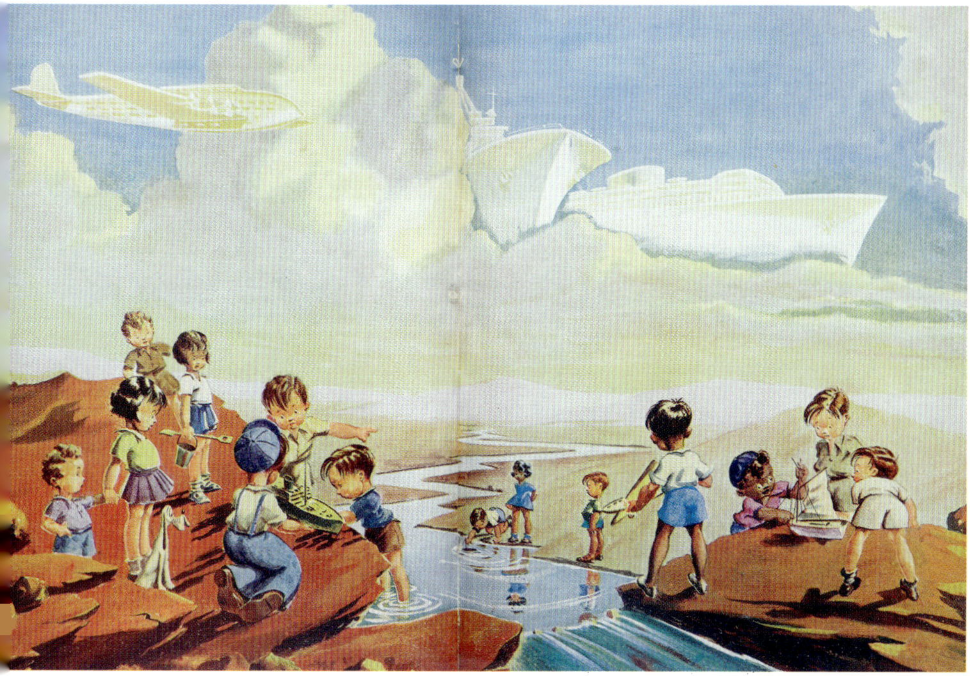

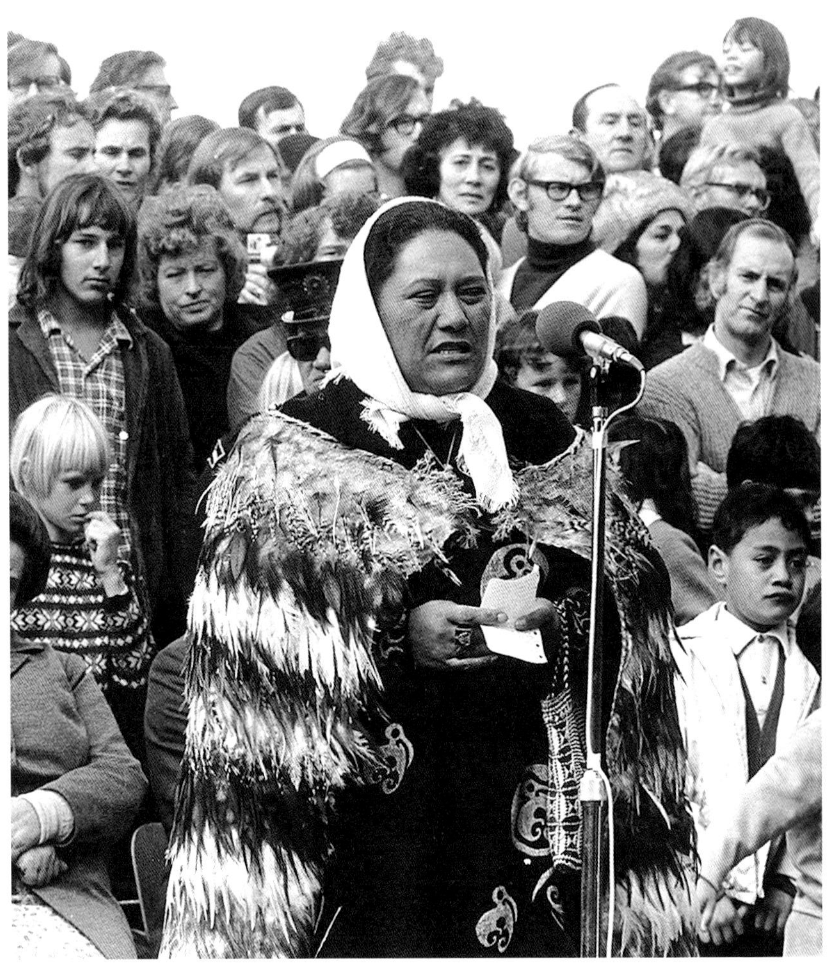

Te Arikinui Dame Te Atairangikaahu, visionary leader of the Tainui people, quietly encouraged the young museum director. Here she hands over the ancient canoe *Te Winika* to Waikato Museum. Waikato Times Collection

RIGHT: Director experiences the thrill of the curatorial chase: Ken takes delivery of the Barry Brickell ceramic piece *Locomorph*, seen here in its natural surroundings – Driving Creek Railway, Coromandel.

Photo Kees Sprengers, Archive of Waikato Museum Te Whare Taonga o Waikato

Reverend Dave Manihera, the knowledgeable teller of stories and singer of waiata (songs), was one of my mentors and guides in matters to do with the Tainui tribe. Here he examines and blesses an old carving uncovered in a Hamilton back yard.

Photo Kees Sprengers, Archive of Waikato Museum Te Whare Taonga o Waikato

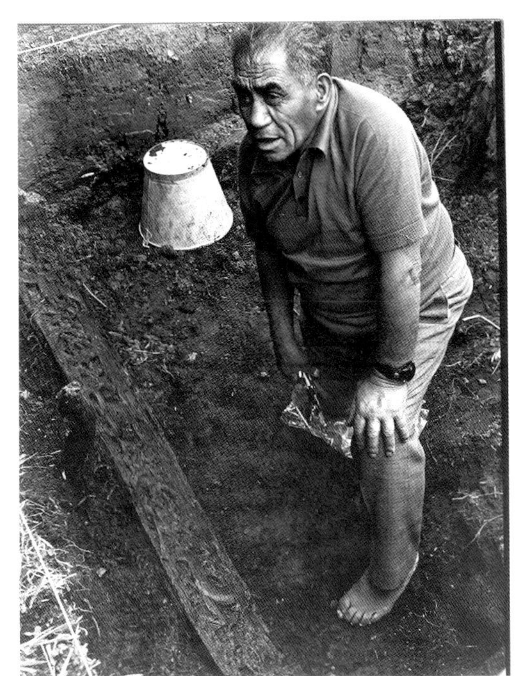

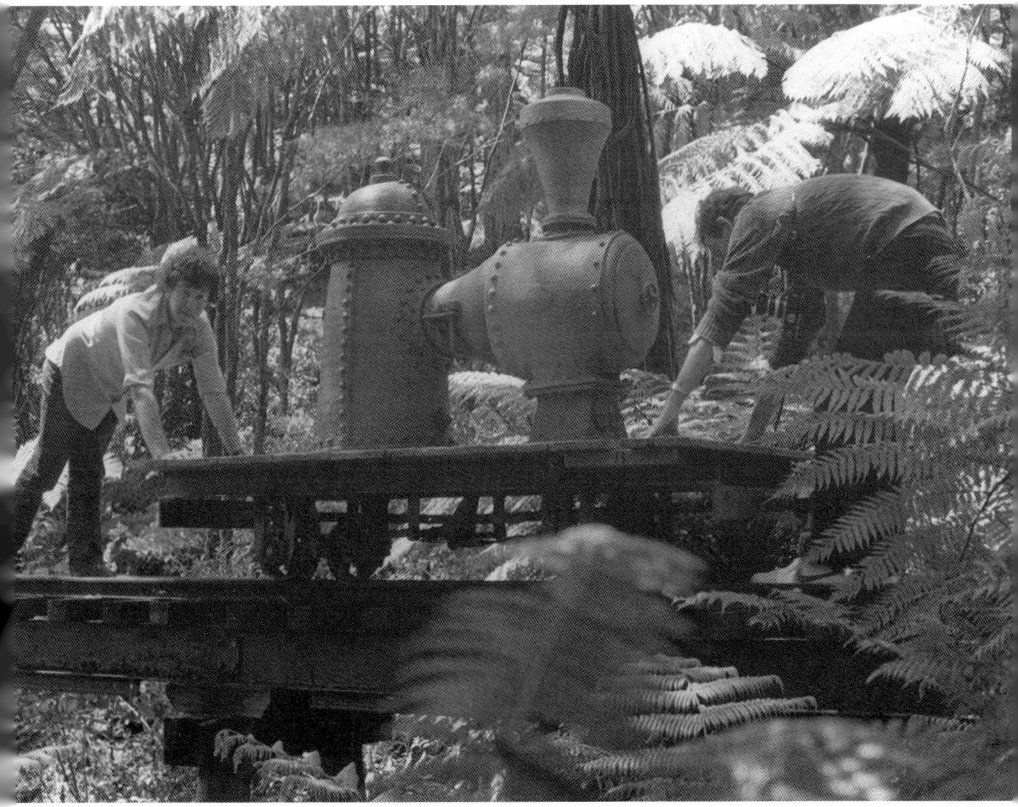

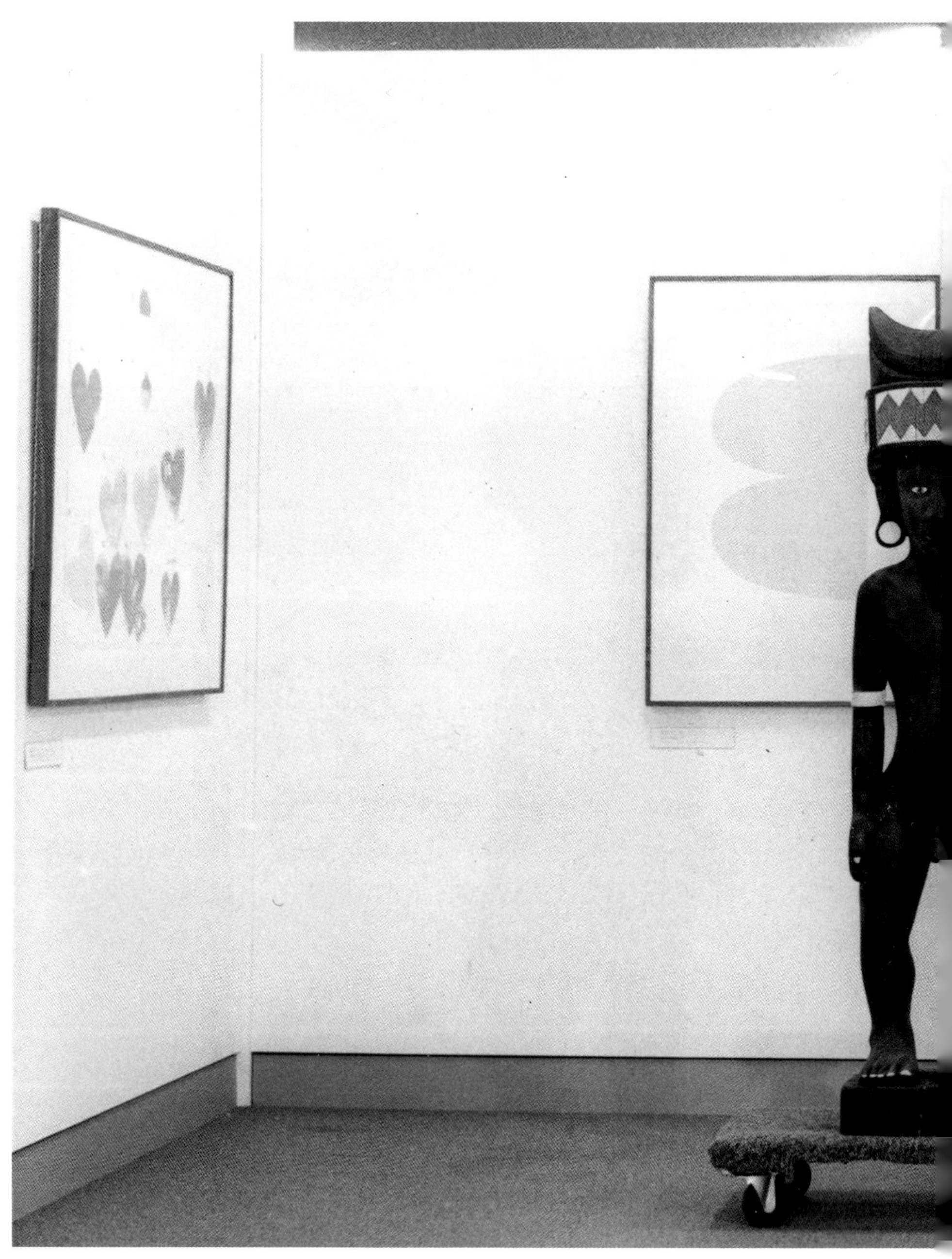

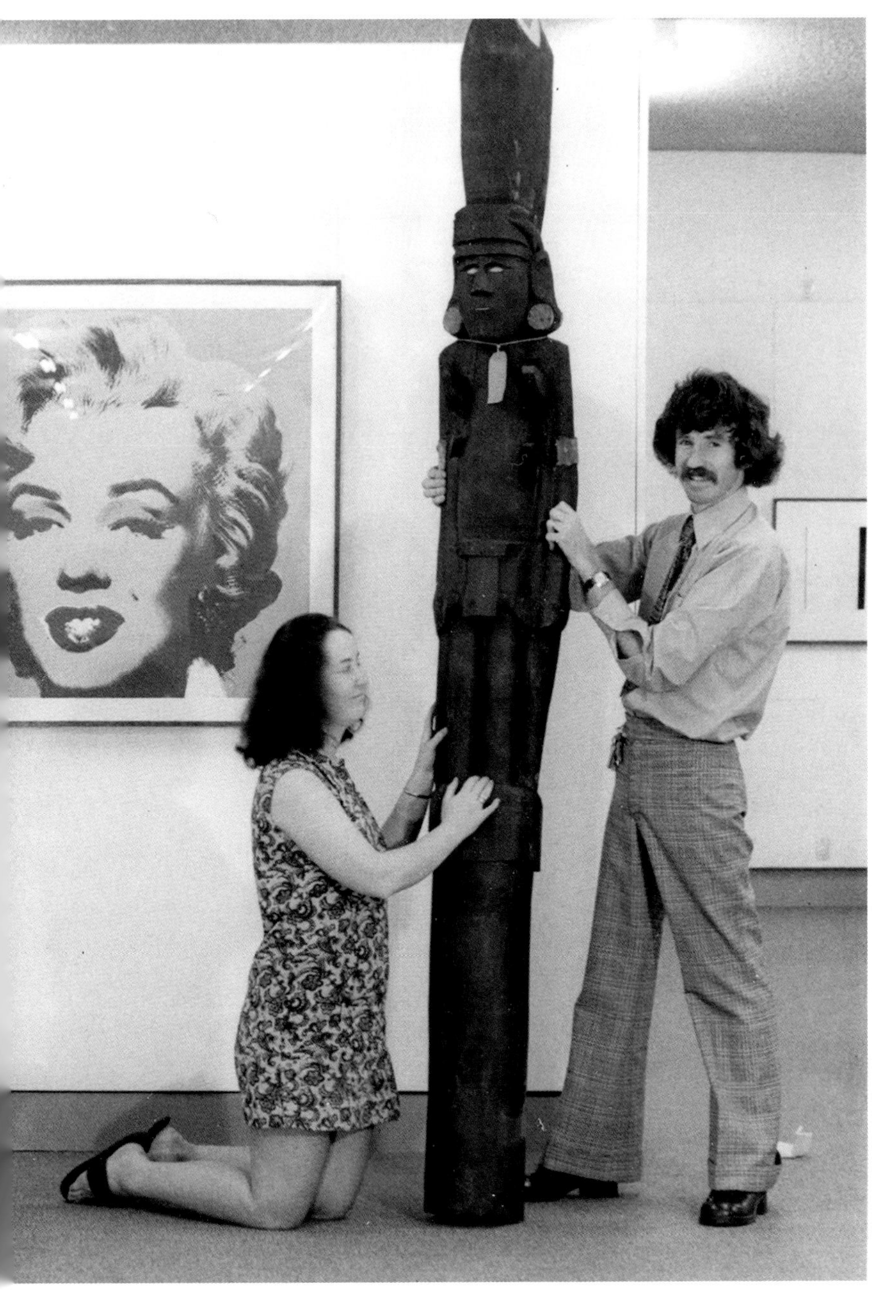

The fashionable Waikato Museum director at work. Note larger-than-life hair, moustache, flares and platform shoes.

Photo James Mack, Archive of Waikato Museum Te Whare Taonga o Waikato

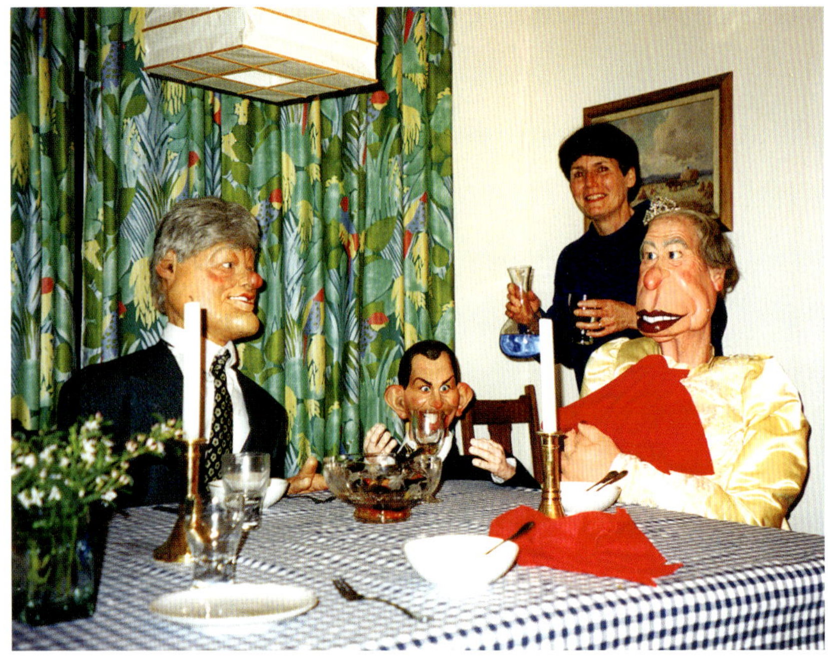

As trailing spouse, I gained access to the wonderful world of political cartooning and humour. I had important roles such as photographer, here behind the camera as Susan Foster entertains Bill Clinton, a small Tony Blair (behind the wine glass) and Queen Elizabeth II. Roger Law, creator of the TV satire *Spitting Image*, sits out of shot. Photo Ken Gorbey

OPPOSITE, TOP: In 1993, 25-tonne blocks of concrete continuously pound the waterfront site to form a solid, earthquake-defeating foundation for the building.

Photo Jan Nauta, MA_F.002162/06, Te Papa Tongarewa Museum of New Zealand

OPPOSITE: The Day One Management Team (D1MT) was my main device for bringing everything together and making binding decisions. Here the second Treaty Exhibition concept comes to the D1MT. It was the third one that was finally built. From left: Sue Harrop, Robin Parkinson, Raewyn Smith-Kapa, Bud Mahoney, Sean Sweeney, Cliff Whiting and Bronwyn Simes. I employed much the same structure at the Jewish Museum in Berlin.

Photo Michael Hall, MA_F.001284, Te Papa Tongarewa Museum of New Zealand

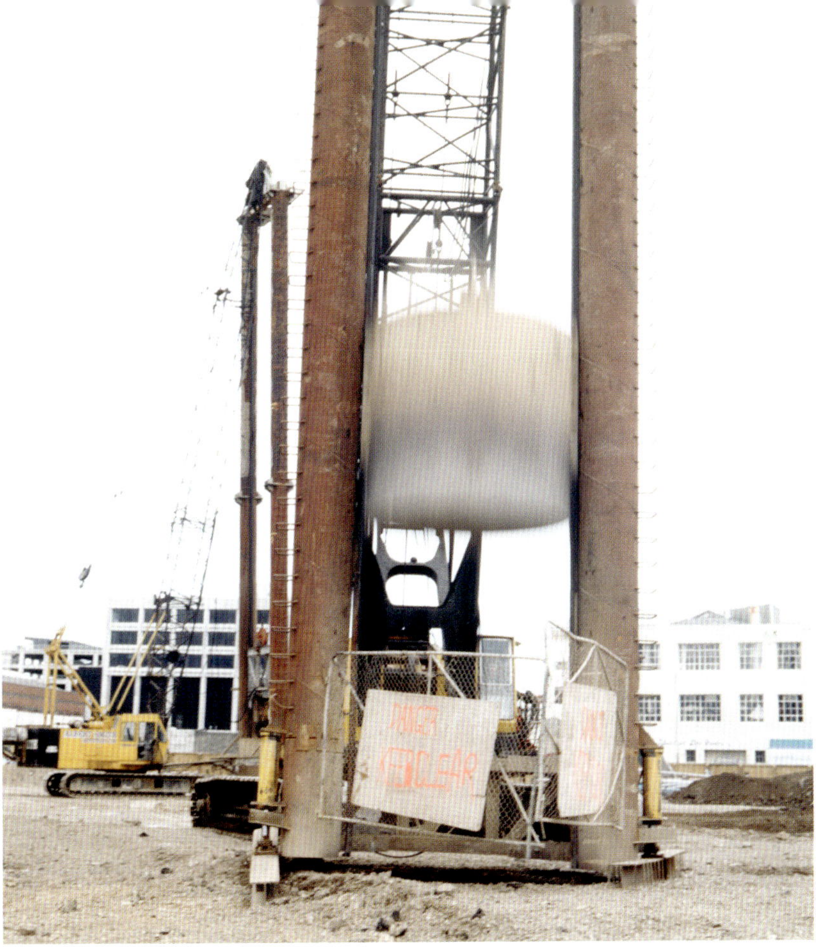

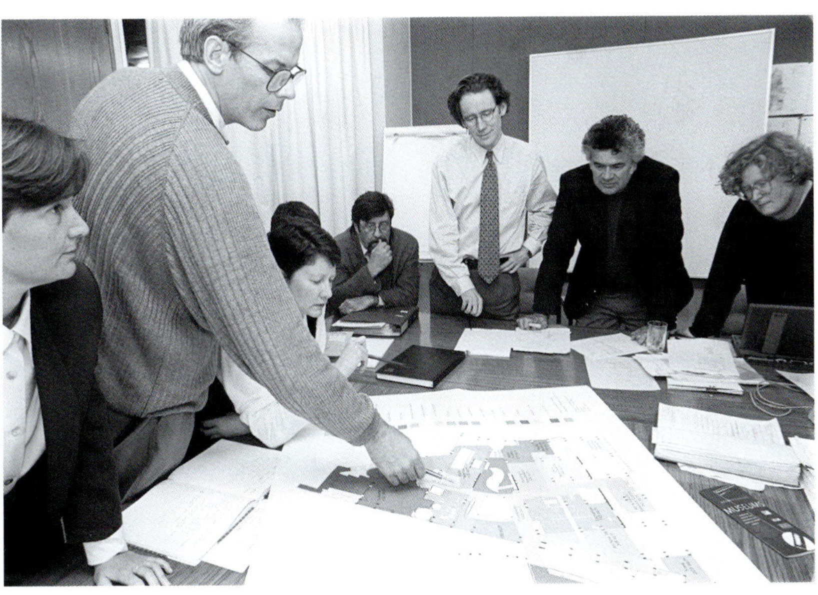
MUSEUM

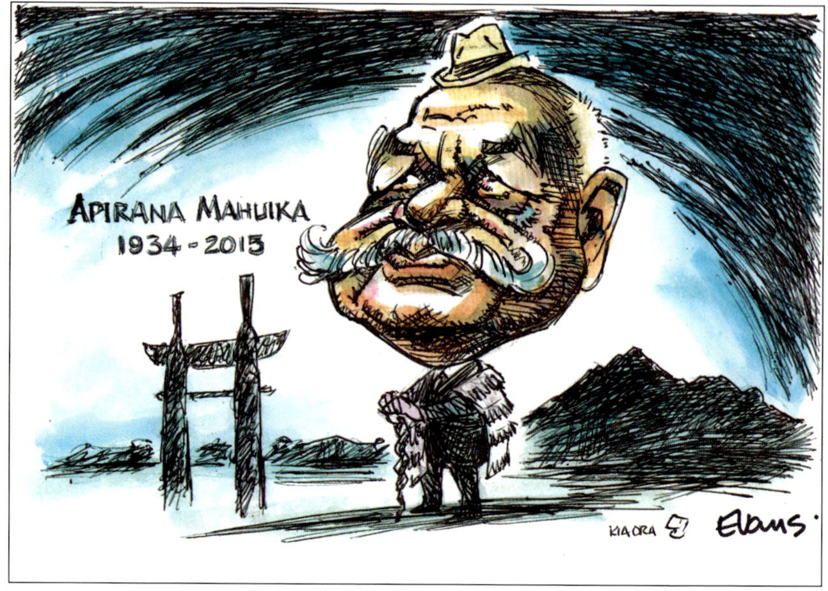

Apirana (Api) Mahuika, respected Māori leader and chair of Te Papa's Ngā Kaiwawao. Cartoon Malcolm Evans

OPPOSITE, TOP: Cliff Whiting's early rendering of the main Māori exhibition concept. This drawing drove all further development work. Cliff Whiting, pen and ink

OPPOSITE: In November 1997, three months before opening, Cliff Whiting – the conceptual leader, creative and practitioner – led the team of carvers within Te Hono ki Hawaiki. Photo Norman Heke, MA_E.001919, Te Papa Tongarewa Museum of New Zealand

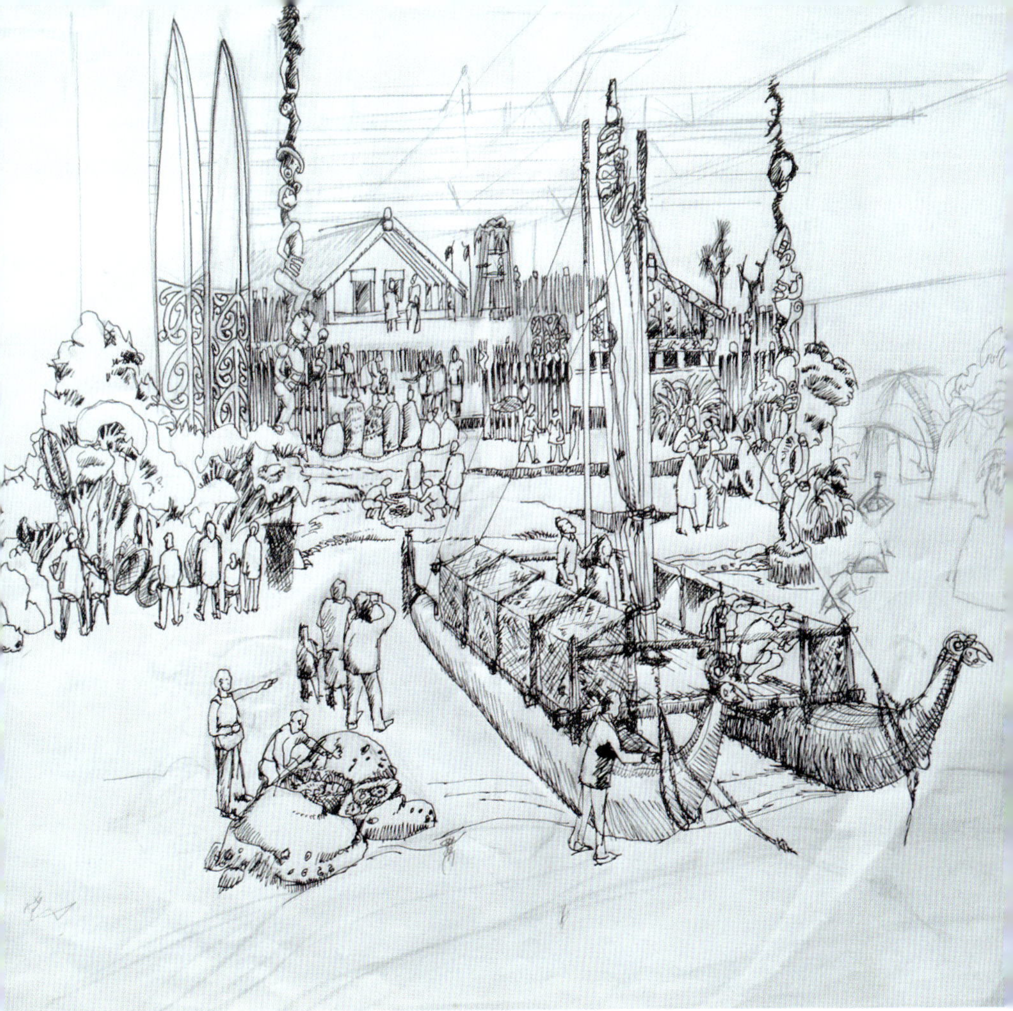

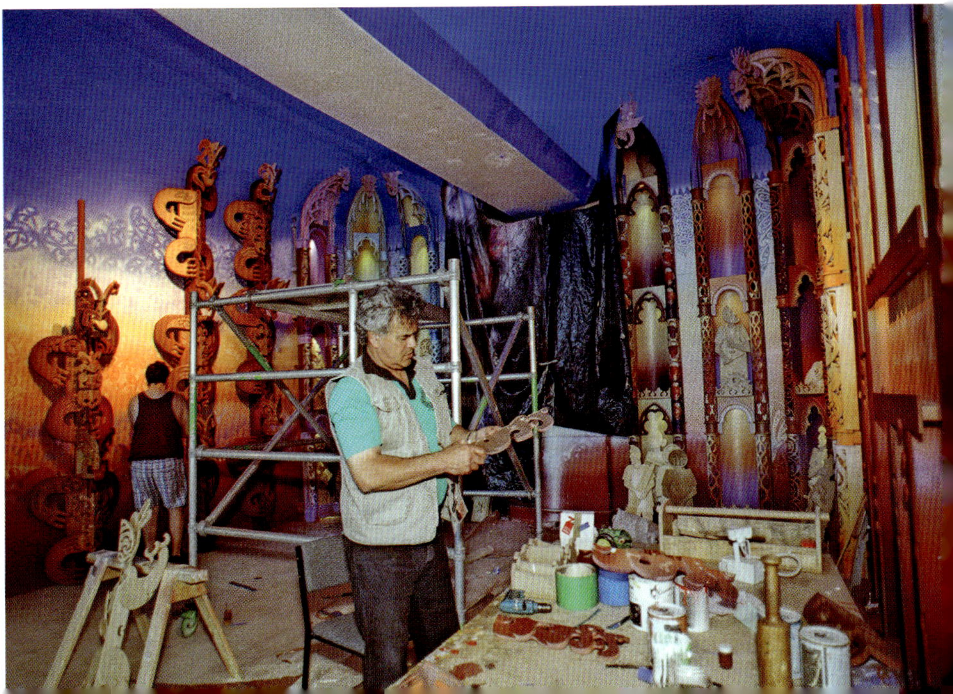

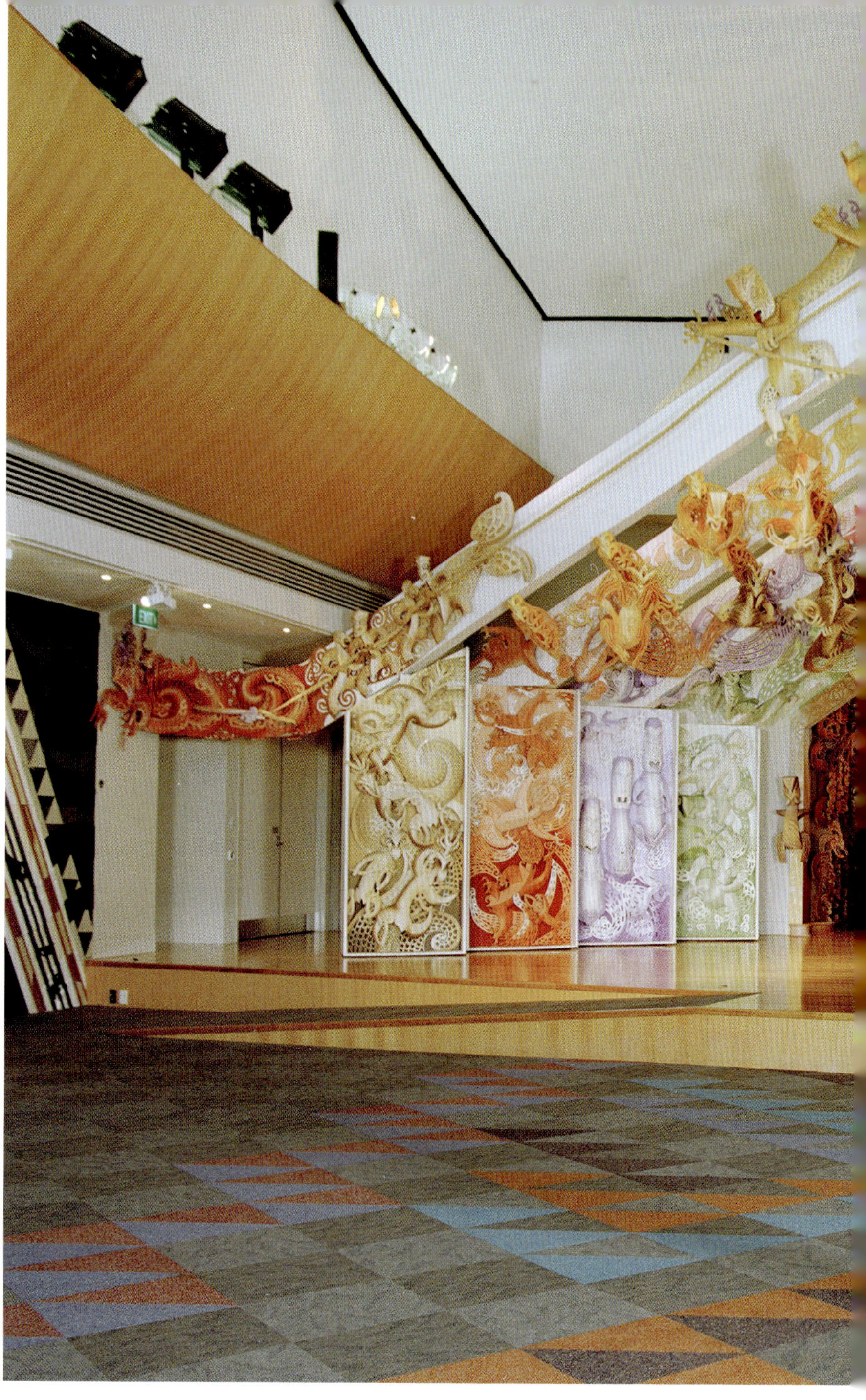
EXIT

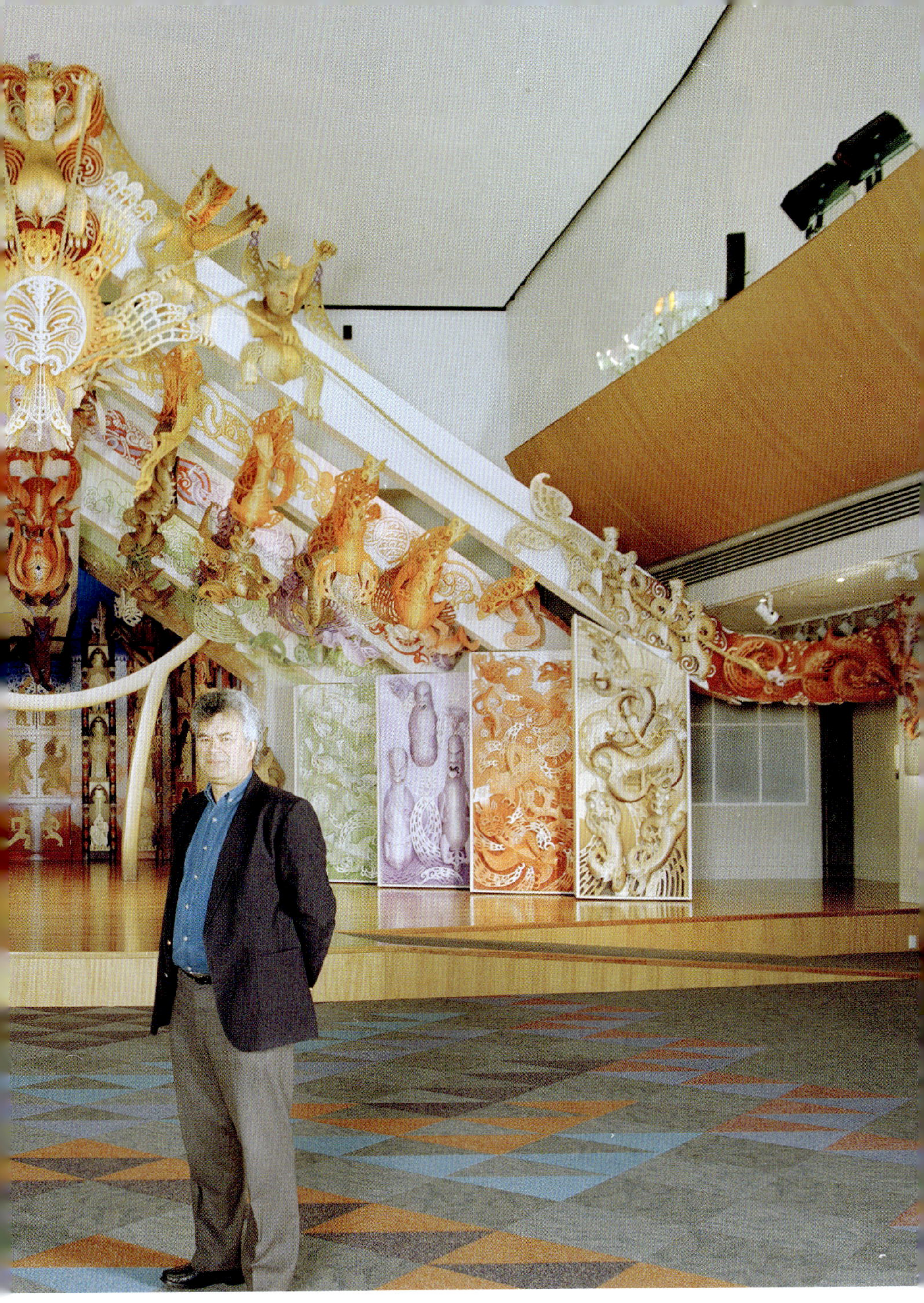

Cliff Whiting stands before his finished work, Te Hono ki Hawaiki, a crucial part of the visual and cultural impact of Te Papa, at Rongomaraeroa.
Photo Norman Heke, MA_F.005426, Te Papa Tongarewa Museum of New Zealand

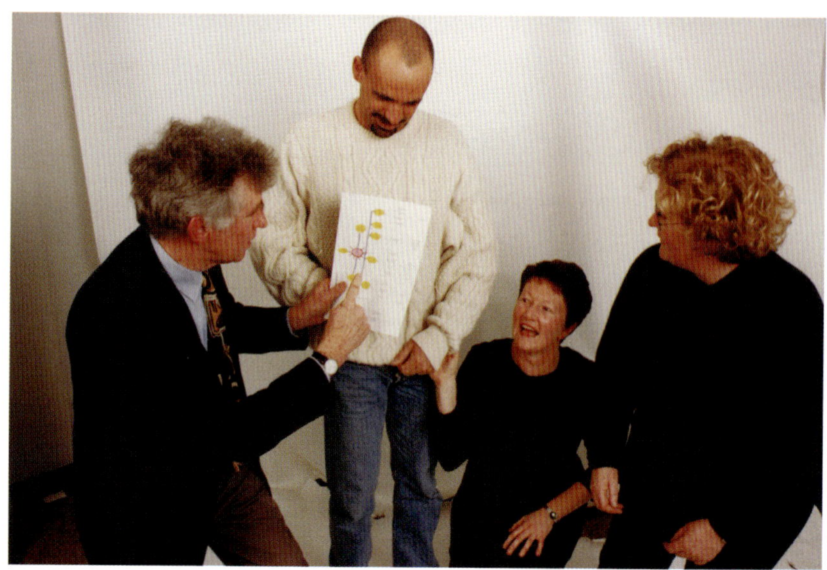

At the wake marking the closure of the project office and the move to the new building. From left, Ken, Neil Anderson, Raewyn Smith-Kapa and Bronwyn Simes laugh over Neil's organisational structure diagram, which always seemed to have him at the top.

Photo Michael Hall, Norman Heke, Jan Nauta, Te Papa Tongarewa Museum of New Zealand

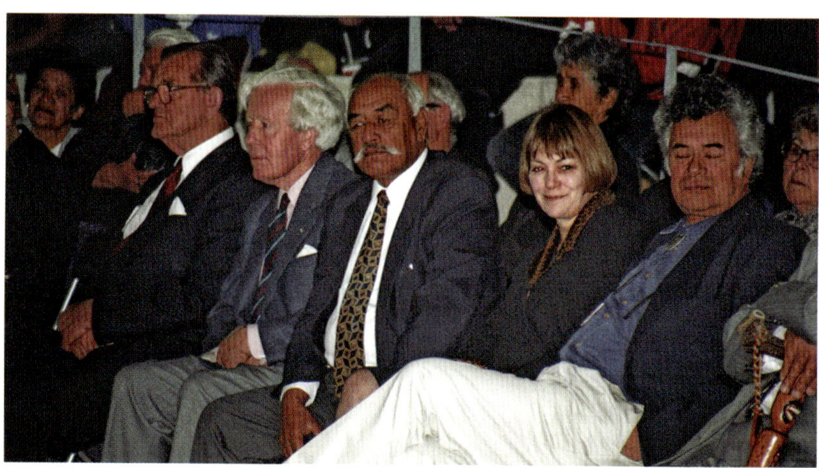

At the ceremonial move of Te Hau ki Tūranga to the new waterfront museum building, November 1996. From left, Sir Ron Trotter, Sir Hamish Hay, Apirana Mahuika, Dame Cheryll Sotheran, Cliff Whiting ONZ.

Photo Norman Heke MA_E.001390, Te Papa Tongarewa Museum of New Zealand

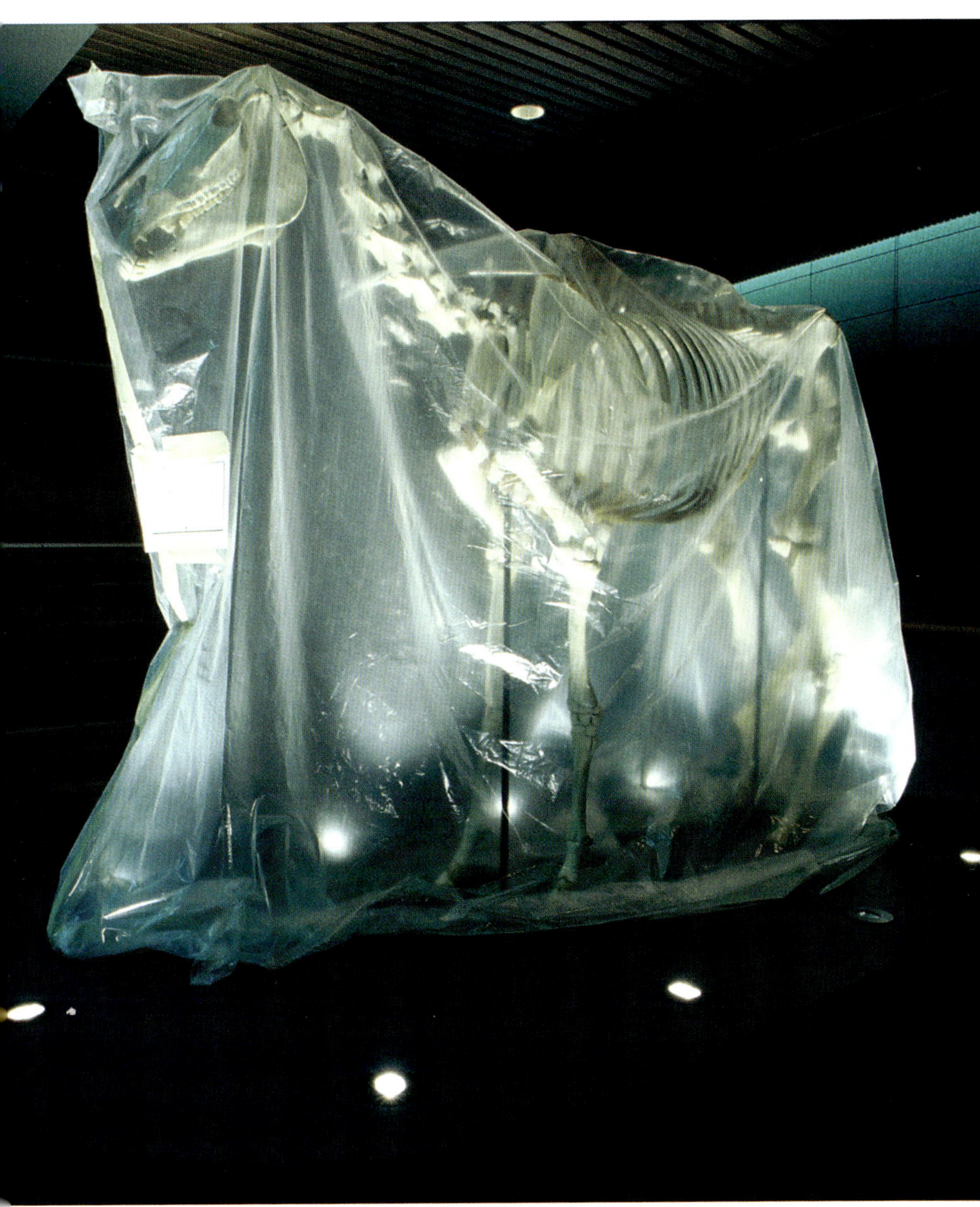

The ghostly skeletal racing horse of eons back, Phar Lap, stands wrapped against dust, awaiting the opening.

Photo Michael Hall, Norman Heke, Jan Nauta, Te Papa Tongarewa Museum of New Zealand

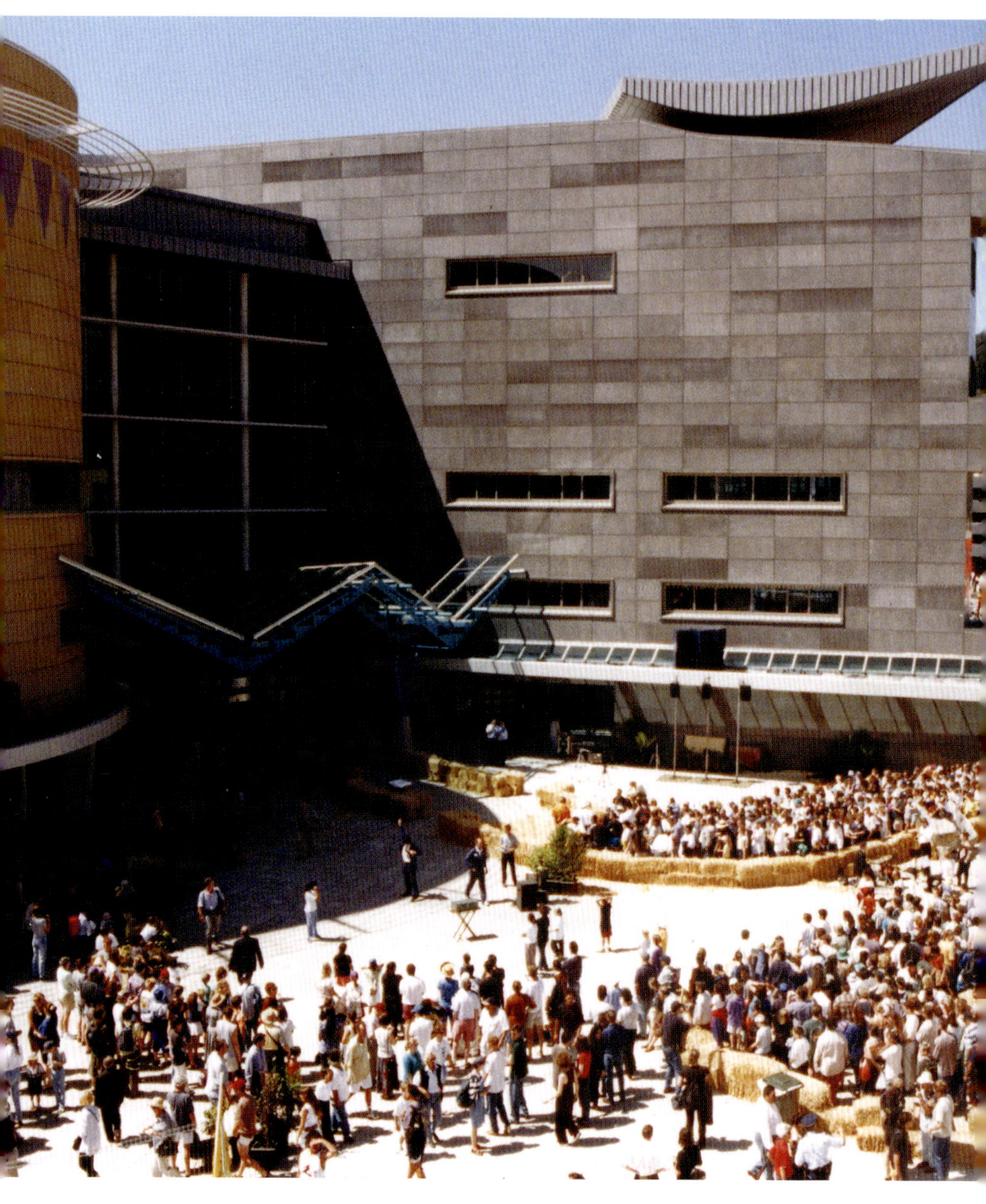

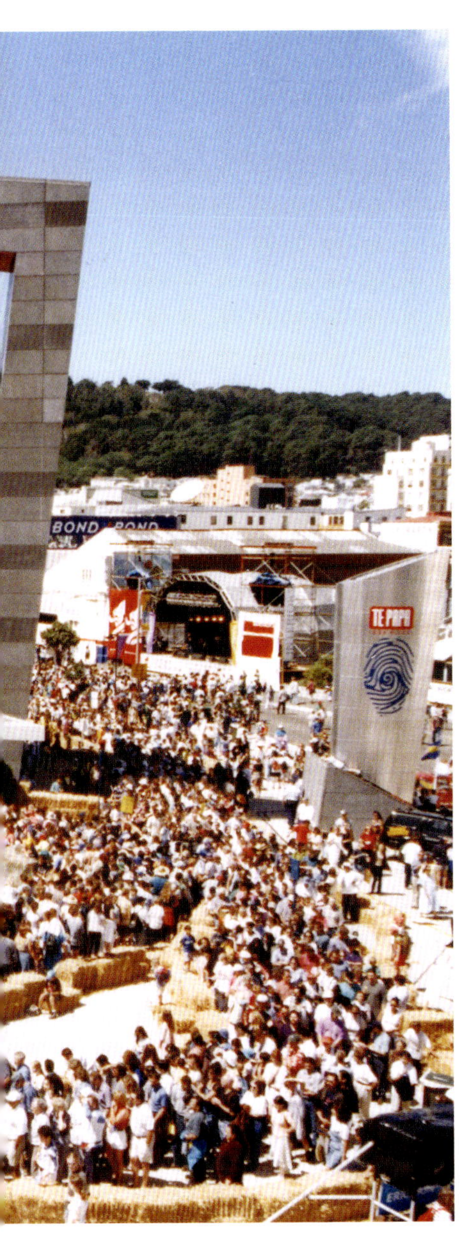

Over 30,000 people queued for a look on opening day, 14 February 1998.

Photo Norman Heke, Te Papa Tongarewa Museum of New Zealand

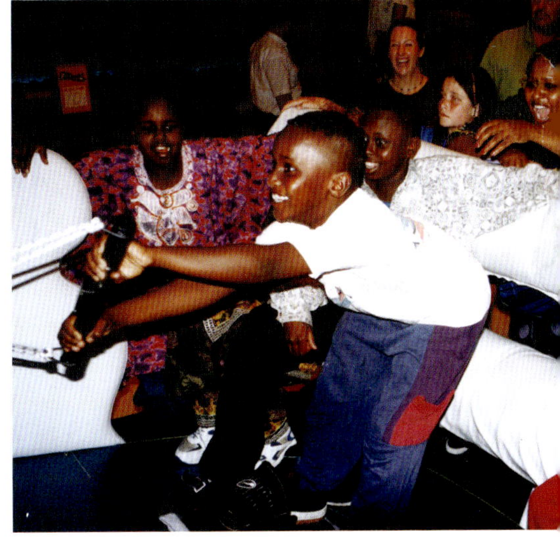

Children play at water-skiing in Te Papa's Time Warp.

Photo Michael Hall, Norman Heke, Jan Nauta, Te Papa Tongarewa Museum of New Zealand

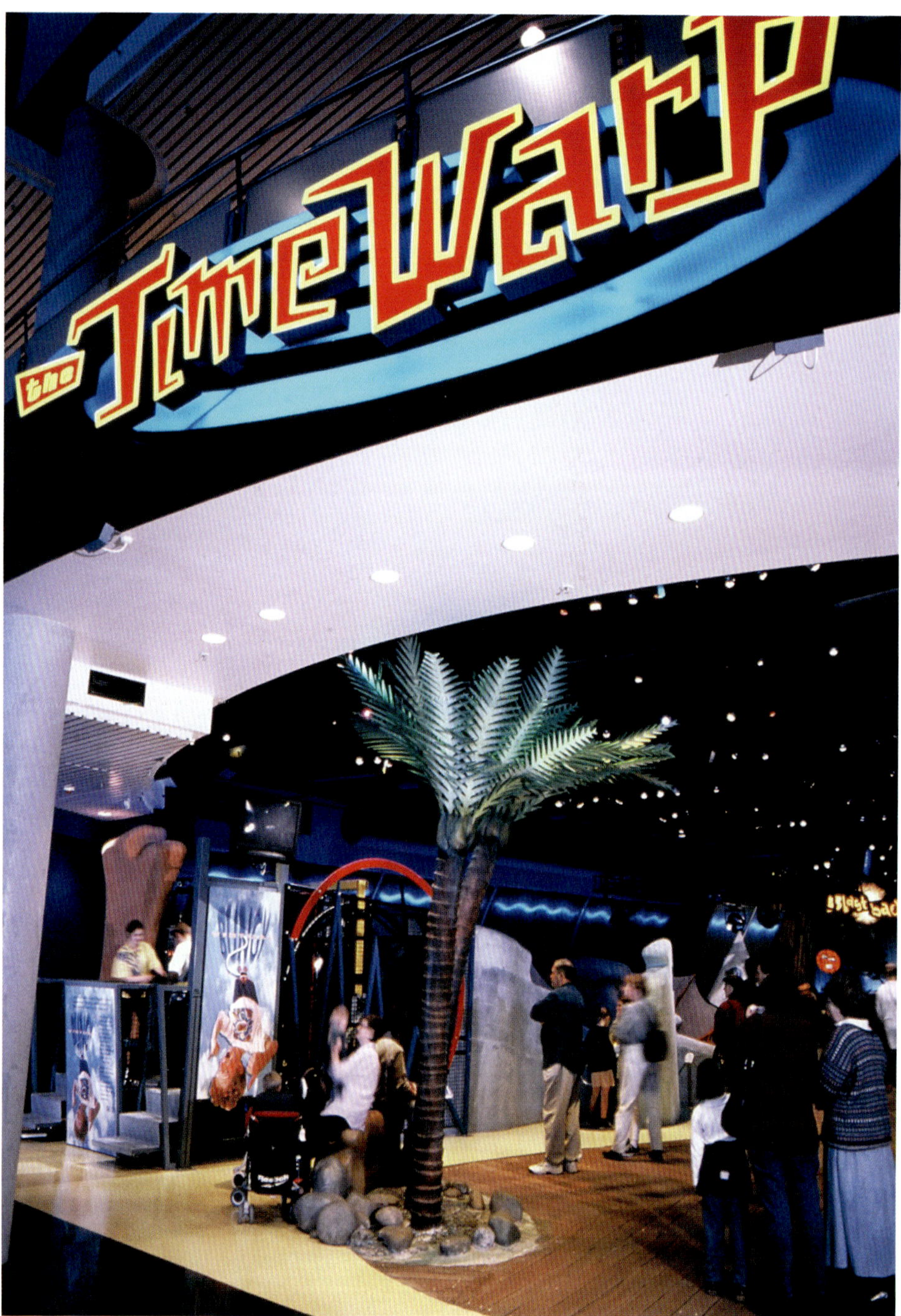

I learnt so much from the leisure industry. Time Warp was our commitment to attracting the adolescent and young adult audience. It worked, at least to a certain degree. Photo Michael Hall, Norman Heke, Jan Nauta, Te Papa Tongarewa Museum of New Zealand

CHAPTER 9

NIGEL COX: WORDS AND ACTIONS

WHEN I RETURNED TO WELLINGTON there was a welcome party around my desk. This was not normal. Most returns would be low key: 'Oh! You're back.' But this was the second time I had been to Germany. My colleagues had noted those strange telephone calls and unusual packages from afar. They knew something was in the air.

In Berlin I had wandered among the sea of cranes seeking two gifts, expressions of quintessential Berlin at the cheap end of the cost spectrum. For Susan a bear, symbol of her new city. The other would stand at the centre of a small piece of performance, the culmination of my struggle with the question of who I would spirit off to Berlin.

I had no shortage of offers. Nothing was official but people had started to drift up to me in the corridors with best wishes for the new challenge, messages of support and quiet affirmations of their willingness to relocate. 'I'll gladly come,' said one. 'It's the most exciting city in the world.'

I needed someone creative, to frame the core story and make it available to a wide audience. The person must also be forceful and organised, to bring everything to the point where the exhibitions could be built. Four talented people fitted the profile; then I got it down to two. Finally, I made my decision. It would be Nigel Cox, storyteller and originator of exhibitions. He would receive the second gift.

I had asked Margarete, Mike's PA and the keeper of local Berlin knowledge, to find what I wanted. The fall of the Berlin Wall had brought not only German reunification but also the Democratic Republic's car, the Trabant or Trabi, to West Berlin streets. The smoky-engined, plastic-bodied Trabi was a high point in the world of failed technology, a frequently immobile billboard for an economic system that had never quite worked. But it now had a new role as nostalgia-hero for a lost way of life. Margarete was thrilled at the challenge and undertook to find just the right one. This took time and, as my departure date loomed, I worried I would leave empty-handed. She assured me the matter was in hand but all the toy Trabis on offer were the wrong colour. 'It has to be green.'

Margarete explained. Citizen Ossi, an informal term for an East German, would go on to the waiting list for a Trabi. Patience was called for but, in several years, official notification would arrive: your car is ready. With influence you might have a choice of colour. Otherwise your new car was green. But tourists wanting to take home a toy emblematic of East Germany required gorgeous colours. Green was not saleable and was now as rare in souvenir shops as the full-size green Trabi had been ubiquitous.

Some years later Susan and I, among a Kiwi audience, would get the joke in the film *Goodbye Lenin*. Mother, kept in the dark about the collapse of her country, East Germany, exclaims in wonder that the newly restored Trabi owned by a West German friend is bright blue. How important he must be to get a car that is not green; he must hold very high office.

Eventually Margarete's search was successful and a miniature green Trabi was tucked into my homeward baggage.

*

'Why, a Hillman Minx,' said Nigel. Later I made my more formal pitch.

'Interested in a job in Berlin?'

He admitted that he had half expected it and had even discussed the possibility with his wife, Susanna Andrew.

'Of course!'

Nigel had joined the Te Papa project to lead the writing team and soon impressed as a creative realist of honest opinion and good sense. It helped that he and I found common cause in museums defined by their social purpose, by their potential to encourage people towards a future that we could all generally agree to be good.

We shared a liking for early starts. By 7.30am, most days, we would be at our desks, each knowing that the other had already arrived by the coffee machine making wake-up noises and that smell in the air. At my insistence the office was open plan, so conversations and commentaries would flow as people arrived. News, the gossip of the day, comments, challenges, concerns, annoyances, plans – all would be out in the open. The most effective meetings, short and to the point, were those held across low dividers. Everyone could have something to say. Job descriptions counted for little until it became serious. Then the rule was, hole up in the glass-walled meeting rooms with no one leaving until the matter was resolved.

In this environment Nigel shone. He was a selfless and thoughtful contributor who got results, and a wonderful negotiator. Elaine Gurian recalls a treaty exhibition crisis meeting with the Māori team. 'It was all about terms and words and emphasis and Nigel kept coming up with cognates and synonyms in a "how about this" fashion. It was civil and eventually we built up words and emphasis that everyone accepted. It was a really important day for me because I learnt the value of word choice as a negotiating tool and I've used it many times since. Nigel was the hero in teaching us all about the importance of words as a bicultural tool.'

But perhaps Nigel's greatest strength was his imagination: his ability to conjure up inspired approaches and then capture them in words and action. His lack of a university qualification was irrelevant. He had proved himself in the real world as a bookseller and then as a novelist. A few years later I was irritated when a US job recruitment person said that they would not even consider Nigel for a project management job requiring drive and experience, because he did not have at least a master's degree.

Nigel was destined to be one of our profession's great leaders. He had the aptitude; he had the talent. But he died in 2006 aged 56, leaving Susanna and three beautiful children. We all mourned his passing. To this day, I think of him often. We had never become really close personal friends, but we worked so well together, gossiped and talked museums and culture. But the other parts of his life he shared only occasionally. I so wish he were here to watch his children grow and to write more great novels.

CHAPTER 10

A HOLOCAUST MUSEUM AS MAGICAL THEATRE

LATE IN 1999 I severed all ties with Te Papa. A courtyard restaurant had hosted the final project office dinner, a full house of the creatives and practitioners responsible for making Te Papa. That night we were all subjected to extremes of emotion, elation to sadness. People who did not normally drink did so to excess. Elaine Gurian flew over especially from her work in Sydney. Neil Anderson and Michelle Tayler made up a song that got no further than 'We want to come!' This caused a mass outbreak of alcohol-fuelled giggles. Graeme Shadwell roasted me on a notable instance where, in front of TV cameras, I had tried to explain some engineering principle that was well beyond me. Stupid stories told, eternal friendships pledged, glowing testaments uttered, undoubtedly to be recanted in the throes of the morning-after hangover. Nigel declared this Te Papa project team to be capable of anything; the next task to which they should apply their talents was world poverty. Everyone hugged everyone.

The official farewell was a sober affair. Senior management people attended and Cheryll offered congratulations and best wishes, her clasped hands chopping at the air. As they were about to depart Bronwyn Simes thanked me. 'Whatever happened, none of the shit reached us.' It was a courageous statement.

A book of farewell messages had been produced with all staff invited to contribute, and as a final gesture the project office presented objects, one from each, packed neatly in an old specimen box complete with scientific nomenclature long faded and insect-gnawed to ancient artefact status. It sits on a prominent shelf in my office to this day.

The new millennium passed. 'Come as your favourite decade.' Strange fashions were dragged from the backs of closets and we danced on our lawn above the harbour.

One moment we were in the twentieth and then the twenty-first century. Computers kept operating. Nothing changed. Except that I had become project director and deputy president at the Jewish Museum Berlin.

Deputy president? The title came up when I commented to Mike that he seemed to have no proper designation. Everyone knew he was Mike Blumenthal of the JMB, sometimes 'general director'. Ostensibly he was beholden to a board, but in reality he ran the show with his friend and minister of culture in the federal government, Michael Naumann.

Late one night in an almost deserted restaurant on Unter den Linden, I suggested that the way he acted marked him as a presidential figure. He liked the idea. It was a good description of his role and demeanour. Director, to my mind, seemed fixed in a role and attending a desk, whereas a president can sweep in and command attention before sweeping out. Despite my simplistic understanding of what presidents do, there was a deep chortle in his voice as he said, 'You shall be deputy president even if there's no official president.'

Of course I had actually been working for the Jewish Museum Berlin since October 1999. New files with JMB in the title had begun to populate my work computer. These were now transferred, via the little floppy disks of the time, to a newly purchased weighty slab of a laptop. And the files grew. Then, suddenly, the screen in front of me shrank down to a brilliant pinpoint of very hot light and disappeared. My personal millennium bug had struck, albeit a few days late. Guided by telephone technicians, my set of small screwdrivers delved into the laptop's innards. I had expected masses of wires but was disappointed. It was a neat array of black containers joined by a few strands of coloured wire to other similarly sealed packages. Unplug, take out, fiddle with wire, reattach. But the device was dead. They would send a new one, to arrive in 10 days. Too late: I would be on a plane tomorrow. I called a Te Papa colleague and carried one of their laptops on the forthcoming long trip.

I remained in good spirits. I was free, and my own boss; the new millennium beckoned. And Nigel, trusted deputy and fellow advocate, was now on board. I had negotiated the outline of his contract in the previous November visit. All that remained was to introduce him to Berlin.

Since quitting Te Papa we had spent little time in each other's company. The previous few weeks had been about practicalities – houses, belongings, legal matters – and a few days' break, plus the last Christmas of the millennium. Suddenly at the airport we were thrown together, in an awkward moment, realising perhaps for the first time that life for the next couple of years would be shaped by a museum in Berlin. We were on our own and the old collegial Te Papa relationship would need to be reset.

*

As our plane climbed out over the Pacific away from a New Zealand summer, a crew member struggled with a seat in the row opposite. It had been an extended, rattling to the point of unnerving, take-off. Now came the instruction to lie back and enjoy. This plane had yet to join the age of flat-beds. Instead, with some button-pushing, plus physical effort on the part of the occupant, the seat would recline into a series of angled parts that had head and neck, body and legs in different, and ultimately back-aching, positions. The passenger opposite reclined his seat. There was a screech of failing connections and the seat collapsed to beyond horizontal, a small mountain range of disjointed surfaces. In vain they tugged and pulled but eventually those nearby were moved to other seats and for the rest of the journey this sad wreck mocked us for our belief in the infallibility of modern mechanical systems.

So began Nigel's first trip to Berlin.

'Let's hope we can do better than that.' He spoke in a low voice as though not wanting to anger the gods that were working hard to keep our aging 747 in the air.

We organised to make enforced proximity work for us, setting up office in the sky. Shunning the films, but not the wine and food, we began serious discussions. It was a moment of suppressed delight. Neither of us was a seasoned traveller but, in an almost sheepish manner, we made much of imitating those about us, who were opening computers and raising spreadsheets that indicated serious money.

For many hours we talked, wrote things down, talked a lot more. Hours of jaunty conversation laced with anecdotes and jokes; oft-told, and frequently retold, tales; then serious observations. I offered a pen portrait of Blumenthal.

'He's mine!' In a moment Nigel had processed Mike, a rich seam of solid gold, a character he was already writing into a story. For Nigel stories were gathered and stored, to be mixed into pieces that eventually might belong in a novel. They were his, shared infrequently.

*

'The Jewish Museum Berlin – it's a Holocaust museum, isn't it?'

I heard this from the first day; I hear it still. Link Jewish, museum and Berlin and it has to be one of the world's great twentieth-century atrocity museums. The first task Nigel and I settled to was classification, forming a simple and consistent response to this notion that the public attached to the Jewish Museum Berlin. Our domain was a lot more than just those years of concentrated industrialised killing from 1941 to 1945. It was also 2000 years of lives lived. We needed the words.

I told Nigel a story of a museum as bank vault. He may well have heard it before, but it was a good one.

In the 1970s I was part of an international museum security group touring the Hermitage in Leningrad, as the city was then. Our translator was an aged and weary academic, dragged in by the Brezhnev regime from her unrelated post to attend our linguistic needs. She understood nothing of museums. We listened to a curator's impassioned discourse, in Russian, undoubtedly covering the aesthetic and historic worth of his collection. When he had finished the interpreter captured the salient point, at least for her: 'In this gallery there are 20 tonnes of silver and three tonnes of gold.'

To our translator this spectacle of grandiose excess, the culmination of centuries of wealth-stripping by potentates indulging their concentrated power and uneven taste, was not a place of high aesthetic worth, or historic value. Like so many museum visitors, she gave way, albeit at a subliminal level, to the seductive appeal of treasure.

This attitude was deeply ingrained in most people's minds by the huge, gorgeous museums of art and their immediate spin-off, the nineteenth-century comprehensive museums. The aristocracy of princes, their supporting clerics and rich officials acquired treasures as endorsement of existing and repressive power structures. They were joined by imperial and robber-baron holders of new wealth, and by the gentlemen of science who travelled the world building archives to advance their studies of history and nature. Driven by bankruptcy and sheer size, their collections steadily flowed toward nation states and city governments, where they morphed into botanic gardens, libraries and museums. These cultural institutions supported the pride and highlighted the wealth that came with industrial expansion, and the trade and growth of empires.

Into our collective thinking went the idea of museums as valuable 'stuff'. The universality of this view was confirmed by a small 'knowing museums' game I had run over the years with new acquaintances and travellers, thrown together in slight, chance encounters. For example, in October 1999 a pleasant Australian was returning to New York, where he worked in the finance industry. On impulse I asked him, as I had asked others, 'Tell me which museums you know.' When put on the spot with little time for thought, most of my captive subjects mentioned the usual suspects: the Louvre, the Metropolitan Museum of Art in New York, the British Museum, the V&A and the National Gallery in London, the various museums of the Smithsonian in Washington. In the shorthand we use when thinking about civilisation, we have in the back of our minds a generic museum model exemplified by the same 10 or 20 great collection-saturated palaces of splendour.

By this definition the Jewish Museum Berlin was no true museum; it had no riches. Instead it would be an identity museum. Yet Nigel and I knew that some would censure us as ignorant imports who would attempt to divert the museum from the true course. We would place storytelling over collections. We had heard these raised voices at Te Papa and knew we would hear them again in Berlin.

*

I had promised Mike that very early in the piece the board would see an expanded description of what the museum was to be, and surely the inspiration could be found in Daniel Libeskind's building. His Jewish Museum Berlin was architectural theatre so why shouldn't the whole experience be theatre? The idea was often discussed in the professional literature, and at Te Papa we had developed highly animated object and interactive areas. Why not lead our whole approach with the idea of theatre?

My interest in theatre went back a long way. When, as a boy, I moved from country to city, I became interested in theatre. I would attend whatever show I could find and afford, be it a D'Oyly Carte Company Gilbert and Sullivan, an Australian musical visiting town or a local production. I was easily captured by what was happening on stage. Once I spent my newspaper delivery earnings on the cheapest tickets in the house to some play that had military people rushing about saluting each other. Totally immersed in what I saw before me, I jumped to my feet and returned a salute. Actors die on stage. That particular evening the solitary teenager in the audience suffered a thousand deaths by embarrassment. A block booking to the Folies Bergère spelt trouble. Tempted by the reward of a free ticket, I pushed tickets as contraband around the school. My clientele were well satisfied, ogling the static tableaus of naked womanhood that were all official morality would then allow. But the following day I was hauled before the school principal. Terrible retribution was about to befall me, until he found that members of his staff were among those who had bought tickets. A few years later the young pre-Pythons of the *Cambridge Circus* revue demonstrated the explosive potential of humour.

By now Nigel had spread an A3 block of paper across the too-small tray table. This would become an ideas map, with words progressively flowing down and across. Emphases and links would be added with a broad sweep of the pen. When full, the sheet would be flipped over. Soon the to-and-fro between us saw ideas starting to converge into circled packages. A lexicon of words and trigger phrases grew. Those that sounded right advanced the discussion. Those that did not were red-pencilled. 'Theatre' was scribbled down and would then appear again in another context.

Of course, theatre is a wider idea than *the* theatre. The word can also denote a dramatic state, larger than normal reality, that nevertheless touches people through their emotions as much as, and perhaps more than, rational thought. Theatre can also, of course, be a device to carry small and grand lies, lulling senses with celebration and commemoration, edging around and glossing over issues. We were very aware of Albert Speer's vast Nazi pageants as theatre in the service of evil.

All these thoughts would come together some months later when I spoke at a conference in Stockholm about museums beyond the year 2000. I explored celebration in museums as a mature consideration of the full span of human history, not as one long joyous parade of triumphant events and heroes. Our 'theatre' must place history's dangerous memories alongside humankind's achievements if we were to properly encompass that universal identity of moral human beings. I gave the example of the darker side of my own nation's history, the strong racism, the New Zealand Wars and the confiscation of Māori land. I spoke also of the fate of the Native Americans, the peoples of the Belgian Congo, even the Enola Gay exhibition axed by politically powerful forces who did not want any exploration of the use of atomic bombs at the close of World War II – and of course the Holocaust.

*

Throughout the night and into the following day Nigel and I talked on, something we had not done properly for some time, about favourite collection pieces and great exhibition ideas, most not realised. Little was new but our talk was concentrated and we now had the time to go into detail. We found words for the drama, the fun, the thoughtful involvement, the ritual, the multiple dimensions that marked off a great museum from the ordinary. We would take all this to our new colleagues and tell them that the Kiwis did not do boring.

Lulled by the engine noise, I slept. Nigel, around two metres tall, tossed and turned. He cursed the lad of small frame alongside him who could curl up and drop off at will.

'Damn you, Gorbey! I can never sleep on planes,' he growled when I woke.

But Nigel had put those sleepless waking hours to good effect. Across the bottom of his ideas map were words: 'Magical theatre that evokes profound feelings.' We agreed. The words worked. A seemingly simple one-liner that spoke of complexity, of inexplicable effect, great depth of feeling, emotion, and the enchanting qualities that are part of any culture. Yes, the fit was right for the German-Jewish story. The Jewish Museum Berlin would be a magical theatre.

CHAPTER 11

BRINGING HOPE

BACK IN NOVEMBER 1999 I had arranged that on my next visit there would be a staff workshop with everyone in attendance. I needed to give the staff a glimpse of what working as a team might look like. We would do this as a sort of play-back theatre, a chance for people to abandon their desks and stand on the project stage. We would also get down to work, beginning the description of the museum to be presented to the board for their final decision in a few months' time.

Eleven days into the new millennium, about 20 of us gathered in the gallery used for the first review three months earlier. The agenda was a set of notes hastily reconstructed after the laptop meltdown. I have the file still: nine headings to be covered, a few paragraphs of expectations and some facilitation ploys.

I stood before them. It should have been a moment of strength, but I was struggling to maintain composure. The museum did not have one of my basic meeting requirements, an electronic whiteboard. On the last trip I had ordered the administration to get the best, the biggest, capable of accommodating many words writ large, with print function: the works. It would be the focus of attention. Instead I was standing before a newly unpacked device, the bottom end of the range and the smallest I had ever seen. In some embarrassment I soon abandoned it. We were back to using sheets of paper stuck up on the walls, as we had done in the original review.

Was the whiteboard saga incompetence or a calculated slight? I was aware that the head of the section responsible for this purchase was a die-hard civil servant who had made it known that these intruders from the far side of the world were causing administrative problems aplenty. He was not pleased. Nigel and I would discuss this over dinner that night. Incompetence was a distinct possibility but, we agreed, more likely it was sabotage.

First I introduced Nigel and explained his role. Then I spoke of honesty: this will be a very risky venture so let's learn about risk and help each other though crises. And, by the way, there will be many. All our discussions would be open; everyone was free to cut across traditional boundaries and venture into new areas. This was an opportunity to tap into the energy and unique talents of our colleagues. We would acknowledge real accomplishments but at the same time learn to spot and admit mistakes.

Much was unstated. This was not the time for a harsh appraisal of failings; these were known, the reason why the Kiwis were here. Nor were there any strong criticisms of traditional civil-service thinking, not yet. I had already noted that a few among us were already casting about for colleagues to blame in the likely event of failure. I needed teamwork. Some had seen me in action on the last two visits. Others had not and initially there was disbelief on their faces as I marched about with exaggerated gestures and expressive antics. I had to break that belief that everything came out of locked offices and protected roles. We were about to create an attraction.

Everyone standing, the tables pushed to the side, where they would stay for the rest of the day. Unable to barricade themselves behind the safety of a desk, the staff milled about on our stage for the day, the open floor.

'Okay, I want to know where we all belong. Where is your tūrangawaewae?' I used the Māori word. The closest German word, I would learn later, was *Heimat*.

'Where do you feel most comfortable and at home? Where is your place to stand? Nigel, you go way across there. That's New Zealand.' I indicated the remoteness of a far corner.

There would be 10 metres of bare floor between the two Kiwis and where all others were clustered, but it represented many thousands of kilometres and, at least at this early point, membership of Clan Other. We were making a point which, as Kiwis, we reinforced throughout the day – we lacked cultural knowledge, we were dependent, but we were mandated to ask the embarrassing questions, to confront issues that might otherwise be politely avoided in order to maintain balance and calm.

'Here's Europe.' I stood in the middle of the floor. 'Germany here. And across here,' I indicated the corner farthest from New Zealand, 'is Berlin. Go!'

This sort of activity was clearly discomfiting for some, but with encouragement a rough line formed across the room. Josh, North America, was off to one side. Mike should have been with him but refused to move. Or did he recognise Berlin as his tūrangawaewae?

'Now, tell me about the place where you stand. Attach a name. Why is it important to you?'

Nigel stood on the rugged Wairarapa coast of his younger years, the setting he would use for his novel *Tarzan Presley*. Not surprisingly, I was under the mountain at Maungatautari. Others were in their home town or beloved haunt. The exercise worked. People began to relax, became animated, contributed.

'Right! Where do we place ourselves along this line in terms of origin group or ethnicity?'

We muddled about. There was some quiet negotiation.

'What are you? I think I'm…'

Finally, I had what I needed. Those of Jewish origin stood around Mike. The Germans clustered middle floor. Kiwis again in the far corner. We explored what origins and history meant for each of us. The three or four people in Mike's group said little.

Later I would question him about the paucity of Jewish employees. At Te Papa we had actively recruited Māori. Why not a concerted effort to have more German Jews on staff? Mike doubted we would be successful. 'Ken, you have to understand they did a pretty good job on us!'

*

Mike made his apologies and left.

'You're just like my wife,' he said as he passed me. Barbara, 20 years his junior, was a management consultant and lecturer expert in non-profit organisations. 'You play these games.'

It was a bit of a put-down, but also an announcement that he was not about to intervene in the step-by-laborious-step process of building confidence, positive working relationships and a sense of urgency within a group that had for too long seen its task as futile. We were all relieved. He would have tried not to intrude, and present his interpretations as definitive, but his would always be a formidable and even inhibiting presence. He just had so much history; had been part of its making. With Mike gone, our slighter histories and book learning could come to the fore, our discussions could be that much freer.

Throughout the workshop Nigel and I made bold assertions about magical theatre and contested the oft-stated primacy of collections. Using scenarios drawn from movies, great novels and, horror of horrors, the leisure industry, we emphasised – perhaps even overstated to get an argument going – the power of narrative.

Generally as a group the staff held back, but fortunately, we had Inka Bertz, who was too much the connoisseur to accept outrageous proclamations from the Kiwis. With a tilt of her head, a small gesture of despair and a slight explosive puff of breath, she objected. 'That's really over the top and inaccurate. That's not what a museum should be.'

Excellent. Inka had a broad knowledge but her certainty invited challenge. Unperturbed, she responded to a colleague with another comment. Her command of English was phenomenal; she would often employ words at the very periphery of common usage that I could only puzzle over. She would sometimes then disappear and return a short time later with her large English dictionary. 'See, it does exist!' Inka-led debates always ended with her throwing her head back in laughter, for she loved a good argument. Very rarely did I give ground on 'what museums should be'.

The workshop was frenetic, bubbling with informality, jest, jokes, interjection, dispute, finally even agreement. Everything was relevant and admissible. Over the years I had developed a checklist of critical areas that always needed to be covered when defining a museum, or anything with a cultural component. Currently it stands at some 25 areas. That day it allowed every contribution, no matter when it arose, to be written on headed sheets scattered about the walls. In this way everyone could see that they had contributed.

As ringmaster my role was to act out, emphasise, encourage, involve, stimulate, even cajole. But I could also make myself small, become the passer of the pen, as others were bold enough to find new ideas and words. Then I could prance about again, so that others had to get up and move. Small work groups would form and reform. It was important that the quieter participants should be part of what was happening, and not just as listeners. Nigel was equally animated, often not requiring any invitation to participate.

I used stock phrases: 'Where and how does the visitor find something quite unexpected?' And homily: 'Never underestimate the visitors' intelligence; never overestimate their knowledge.' Frequently someone would support their position by announcing that 'all Germans' (or Kiwis, in the case of Te Papa) 'think/read/act like this'. I would respond, 'We and our professional colleagues, with our specialist knowledge and commitment to museums, are the worst possible model of the broader audience.' In due course market researcher Christiane Birkert was available and Nigel or I would demand that a test be run. Inevitably she would come back with a result which established that Germans shared very many of their behaviours and expectations with the citizens of the United States, Canada, Britain, Australia and New Zealand. The idea of the universal citizen was alive and well.

*

The workshop made progress. The headed sheets of paper spread across the wall began to look like an outline of our board paper.

'Who is our audience?'

'Everyone,' responded some wag, with a broad grin.

'True,' I said. 'We'll exclude no one. But we need to be much more specific so that our writers and designers can focus on the needs of our target audiences, some of whom will be new to museums.'

This was a somewhat devious discussion. Months before, Mike and I had agreed that we would be seeking a cross-generational audience. He had demanded that the museum should not be formed in the 'tradition-bound German model'. Although he was not a great museum visitor, he knew the United States Holocaust Memorial Museum, and his thinking was increasingly influenced by Te Papa market research. He saw extraordinary results in those museums. 'I see the JMB as a modern museum like the best of those in America, something I can take young Michael to.'

That addition about his son was important. We were to create an attraction, a place of interactivity, bustle and noise, even fun, with whole families engrossed and participating. I had explained this meant we would need to join that brash and noisy entity that is the market. We would be competing openly for the families' time, against all other available attractions. Nigel and I were thrilled. We would make this Jewish museum unexpected, not a boring place but an experience that demanded a visit.

When we arrived at the right place in the workshop, I announced that Mike wanted the cross-generational audience and we defined it: family or family-like group of parents or caregivers and children, moving through the museum together, feeding off each other's responses and insights.

Nigel warned, 'It's not as easy as it sounds but it does allow us to shift the whole museum to a different plane. No one is allowed to be bored. We'll emphasise interactivity so that visitors of all ages can get their hands to work as well as their minds.'

'Sounds a bit juvenile. A museum of buttons to be pushed.' The wag again. 'Isn't this just part of the current rush to dumb down museums?'

There was a murmur of approval at this intervention, but Nigel was in his element. 'There are many different ways of achieving interactivity, and it has nothing to do with museological fashion. There'll be nothing dumb about what we'll be producing. Our museum will be a complex, information-rich experience for those who wish to spend more time. It will engross people in the task of seeking information in their own way and at their own pace.'

Mike had heard all this from me, and it was a done deal, but it was important to talk this aspect through, since we knew soon some critics would make the same points.

After 'Audience', my heading 'Museum Philosophies' gathered words and one-liners. Then came 'The Conversation', the style of our communication with visitors. Nigel, novelist and storyteller, led with something very new to our colleagues, the tone of voice that would best serve our purpose, including humour. We outlined an 'Exhibition Plan', perhaps the simplest of our tasks, for it was essentially the current historical framework expressed as exhibitions. Simplest, but also what worried me most. Finally, the workshop talked about, and acted out, how we would run the museum. This, I insisted, was more than just employing a few cantankerous guards who would focus on infringements, berating visitors for having backpacks and children for being rowdy. It was about welcome and assistance. For the first time I pressed the idea of life as one of the defining characteristics of our museum.

At the end of the workshop I asked each participant to tell their colleagues what they had gained from this day. All agreed they had learnt much and that the whole experience had been positive. In various ways they talked of being on a new plane, moving away from the docile and the deferent towards greater honesty. Also, it had been fun. My closing observation was about the confidence we had found in working as a team. Together, we would open this museum.

Back at the hotel Nigel and I went over the next steps in detail, defining major work streams and laying out a work plan for the next few months. One stream would be Nigel's responsibility: developing the exhibition plan. I would take the directorial role, keep Mike up to speed, compile the concept for the board, review and approve, create a museum culture and string the whole operation together.

*

I would also be building a new staff and strengthening both their project skills and their resolve. I had been surprised to find how restrained my new charges could be. Our New Zealand German friends were masters of strongly held and expressed views. They would tell us if an idea or suggestion was good or bad in a manner that left us in no doubt as to what they thought. I had expected more of the same in Berlin. Instead I had found studied evasion, even avoidance. That is, Kiwi behaviour, the fudged response and complex linguistic manoeuvre, all in the name of not being seen to give offence or raise a shadow of disagreement.

At first, I took this reticence to be the result of feeling trapped within a failing project that would be harshly judged by their international peers, but I came to see it as much more. It was plain that these young German academics and practitioners carried the inherited guilt of a war fought and genocide practised decades before their birth. They were open and knowledgeable about their nation's dark history and I admired and respected them for this.

But at the same time, I began to worry that embracing blame for the Holocaust was also an avoidance device – a protection against the sometimes dangerous nature of their own family and community histories. Only once did I hear a family story, and that was from a staffer whose parents were Jewish. In New Zealand the Te Papa concept had been a deeply personal exploration for everyone involved and a bunch of Kiwis had shared their family stories. But this did not seem to be the case in Berlin. To reach beyond this would require my new staff to undertake a personal enquiry into their family history, and that carried terrible risk.

So often the only lively conversations were about self-blame, born of the Holocaust, despite the fact that we were telling the history of 2000 years of life and that in an early academic review historian Professor Reinhard Rürup had stated, with some feeling, 'the history of the Jews of Germany is *not* a prehistory of the Holocaust'. Interestingly, some of his colleagues disagreed.

*

The workshop had the desired effect. In the days that followed every hour was filled, setting targets for the next two years and allocating workloads. The fear of failure was in retreat, but that dangerous fog, euphoria, was in the air.

Euphoria is the bane of all projects at that early anything-is-possible stage. It blurs vision, dulls thought processes and causes the problematic to be underestimated. In such a state we skip the forthcoming grind, the many months of hard work, to stand calmly on opening day accepting the plaudits of the crowd of luminaries gathered to wonder at the great thing that has come to pass. People in their thousands visit our environment of delight and wonder. It is a daydream, one that I must admit to having many times. Perhaps there is worth in these dreams. Perhaps they motivate. But in Berlin I had to remind myself, once again, that euphoria had no place, not yet. Instead we would harness passion, which separates the driving, achieving cultural institution from those that exist in a state of routine ordinariness.

Mike had planned a lecture for the evening before the Kiwis would turn again for Wellington. We would tell everyone, staff, colleagues and museum friends, about what lay ahead in the next 19 months. Some 60 people gathered in the room. Mike sat in the front row. At my persuasive best, I began with the heady stuff, the words that flow so readily early in a project.

'The Jewish Museum Berlin will be a magical theatre that evokes profound feelings. We can make this one of the great museums of the world. But don't underestimate the challenges we face.'

Next Nigel dwelt on the need to know the ordinary visitor's mind, their needs and level of experience. He told a group, used to writing the final text, that things would be done in quite a different way. From now on they would produce content briefs full of the scholarship, but the actual words that would communicate the narrative would be the job of professional writers.

Then came a warning. These people were about to invest a part of their lives in a taxing project and they needed to steel themselves against what was to come – frequently unfair, even cruel, comments capable of inflicting hurt.

'Well before the opening, naysaying critics of limited understanding will appoint themselves as all-knowing commentators. There will be dire warnings of tasteless presentation, inappropriate ideas, lack of integrity and imminent cultural failure. They won't be interested in what's actually happening in the museum but will act as oracles with a message of impending doom. We must prove them wrong!

'Even after a successful opening, the voices won't be quiet. They'll point out how easy the project really was and how it could have been done by anyone. Why can they be so certain? Because it's open, isn't it! It must have been easy! Indeed, they'll say that it could have been done better.'

I hammered away at the many things that could go wrong if we did not keep the pressure on. Some bemusement was evident. What was the new project director saying? They all had things to do. Here in Berlin and from afar he had plied them with tasks and plotted a steady progression to opening. They had a new colleague in Nigel. Why the doubt?

I slapped my final sheet on the overhead projector, this being long before I had conquered PowerPoint. It set out the six stages of project management. Everyone expects these to be technical, but these were different.

'Euphoria' was the first stage; we feel elation and everything is possible. During the second stage, 'Diminution of Dreams', reality starts to bite; everything is not possible. Our spirits sink further in stage three, 'Disenchantment', as a harsh timeline and tight discipline takes its toll. Things get nasty in stage four, 'Search for the Guilty', when those outside the project broadcast their worst fears, and nastier in stage five, 'Punish the Innocent', when project workers carry the can for those fears. Finally, in stage six, 'All Glory goes to the Uninvolved', the museum opens magnificently and everyone discovers they were supporters all along. Project workers are largely ignored. 'And note, you won't be invited to the opening.'

After a slight pause there were hesitant, disbelieving smiles. But Mike slid around in his seat to face the audience of museum people about to experience a very, very tough ride. 'You'd better believe it!' he growled.

*

There are many traps hidden from those with little historical knowledge. In the workshop I had lined people up across the room according to ethnicity. A couple came up to me afterward and told me how instructive this exercise had been. For the first time ever there had been a discussion about origins and the paucity of Jewish staff.

Then a few months later Cilly Kugelmann, the new head of education, arrived at the museum. Mike had recruited her before I had joined. She was a talented woman possessing a wicked humour. We were destined to become firm friends. At our first meeting, however, Cilly indicated she had heard about the workshop and, in a quiet voice, she pointed out the chilling irony of my game: 'So you're the one who caused the Jews to be lined up to the left and the Gentiles to the right.'

CHAPTER 12

CITIZENS OF BERLIN

BACK IN NEW ZEALAND, early in 2000, I had to confront the nose job. When Susan came into my hospital room her face said it all. I had thought of delicate blades deftly handled, but now I knew otherwise. Nose Renovations Inc. must share drilling equipment with the local automotive engine reconditioning factory. I was a battered mess.

Recuperation meant desk time. There was no break in the flow of faxes from across the seas, information that fed into business plans, staff requirements, a budget, planning schedules and building briefs. Nigel and Susanna went ahead. Then, with our home above the harbour let to a delightful couple of German academics, Susan and I made the move to Berlin. During each of the 12-hour flights across the globe I wandered about the sleeping plane, the pools of light where some insomniac was reading reminding me of the 'Lili Marlene' street lights that foggy Berlin morning months before.

In February, Nigel and I had flown via Asia. This time the route was via the States. It mattered not. New Zealand was one side of the globe and Germany the other. Turn left or right, the distance was much the same: 18,000 kilometres.

*

It was early spring 2000, and Susan and I took joy in learning how to live in a new place. With exploration came discovery and frequent misunderstandings, the cause of much laughter. It is the oldest one in the stranger-in-Germany book, but I couldn't find Einbahnstrasse (one-way street) on the map and wondered aloud who Einbahn had been. Our newly purchased bikes revealed the city as a car never could. A surprise was the green, with trees and parks everywhere. We found our 'locals', including the Deutsche Oper. On our first investigatory stop we came away with a wodge of opera tickets. We puzzled at the intricate and coloured pipe system that criss-crossed the city, above our heads one moment and, at our small local park, Olivaer Platz, snaking across the ground. We learnt they were part of green Berlin. Construction companies that breached aquifers below the city were required to pipe the water back underground. The pipes never seemed to have a beginning or an end and for all we knew were their own closed world of endlessly circulating water. Then the graffiti, everywhere. On our first day we found graffiti as artwork on the banks of the Landwehrkanal.

Susan took responsibility for finding an apartment. One agent had a quality prospect. We were foreigners, Ausländer, perhaps in banking or some other well-paid pursuit. It was in the new Sony Centre. Would we like to see it? This was the wonder location of Berlin, well beyond our means, but we were not about to admit this. First deep into the multiple descending levels of a carpark, then a lift to emerge, looking straight out at the immense upside-down suspended hook that gathered up the network of cables and seemed, in a gravity-defying reverse act, to hold up the vast canopy roof over the central court. The apartment was 90 square metres and glass-walled, all the better to get the best vistas back into the centre one way and out over the Tiergarten the other. It was a science-fiction film set, sterile. A bit beyond our allowance, we told the agent. The truth was it was roughly four times what we had allocated for an apartment.

Then we had one, light and airy, and bigger than the house back home. In its time it was probably an artist's studio. The room facing the street was double height, six metres floor to ceiling, with huge windows and a narrow gallery on two sides, accessed by a staircase so steep it made better bookshelves than steps.

As with so many others, war had torn at our building's façade. Once it had been decorated in Kudamm-style, flowery decorated façades of apartments for the rising German bourgeoisie and in its day much loved and derided. But Konstanzerstrasse 63 was now blank, with just a couple of balconies. We only ever used ours as a cooler when it snowed, since we were worried it would not bear our weight and could plummet to the ground, something that did sometimes happen in Berlin. Across the street a building had survived intact. Then, immediately next door, a crude modernist infill plugged a hole left by the bombs. Several hundred metres away an almost picture-perfect set of old buildings stood beautifully preserved on tree-lined Giesebrechtstrasse, testament to the roll of the devil's dice that was carpet bombing.

I would come to understand the completeness of destruction wrought upon the city during that ordinary, day-to-day thing that was the walk to work.

*

Very early morning; my reconditioned nose would detect an apartment smell, and then lose it in familiarity. Cooked food was only part of it; more the aroma of history and a space lived in for a very long time. The little house on the hill in Wellington had no such smell. New Zealand air is always on the move from one ocean to the other, flushing away any lingering fragrances. Each morning I was reminded that I had awoken into a different world.

Automatically I would check the chestnut tree. Its green canopy softened the view from the Berliner Zimmer, the long room that connected the front of the apartment to the back. In winter it was a skeleton of dark branches. The resident crows were good to wake me with their raucous squawking. At the large windows fronting the street I would squint at the temperature gauge on the shop below. How far below zero was it this morning? Had the temperatures slipped to life-threatening levels, or were we heading for a heat wave? Berlin, like London, is not a hot city; it is best muffled up in a soft comfortable blanket of snow. The summer worked, as long as northern European conditions prevailed. But as soon as the city tried to be Mediterranean it became stifling, the famous Berliner Luft, air, telling of drains not working as they should. In the first few weeks of our residence the temperature hit and stuck at 38°C. Heat was everywhere and, dressed for official duties in a suit, inescapable. It permeated the museum, despite air-conditioning. Susan was co-opted to write business plans in areas outside the experience of staff. Early bright mornings might be cool, but returning to the apartment at the end of long hot days was particularly difficult. We would try the U-Bahn, but underground the still and oppressive heat was relieved for a moment only by a rush of air as the train raced into the station. Then, forced to the surface, the heat would reflect off every surface. The buses were fetid and sticky heaps of humanity. That week we walked long distances searching out scraps of shade.

But most days were not like that. Shower, light breakfast and walk to the U-Bahn. I stuck with the route I knew from my first hotel, through the old ornate Wittenbergplatz station with its murals of all things early-twentieth-century modern. Then the ride up toward the light before Gleisdreieck, where I puzzled at the archaeology of former lines marked by old brick archways going nowhere, and checked the construction of the new high-speed train line where it burst out from under the city. Then followed a picturesque elevated route, steel wheels squealing against rails on tight curves close between buildings in which people could be seen living and working, past the Technology Museum, over the Landwehrkanal to Hallesches Tor, and the walk to the museum.

A few weeks on and travel time mattered. The fastest was another U-Bahn route from Adenauer Platz to Mehringdamm. From there I would walk. At first I did not know what I was looking at. But, armed with new knowledge, I began to understand that, morning and evening, I was walking over ground that had been a battlefield within living memory.

I turned towards the Landwehrkanal and its handsome stone bridge. Above was the early twentieth-century battleship-like bulk of the elevated Hallesches Tor U-Bahn station and its substantial riveted girders, the best Siemens technology of the time. It was probably once deemed to be ugly but now it had matured, was part of urban heritage. Ahead was Mehringplatz. This was a new name and I much preferred the old, Belle-Allianceplatz, even if the 'belle' had long been lost.

Fifty-five years before, Stalin had decreed that his final goal in marking the end of the Nazi state would be the Reichstag. He set up a crude competition among his generals to be the first there. For the army approaching from the south the waters of the canal had been one of the last physical obstacles to be overcome. At various points soldiers had scrambled across amid heavy gunfire, taking and inflicting terrible losses. Immediately beyond the canal was the Platz. Already badly damaged by bombing raids, it lay on the route to the Reichstag. Over a couple of weeks in late April and early May 1945, Soviet artillery poured almost two million high-explosive shells onto Berlin, completing the destruction of a city already battered by bombing.

I saw the photos, and read the accounts, of the buildings of Hallesches Tor (tor means gate) when it was a true, formal portal to Berlin city, of the finery of the encircling apartment buildings that had been Belle-Allianceplatz, and of the grand avenues that flowed into the Platz from the old city. Equally I came to know of ruined streets and bridges, and the buildings as smoking shells. Amid the destructive force and noise of constant artillery fire Berliners had tried to save themselves in the cellars, fearing, for good reason, the advancing soldiers bent on terrible revenge. The remnant German army, supplemented by boys and old men, would fight on with senseless determination when everyone but a few fanatical leaders knew that all effort was futile. They would die. Some would try to desert and, if unlucky, be caught, tried and executed on the spot. Survivors would be shipped to prison camps in Siberia or melt back into the population. My Belle-Allianceplatz was ugly. The circle of once elegant apartment buildings and shops had been replaced by cheerless modern apartment buildings that sought to capture the form, if not the former glory, of the Platz. The grand avenues had been diverted. My imagination would overlay images of devastation upon this now peaceful scene.

It is for this reason that I am miles away as I cross the Platz. A couple of kids kick a football into the air and it falls from a height, brushing my face and suit. Some older women, old enough to have huddled in those cellars, tut-tut and shout annoyance at the young tearaways. One of the boys stands in front of me, aware that this had been a close thing. As the ball descends, second bounce, I move into it and kick a perfect half-volley, firmly. The ball slaps into the boy's chest and he gives out an involuntary grunt. The tut-tutting women applaud and loudly praise my skill. But that kick is so perfect in its execution it could only be a fluke.

The final approach to the museum from the Platz was a short walk along Friedrichstrasse, then a right turn and that charge, always, of seeing the Libeskind building through early-morning sun, or gloom, rain, fog, snow.

It would be sometime after 7am when I pressed the button next to the heavy door at the staff entrance and announced my arrival to the guard on duty.

'Guten Morgen.' Sometimes it was a new guard and I would give my name and try the title in German.

But in reality my language was juvenile. There was a market in the Platz every Wednesday and I tried to learn some shopping words. 'Zwei stück Lachs, bitte.' I would point to the two pieces of salmon I wanted. 'Ein kilo Spinat, bitte.' I was a spanakopita man and determined to continue my habit of making a large one every week that would spread over a couple of dinners and a lunch or two. The first time at the local market I had my well-practised phrase ready, but in front of the vegetables, with a commanding woman awaiting my order, I froze.

'Deutsch? Russe? Englisch?' No 'Türkei'; the stall was Turkish.

'English,' I admitted, ashamed of my lack of languages. But by the next time I had conquered those few words and gradually became a local, greeted with smiles from the multinationals fronting the stall and my kilo of fresh spinach already being gathered and wrapped as I approached. It was a nice feeling, but nothing would overcome the fact that I was a foreigner and did not speak German. At least I could tell people this. I had learnt it to the tune of 'She'll Be Coming Round the Mountain When She Comes': 'Ich bin Ausländer und spreche nicht gut Deutsche.' There was great hilarity when I sang it to Mike and a few staff late one evening.

The desk I called my own had a window that opened in defiance of the air-conditioning. It was a comfortable distance along the corridor from Mike. My arrival had been a territorial worry to some. It had been suggested that I should commandeer a large office, one capable of housing an appropriate-sized desk and a personal assistant. I would require one – yes? Well, actually, no. The last thing I needed was a PA; I had never had one in my entire career and I did not plan to change that now. The exceedingly bright Josh, allocated to me on my arrival, was too valuable to the project to crash about doing my bidding. He would soon find himself in a production field far removed from, but drawing on, his considerable historical research expertise. He loved this change of direction so much that we would all ultimately have to pressure him to go back to Princeton.

I was not about to disrupt people who were established and happy in their places of work, surrounded by their books and personal items. I would take the small office, the one that was vacant and available.

Often at the start of the day Nigel and I would meet for an uninterrupted 90 minutes to discuss what was on our separate and joint agendas, actions required, or just to catch up. We would share news, at Te Papa? In New Zealand? In the world? He would have been awake since 4.30 and have already written another 400 *Tarzan Presley* words, perhaps more. He gave out little, but once, under pressure, he summarised the storyline, protesting that I would hate it. 'It's about a child raised by a troop of gorillas in the jungles of the Wairarapa, threatened by huge wētā, who is found by Jane and grows up to be Elvis Presley, who is still alive and living in Australia.' That sounded okay to me and I loved the book when it was published. Those early months in Berlin coincided with the publication of *Skylark Lounge*. Nigel was chuffed when I arranged a Berlin launch of the novel as part of the normal Friday-night staff drinks.

*

In moments of reflection I would look out my office window and see foliage I had not expected. This was a city of many open spaces; a park surrounded the museum and the school opposite, set against a backdrop of the tall buildings of Mehringplatz, evidence of rational master planning. It all seemed so reasoned, yet I came to feel that the landscape I observed camouflaged chaos.

Look at the trees, all of a certain age. It was nothing to do with decline – they were healthy and full of vigour come spring – but the oldest among them had been around for no more than 50 years. Their parents had been cut for firewood in the harsh winters just after the war to form a barren urban wasteland. The trees had returned but what I saw was a thin membrane of growth laid across the foundations of ruined apartments, shops, industries, even the occasional unexplored bomb or artillery shell that would cause much fear when uncovered after decades of rest. This was a place still in the process of healing.

But what of the citizens of this city under repair?

Frequently there was some awkwardness when people found why we had shifted to their city. They knew of the Jewish Museum Berlin, but that these Kiwis should be part of it came as a shock. There would be a pause, a resetting of expression, a search for the next response, for any interaction that might lead, yet again, to Germany's history being revealed. And part of that history was personal.

We came to hear family stories that encompassed the Nazi era. Was there any other past that could be talked of? The accounts would be told sometimes in snippets, sometimes as a more practised statement. They had no explanations for what had happened in their parents' and grandparents' time but would tell of how that past era touched them all at a very personal level. The family that benefited from Jewish property confiscation, the quest to prove the purity of Aryan ancestry, the 'terrible death' of the uncle, even the religiously motivated ('naïve' was the word used) resisters. The relationships we forged were not based on the past and my role in creating a history museum, however, but on friendship. These new friends enriched our lives. We told jokes, talked politics and enjoyed one other's company.

'It's the funniest film I've ever seen,' Olaf Brosig explained, 'but I don't understand the game.' He had just seen the Bollywood spectacular, *Lagaan*. Central to the plot was a cricket match between the dastardly and devious English tax collectors and the much-put-upon villagers. We were in our local Greek restaurant, Samos. I cleared the table and used various utensils to explain this strange ritualistic rite. The owner, Christos, contributed free shots of ouzo. Later I would see this film and only then realise just how impossible it is to truly understand cricket unless you are born to the game. The *Lagaan* 'game' depended on a deep knowledge not just of the rules but also the unwritten codes and traditions of fair play (the province of the Indian villagers) and foul (the English tax collectors).

Berndt and Robyn would suggest a Sunday afternoon trip to search for, if rarely find, some restaurants – most of them now long closed – from their days of early marriage and children. As he searched among rundown lines of lakeside buildings – 'It has to be around here somewhere!' – Berndt talked of the frustration of increasingly affluent West Berliners taking their new cars out on weekend jaunts. Everywhere beyond the city limits was the East and therefore not available to them, so they would head for the Grunewald Forest to join a six-hour, and increasingly angry, traffic jam, with the picnic lunch happening where the car became frozen solid at a roadside not of their choosing. There would be no movement until the tangle slowly cleared toward late evening and they would grump their way home.

Olaf and Maria took us into rural East Germany accompanied by their dog, a border collie called Moira. She was a constant reminder of New Zealand farms. We edged along an old military road, just narrow slabs of concrete laid on the bare earth with an eroded half-metre car-destroying drop on either side. Finally we arrived at the fish farm destination and with much glee read the sign that did not welcome but instead warned of the dire punishments, including the confiscation of all tackle, that would attend a long list of transgressions.

We were welcomed into homes for New Year's Eve celebrations and dinners. Francis and Boris, who lived in our street, invited us to their country cottage and showed us the medals and Nazi paraphernalia found in the garden, obviously buried hurriedly before Russian tanks rumbled up the road. We took trains to visit the towns of Germany. Dresden became a frequent destination, to glory in the museums and learn of the restoration of this bombed-out city. We attended exhibition openings, tours, lectures, concerts, the opera and met artists, becoming in a small way part of the cultural depths and social life of Berlin.

We began to discover the East. Helmut listened as we pined after our New Zealand coast and promptly arranged a few days in Heringsdorf on the Baltic Coast. Gigi and Kallo Jaspers owned a hotel there and we would find what we were looking for. The weekend was wonderful and the chef put on a special meal, the biggest plates I have ever seen loaded with food. The beach was long and we walked to Poland. But it lacked the scale of Pekapeka, that occasionally stormy endless stretch of sand. Here the waves were measured in centimetres, not metres, and where our beach was marked by the occasional storm-delivered tree trunk, this one had dinky woven wind shelters like large baskets. We came looking for New Zealand in Germany. Instead all we found was a part of Germany, thereby taking a step toward embracing our new *Heimat.*

We attended an exhibition at the Martin-Gropius-Bau that made thoughtful historical links between Germany and Russia, enabling a better understanding of that part of the world. But the failed utopia of the communist experiment was laughable, in a sad sort of a way. The 1930s film clips made a dangerous and heroic drama of the workers' struggle against reactionary wrecker Trotskyists to bring electricity to the new Soviet town; Stalin was portrayed as a god-like figure in a clip culminating in applause that went on and on and on and on. How the filmmaker had struggled with that key question, when to close off the cheering crowds. In another circumstance a regional leader had indicated, after 15 minutes of hand-numbing applause, that it was time to finish and get down to business. But too soon, and he had earnt many years in the gulag. With hindsight I can say that this exhibition was the beginning of a change in my views of the world.

*

Berlin sits on the edge of central Europe. In one direction the world is the West. But to live in this city is to feel a pull, a periodic tug, towards that cultural and moral construct that is the East, that vast physical and cultural territory stretching away to the distant Pacific Ocean. I resolved to delve deeper into this new 'other', in order to develop a greater understanding of the relationships that ordinary people around the world are bound to forge if we, and our planet, are to survive the threats of the next one, two, three, perhaps more centuries.

The beginning of the East was a bicycle ride away, a part of our new city. There we found, in the seedy and deteriorating fabric of East Berlin, a metaphor of the power of the state crumbling towards eventual demise. More than most, the communist East was an artificial construct of a state – its citizens lived within a political and social culture imposed from afar. Immediately after World War II, aka the Great Patriotic War, concluded, a cadre of disciples carefully trained in the ways of Marx, Lenin and, in particular, Stalin descended. A grey communist regime became the reality for the next 40 years. This state could survive only via rigged elections and a massively intrusive police state in which your friend was also likely to be your betrayer. Some millions chose to leave until a barrier wall contained them. Not for want of loudly shouted slogans, it was a system that steadily ran down and down towards collapse.

It was so unlike our part of town, Wilmersdorf, where we lived among a concentration of apartment blocks layered on the land by history. Our pavements were full of the people who occupied those apartments and who jostled in the shops immediately outside our door. Although the East was the same city it was a different place, where the regime had completed what bombs and artillery had started. The old and narrow had been swept away to accommodate the parades of orchestrated precision by which the always glorious state apparatus demonstrated to itself how much its caring leadership was loved. To either side stood the buildings, the Plattenbau apartment blocks, standard factory-made components of dubious quality piled atop one other, formed to provide an appropriate frame for propaganda photos that recorded the flags, the lines of soldiers and military hardware, the bands, the happy factory workers, the saluting platform. It all had purpose, at least for the authoritarian state.

But by the time we came to East Berlin history had passed judgement. The state had crumbled. One night in 1989 long-denied people streamed through the breached wall. The parade grounds became just streetscapes, putting excessive distance between active living zones, across which people scurried. The memorials became incongruous, but their very presence demanded our attention and further interpretation.

Perhaps the grandest of them all looms in Treptower Park. A Soviet soldier, in heroic pose and many metres high, cradles a small rescued child. Surely a fitting tribute to the men who had lost their lives in the battle for Berlin, it was impressive, but we already carried with us the black Berliner joke that this monument was the 'tomb of the unknown rapist'. Oh, the cruelties of conflict. On one side the liberating Soviet soldier who had defeated the fascist beast; on the other, less formal side, this was the person who visited rape upon the women of the city. Both, in their own ways, were accurate.

Further, the soldier portrayed in that memorial is a heavily romanticised construction written in slogans by the communist party back in Moscow. There was but one sanctioned story, Stalin as military genius, the architect of victory in the Great Patriotic War. But this was a mask to cover the faith-shaking slaughter and the incompetence that attended so much of the Soviet war effort. This tall bronze figure bears no resemblance whatsoever to the Russians who arrived at the gates of Berlin and fought their way in. Carrying the greater part of the fighting burden throughout World War II, they were pressed in suicidal waves upon the enemy. They died in their millions, way beyond the death toll of any other fighting nation, including Germany. In the process they were dehumanised by the vicious battles they fought and the demands of Stalin and his generals. They were exhausted physically and morally, and outraged by the atrocities committed by Germans. Rape was part of their practice of war, especially as they crossed into Germany, and after four long years of cruel battle they plied that art with official encouragement until finally called to heel. Now that vast body of men (there were some females but mainly it was an army of males) is represented in Treptower Park by a monument that is a falsehood.

Across town Ernst Thälmann, the German communist leader murdered toward the end of the war, has his own huge sculpture. He looks out toward the ultimate victory, fist held high against a backdrop of frozen bronze flag. His nose is heated. Other sculptures, and cold animals in the zoo, could accumulate caps of snow in winter, but not a hero of the DDR. Too big to be cut up and ground down, Ernst was now good only as a canvas for graffiti.

Our first encounter with the Ossis of East Germany was equally sad. On the same day we had encountered the Soviet soldier memorial at Treptower Park, we stumbled upon a market. We had visited others, all lively with interesting trinkets cunningly presented as unique objects, but this one was different. Each stall had a puzzling array of goods, all essentially useless and from a different era. One stays in my mind. A stall owner, a tall but wretched man, sat hunched over, surrounded by many hundreds of brass pipe valves of all different sizes to fit all situations. Somehow, they made no sense and melancholy hung in the air.

It was another cultural enigma to take back to the staff for explanation. Thomas Friedrich, an expert in the social life of Berlin, had a suggestion. In all probability this man and his collection had been stranded by the collapse of the communist regime and its economy, or more correctly its two economies. The official command economy functioned at the level of a state-controlled money system and official decree, coexisting with a vast network of hidden under-the-table transactions. In this second economy, the true entrepreneur would find and fill a special niche.

Thomas explained. 'Suppose your car needed a new tyre. The state might supply it in some months or even years. Better to mention what you needed at the local pub and soon you would find who specialised in your particular tyre. Likely they would have an apartment full of them and a deal could be made.' Thomas could only conclude that the man at the market was such a specialist. He may even have been rich in DDR terms but he had been overtaken by new ways of meeting demand, and by PVC pipes.

*

Beyond the city that had been East Berlin was the country that had been communist East Germany. Our first expedition had taken us to the Baltic coast, crawling at 30 kilometres an hour along motorways whose concrete sections, now aslant, had been laid directly on the soil beneath. We could speed up when our route took us down picturesque tree-lined rural roads through a landscape of old industrial buildings and derelict houses with storks nesting on abandoned chimney-tops.

Then we had professional reasons to visit Eisenhüttenstadt, a town created by planning decree to produce steel. The drive took us through fields of sunflowers, bright yellow against a sculptural horizon of huge blast furnaces. This was picture postcard, so very European, so very different from New Zealand. Official artists of the regime had been required to evidence modernity with smoke pouring from those tall stacks of reddened steel, but now only two were working. The rest were dead.

We had expected communist drab but the town was special, everything that the political propaganda of the early 1950s said a socialist enterprise should be. The buildings were well proportioned and crafted, an early promise of urban environment that soon would be set aside as the command economy sputtered and failed. There was a certain humanity about this sun-soaked, but much-reduced, corporate town.

'When all these furnaces were going full blast the works employed 12,000 people. That number included all social services, medical and the like, even a brass band and professional football club!' shouted our guide, one of the many made redundant by the new capitalist order that came with the collapse of the DDR.

He seemed unable to talk quietly, perhaps because he had worked around noisy machinery all his life. Cilly translated, racing to keep up.

'I know now it was terribly inefficient,' he admitted. 'The place has been sold to a Swedish company and now there are only 400 people employed in the entire works.'

Here we could see the huge unemployment problem of the former East following reunification. We stood on a platform above the newly opened high-tech robot-like roller mill. A 20-metre-long slab of white-hot steel emerged from the furnace. Even at this distance it was difficult to withstand the heat. It was rolled this way and that, becoming longer and longer, faster and faster.

'Watch! Watch!' shouted our guide. Then, an astonishing flash of magic and the hot steel wrapped into a huge roll. It was exhilarating.

Two women crane drivers worked high above our heads, lifting the rolled sheet metal onto railway trucks. A solitary man at the end of the process recorded and marked the rolls. Beyond those three there were no other workers in this vast hot hall.

The visit to a museum of everyday life, our official duty, was quieter. Much there reminded me of a New Zealand beach cottage frozen in the 1960s.

CHAPTER 13

DANIEL LIBESKIND, ARCHITECT

'HELLO – YOU'RE THE FIFTH DIRECTOR I'VE WORKED WITH,' and Daniel listed them.

It was early in our Berlin residency, spring 2000, and I had arranged to meet architect Daniel Libeskind. Susan and I were uncertain what to expect. I had already read of Libeskind described as Woody Allen on speed. And I had it from colleagues in the international museum community that he was no 'loving child', the literal translation of his name, but, rather, a harsh infighter and a person to be wary of. Mind you, none of these commentators had ever met him and that reputation undoubtedly came from the vicious fight some years back to make sure the museum was not cast upon the scrapheap of bright, never realised architectural projects. Even now, with the museum built, the hurt of that campaign was still fresh.

We stood outside the museum. It was a Sunday, one of those brilliantly fine early spring days when the sky above Berlin does its very best to be blue. Few people were about. I was tense, even anxious.

Libeskind arrived with his wife and business partner Nina. They were a short couple but up close their bright and open faces dominated all else. There was a generous sparkle as Daniel put names to those who had gone before, evidence of various executive arrangements tried, failed, rejected. We relaxed, and in no time were joking. I am sure that this couple could be very tough when required but right from this first meeting it was humour, as well as Daniel's building, that bonded us. It was the beginnings of not just a partnership but an easy friendship.

'We were crossing this street after the competition award ceremony.' Nina indicated Lindenstrasse. 'I turned to Daniel and said, "Do you really want to build this thing?" and he said, "Yes", and I said, "Right, let's do it!" At that time we were in the midst of a shift from Italy to the States. Daniel had a new position. Our household stuff was already being shipped, but I took charge and organised everything to be reloaded and moved to Berlin.'

Daniel was architect as academic. The Jewish Museum Berlin was not just his first museum, it was his first building. Photos show the professor in front of his students, engaged in architecture as theatre, perhaps the Woody-Allen-on-speed reference. The chalkboard behind him full of powerful, if obtuse, diagrams.

*

The Berlin City Museum, on the other hand, was no theatre, nor did it have a single driving idea that captured attention. Levels of excitement and expectations were set low and nothing lifted it above the noise of other cultural happenings. Its collections were slight, of interest to a limited group. It had no champions. As a result, the economic recovery of Germany after the war, the Wirtschaftswunder, had not touched this place. Other cultural institutions, opera, music, theatre, dance and museums, had new buildings to replace bombed-out ruins. But the Berlin City Museum, infrequently visited and with minimal profile, was bypassed and could only wait many decades until the grinding official process finally brought an extension project into the city budget. A competition was announced. Daniel Libeskind submitted an entry, and everything changed.

Within the Berlin City Museum was a small department of Jewish history. Daniel was a Jew. His father was one of that small percentage of Polish Jews who had survived the Holocaust. The rest were murdered. All this he poured into his competition entry, along with an architectural vision uncluttered by tradition and the strictures of practice. The result was not so much a formal response to a competition brief as an art project in which a shining metallic thunderbolt was cast across the site, pierced with walls thrown about and thrust over it at precarious angles. It had spaces that seemingly made no concession to purposeful function; they were just shapes and voids that spoke to the emotions. It tapped into the Berlin ghost culture of the bunker in an audacious manner as it drove underground to link with the Kollegienhaus.

Most entries paid homage to the adjoining entry building, the baroque Kollegienhaus, stepping back, deferring, placing an appropriately sized box here and a rounded surface there. Animation and impact figured little, as though any architectural excitement might be bad form. I know nothing of their deliberations, but in an act of great bravery the judges picked Libeskind as winner, looking beyond design norms and museological function to select a building that captured an important element of past and evolving German society. A few years later I would talk with a professor who chaired the panel of experts that awarded another project, outrageous in form and marginal in buildability, to rising star of the avant garde, Zaha Hadid. 'A competition committee is allowed to dream,' he said. 'It was about time Zaha got a major commission.' He might have added that perhaps they did not expect it to be built.

Dreams can be very difficult to translate into reality. Shortly after the Berlin City Museum competition the wall fell and, in the face of the likely costs of reunification of the two Germanys, the extension was threatened with delay and even abandonment. A campaign of powerful voices took up the cause. 'There was a relentless playing of the Jewish card on the political stage,' said Mike later. 'They used the Jewishness of the building to best advantage. This was Germany and that idea was worth a lot.'

The building was completed but the question of what type of museum it would house was left open. Enter Mike Blumenthal. It was 1998 and Berlin politicians went to their now famous, once spurned, refugee son.

'Herr Professor Blumenthal, pray tell us, should the Libeskind building be just an extension to the existing Berlin City Museum or a new Jewish museum?'

His conclusion was that this powerful piece of architecture would be wasted as the home of such a slight cultural enterprise as an ordinary, underachieving city museum. No, such deep symbolism meant that the architectural tail must wag the museological dog and Libeskind's building could only be a museum of Jewish history.

*

The Libeskind building had an unrelenting physical presence that challenged and defeated any fondly held beliefs about what an 'ideal' museum should be. To look at it, to walk through it, was to feel an awe that trumped the professional certainties of decades. A few concentrated hours of discussions and I began to form new understandings. The museum occupied anything but neutral ground. This had been a battlefield; a few kilometres away was the site set aside for Hitler's huge domed grand hall, a temple where 180,000 of the (standing) faithful would come to the renamed capital Germania to celebrate their Führer and his Thousand-Year Reich. In short time I saw the Libeskind building's landmark features as an extension of that history.

It was a bewildering anti-structure of brooding dark history. A commentator described it as 'a disassembled Star of David', a place of knife-edged corners way beyond the predictable right angles of a well-mannered edifice. It was rendered in the materials of industrial processes, its façade cut about by irregular and seemingly haphazard windows. The interior was as challenging: the descent underground, the long main staircase, Voids where a concrete-faced thickened line was drawn across the weaving zigzag of the building, and of course the long galleries. Disorienting. Discomfiting. But then there were parts of the building so beautifully evocative they took my breath away.

I struggled, though, to comprehend it as a whole. It took some weeks before I understood that the Libeskind extension to what was now the Jewish Museum Berlin was not a malleable thing, but a universal proclamation about suffering. It said, 'I am grievously damaged in ways that the human race should never endure. I do not forgive.'

*

That spring morning Daniel led us off Lindenstrasse and through the building that had made him an international star. The entry area was the best place to start on my main objective for the morning: the extensive modifications that would be called for. We stood in the Kollegienhaus and Daniel listened to my concerns.

'This mean little revolving door at the main visitor entry is good for one person at a time, not the crowds we're confident will come. There's no place for ticketing, the garderobe is far too small and the journey through to the museum exhibits is confused. What's more, the bookshop is a meaningless mess that just doesn't make commercial sense.'

I half expected a defensive response. But no, Daniel positively glowed when I described the new Jewish Museum Berlin as an attraction with an important story to tell, one that would draw at least 600,000 visitors each year, perhaps even 750,000. Immediately he was interested in the solutions. We, Blumenthal's new guard, proposed a museum as a grand international event, not the inconspicuous little city institution with a mindset out of the nineteenth century. Daniel had been told to design a museum for 150,000 visitors and minimal impact. Now I was telling him the museum would attract many, many more people. He understood, so it was straight into the minutiae of making it work: circulation, door widths, security, ticketing, coat racks, direction signage and much more. Deeper matters of philosophy and intent would come soon enough; in those first exchanges we talked of an extensive rebuild of some parts of the museum.

The tour continued. The steep steel staircase to the underground level and the three tilted Axes, Holocaust (murder), Exile (the diaspora) and Continuity (life moves forward). We stood within the tall Holocaust Tower with its sliver of sun high above. The brutal look and texture of the concrete had been important. It had to speak of inhumanity, a bunker mentality. The authorities had demanded a fire escape so he had turned it into a sculptural element. I became aware of the importance of sound and the amount of work that had gone into the deep click that marked the closing of the door as people were confined within. Later, when we did an operational test before the opening, a small girl would hear that click, turn to her mother with some fear and ask, 'Mummy, are they going to let us out?'

Daniel introduced his Voids: a single line of contained space the full four-storey height of the building, and the full length. Heavy concrete walls, the materials of bunkers and extermination. Void with a capital V: a physical expression of nothingness.

We entered the Main Void. Again, every sound reverberated back. This, along with the Holocaust Tower, was the only one that could be accessed. The others were only for glimpsing from narrow slit windows, never the full Void, only part. At the top of the steep main staircase the corridor-like galleries. where mind-games were played by awkward corner effects and dead spaces.

I began to notice that the Libeskinds employed two quite distinct levels of discussion. One was superficial and not entirely convincing, perhaps a practised campaign spiel formed as part of the battle to get the museum built. But then there would be moments when architect and architecture came together with a single passionate voice: 'Listen carefully and you will hear of a deeply felt need to disorient, to throw up obstacle. My very form is defined by the symbols of violence and exclusion. Enter only if you will undertake a traverse that demands the exercise of empathy to the point of discomfort.'

There was, though, a huge problem for a visitor-experience man like me. Visitors are intelligent and able to be challenged, but at the same time they do not wish to be confused and disoriented, to lose control of their visit and even feel belittled. We would need to draw soft boundaries between the discordant elements of Daniel's stunning architecture and the needs of the ordinary citizens who would come to this museum.

I had been told that Daniel required the Voids and surrounding areas to be unsullied by any form of use, to remain absolute expressions of nothingness. I wanted to explore this further.

'Are the Voids and their walls taboo?' I asked. 'Could these walls frame exhibits? Could the Voids contain something, or must all exhibits maintain a respectful distance?'

His response was nuanced; he had ideas; we had plenty to think about. Also, we would work on an accord that stated our respective positions, just as Cliff Whiting and I had done at Te Papa. I was delighted that Daniel was open to opportunities. His architecture would be an active participant in the special, even transforming, experience we were creating. But everything he talked of, every built symbol, shouted out Holocaust. I could not take my mythical chainsaw to this building; the depth of the longer and larger history would have to be achieved in a building made out of those few horrendous years.

Back at the museum I talked with Cilly and Inka. We must expand our vision for the Main Void. In exchanges at office doors we tested out various ideas. How about this? I know this sculptor. Then Inka came up with the unique piece that would change the nature of the Jewish Museum Berlin. Collectors Dieter and Si Rosenkranz had offered a major Menashe Kadishman sculpture, some 12,000 iron faces/masks to be scattered about a floor area in different numbers and configurations. This work immediately suggested itself as an ideal solution for the Main Void. I tried it out on Daniel and he extended our thinking into having this work occupy all the Voids, even those that were not accessible.

Kadishman's *Shalekhet/Fallen Leaves* arrived at the museum, many tonnes of it in several truckloads. There followed a fascinating meeting in the Main Void: Menashe Kadishman, small and gnome-like, in a flowing nightdress and seemingly little else, and Daniel, equally small but attired in the latest designer fashion. Arms waving, they marched about, talking volubly and, in all probability, past each other. Smiles all round; we had agreement. *Fallen Leaves* would inhabit the floor of this tall and narrow concrete emptiness. The staff cheered silently from the side.

The work is still there. It has become a key reason to visit the Jewish Museum Berlin, as one of the *Guardian* newspaper's 'thousand art works to see before you die': 'a moving, unforgettable experience.' Most would agree. Thousands of heavy, roughly cut, open-mouthed iron masks scream in the face of death. Each is an individual, the detritus of extermination. They lie where they fell. The visitor is invited to traverse the space, to walk over them. The clinking sound fills the Void. For many, including some staff, it is abhorrent to step on the faces of these 'people'. Elsewhere in the museum we would honour the achievement of many generations of German Jews. We would be rational, even use humour. But the Kadishman work in that Void was about inhumanity. In no other museum I have seen are visitors brought so close to the direct experience of human suffering.

Often I would encourage fresh thinking by challenging a wider staff group to suggest ideas outside the scope of their exhibition responsibilities. Usually I would float something that I thought to be particularly ingenious and invite comments. Before settling on the Kadishman, I had done this for the Main Void. In that case my initiating notion had been based on sound, so important in Daniel's building. In the Main Void in particular, any tiny noise or whisper would reverberate back and back, until seemingly absorbed into the concrete walls. Perhaps we could commission a work from Scottish percussionist Evelyn Glennie. She might be asked to respond to the acoustic qualities, giving visitors an extra dimension in a building designed with sound very much in mind. She could even work with Daniel on the piece: in his youth he had been a talented, scholarship-winning musician. I ran out of time and it came to nothing. To this day it remains a disappointment.

*

My accord with Daniel was only two pages but of long title: 'A Partnership Based on Mutual Advantage for the Licensing of the Libeskind-Bau Design and the Development of the Museum'. The museum would recognise the status of Daniel Libeskind as a mature artist and one of the great architects of his age, and his building as a major work of art. We could also agree that 'the concept of a work of art evolves over time when subject to usage, research and reinterpretation'. The building would be reinvented as part of a thought-provoking exposition of German-Jewish culture and history. Importantly for me, it was recognised that the 'Museum Director will have the final approval for exhibition design concepts'.

The accord worked. I would take any new idea that impinged on the building directly to Daniel; we would negotiate; an agreement would be reached. Mostly, anyway. But there were times when staff in the Libeskind office would worry about a change. It was as if they carried an authorised version in their heads and this Kiwi was bent on challenging a larger architectural truth. But generally, Daniel and I could find a place where building and exhibition concept drew strength from each other.

*

Defending and endorsing the Libeskind building was part of my job description, but the place had captured me. Early each morning I thrilled at that first glimpse of the museum and delighted in my good fortune to be so closely associated with its future. Within it I found places of refuge where I could take myself at stressful moments to be lost and calmed. I formed a deep respect and even love for Daniel's creation. And I was not alone in my enthusiasm. The building had opened to international acclaim and had been acknowledged for its ground-breaking design. It was on the cover of every architectural, and travel, magazine. In the months before the opening, buses would draw up and disgorge tourist bent on getting photos of themselves in front of a building to be talked of and puzzled over. Those in the 'see the city in three hours' tours would crowd the museum-facing windows, their cameras clicking as their bus drove slowly past.

But, for many commentators, the museum was good only to be dismissed. One international journal stated the usual criticism, that the Libeskind building was not fit for museological purpose and that all those who liked it were 'perhaps a little gullible in their acceptance of the new'. In my response I wrote that 'the spaces of the Jewish Museum Berlin are not a series of sound stages waiting obediently for academics and exhibitions designers to strut their stuff. Rather these spaces, and their component elements, are active contributors to the telling of arguably the most fraught history of any cultural relationship the modern world has known.'

On three separate occasions I sat on panels where famous architects dismissed the Libeskind building.

'It's kitsch. I don't like it,' said one. He thought the design too obvious, too singular an idea. Another convoluted dismissal seemed to be based on changes in functional spaces, as though this was something that never happened in the refining of any design. Yet another said, 'I find it too …' and then, lost for the right word, showed the audience a face full of disdain and made a vigorous arm gesture, which he left them to interpret.

These were all architects whose designs were more nuanced than anything Libeskind might produce. They rejected his architecture as too direct, somehow not subtle enough, and certainly infringing every canon of building as functioning machine. In these exchanges I often found that the critics' negatives were my positives. Perhaps we could never cross this particular divide.

*

One discussion did not involve me but I followed it with interest. Daniel's building was opened to tour parties two years before any moves were made to install the exhibitions, and visitors began to comment on the impact of the interior. At that time the news was full of plans to establish in Berlin a monument to Holocaust victims.

In general, unlike some other states, the German nation had made the effort to confront and make amends for this past, despite frequent expressions of 'shame fatigue'. They had done this with reparation and education, in some cases through memorialisation. In sculptural and architectural form they sought to understand their ignominy and make some form of redress. American architect Peter Eisenman had designed a monument, the Memorial to the Murdered Jews of Europe, a sea of tall steles to be sited on a full city block up the road from the museum. We stood about a barbecue in a Berlin suburb, a gathering of friends. The subject of the memorial arose. To a person these socially conscious citizens expressed their distaste at what they saw as a static thing not of their culture, an imported idea. Someone dubbed it a carbuncle. They went on to explain the responses they had made as a community to address their Nazi, and colonial, history, thereby shaping a better world. They worked with refugees; they had set up a training programme for African doctors and surgeons in the local hospital. There were other initiatives. Later it would be such people who would welcome to their country 1.2 million Syrian refugees.

I felt that the memorial was an imperial imposition on both the cityscape and German society. On sombre snowy days it seemed to work and the underground information centre provides context that the memorial itself cannot. But only a small proportion of those who came to the memorial visited the centre. On a fine day, the memorial had too many of the qualities of a playground. Adventurous souls would laugh as they jumped far above the paving stones below from stele to stele, always pursued by exasperated guards. The day I was there, with children, the memorial did not speak of reflection on harsher matters.

One response was that the Libeskind building should be that memorial, that it should become sacred ground. I could understand this: the empty building had an intensity approached by few others. But at the same time, I was forming the view that this building was not so much sacred as magic, a place of dramatic experimentation.

The building as memorial was not taken further, and I was glad, not just because I was in Berlin to open a museum but more because I have always worried about memorials. The Vietnam Memorial in Washington works so well as a single idea beautifully realised. It draws forward the names of Americans lost in a futile and destructive war. Each and every day people come, searching for a family member or friend, leaving a personal memento, reflecting, mourning. I have been fortunate to see it as a dark gash in a snow-covered landscape and it strikes at the soul. In New Zealand, and Australia, our Anzac memorials are designated sites that each year are used for services of commemoration. The Angel of the North in Gateshead was not meant to be a memorial, but ordinary folk had taken to using it for ceremonies of their own making, from weddings to commemorations for traffic accident victims. When I visited, there was a bunch of flowers at its base. These are all sacred places that are about personal and community identity, and they are bound together by their role as elements of a moral society.

If only they were all like that: other memorials carry messages that do little to shape a better world. The Congo memorial in Brussels lies about a cruel and exploitative colonial rule. Others seek to legitimise the oppressive regime, glorify the brutal leader, or carry divisive messages that tear peoples apart.

My objection, then, to a memorial in the centre of Berlin that certainly attracted visitors and focused on a critical part of world history? It was the fact that a tradition of the 'large', developed in more authoritarian and fascist times, should be perpetrated in this modern age. Its size, bigger than anything the communist regime had managed across town, seemed to come from a need to shout louder, to make up for the enormity of the crime. The scale of its conception dehumanises a very human crime against the notion of humanity.

*

My role included architectural guardianship. A good example was the saga of the fence. It was proposed that the Libeskind-Bau and its garden be encased in a tall steel barrier. This, the proposers explained, was required of all Jewish institutions in Germany. It was true. Most such buildings throughout the city stood behind heavy fences. Where it was not possible to build a fence, one had an armoured car parked outside permanently.

I returned to the plans. Because I had, for a time, been a member of an international museum security committee, I had a few analytical skills in this area. A very brief search revealed that the proposed fence had two very obvious holes, through which the proverbial, and actual, bus could be driven. When I pointed this out to the police security expert, he knew what I was saying, but would not comment. He did not want to get embroiled in a Jewish matter. 'It is up to the museum to make the decision,' was all he would say.

I had a further objection to the fence. The staff and I were deeply involved in branding the JMB as a friendly place, not cut off from the local community, city and nation. We would set aside the fortress mentality that typified so many of our sister institutions. Yet here was a barrier that flew in the face of these values.

I came to see that the fence had little to do with security but was more a manifestation of how members of the local Jewish community positioned themselves within contemporary German society. I knew I was treading sensitive ground: there were, and still are, extremists out there who would harm these people, but the fence did not work. Eventually, to my great relief, I prevailed and the project was shelved.

*

It is after the opening of the Jewish Museum Berlin. Daniel's building has been a large part of the general perception that this really is an outstanding institution. We can celebrate. Daniel, Nina, Susan and I meet at a fine little restaurant not far from our apartment. The theme for a memorable dining experience has become Woody Allen's double album, *The Nightclub Years*. We have known for some time that four of us are well versed in his early stand-up performances from the 1960s. Nina recounts how they once whiled away a long drive across the American Midwest listening to and reciting the best of his jokes. Soon we are sharing them anew, fuelled by a couple of bottles of chablis. The telling descends into trading punchlines.

'And the joke is on them because they don't allow Jews!' Raucous laughter. This is the one where the Berkowitzes, a couple at a party dressed in a moose suit, are transported unconscious to the forest, shot, stuffed and hung in the New York Golf Club. Other diners are not amused.

'Keep the kid' – the most memorable line in 'Woody Kidnapped'. The police negotiator and kidnappers trade demands and finally agree that the crooks will not get much of what they want but they can hang onto the abducted Woody. Though there is also the lovely moment when his parents, after finally getting around to reading the ransom note, 'snap into action immediately – they rent out my room'.

The chablis is excellent, one of the best on the list, but is challenged by the museum administration. I plead that this was a serious evening of critical relationship-building, and I do so without even the suggestion of a smile.

CHAPTER 14

REACHING FOR THE UNEXPECTED

BUT WE STILL HAD TO GET TO THE OPENING, and that meant convincing my new staff that the Jewish Museum Berlin would succeed as a magical theatre. To demonstrate this I required some memorable occasion, a piece of drama. This would be my one moment on the stage, after which I would retire from the boards.

In our first weeks in Berlin, Susan and I had discovered an English-language bookshop, and one of the first titles I bought was a recent book by Fritz Stern, *Einstein's German World*, which considered Einstein and his cohort of outstanding German scientists. In a long chapter, Stern explored the relationship between scientists and correspondents Fritz Haber and Albert Einstein. Both were of Jewish origin, both rational men of science, but otherwise very different.

Haber was quintessentially Prussian in his embrace of nationalism. As well as receiving a Nobel Prize for his work on synthesising ammonia from the air (the process on which so much of world agriculture is based to this day), Haber had willingly joined the military efforts to make Germany great, including taking a leading position developing gas warfare in World War I. Ironically it was at Haber's laboratory that Zyklon, the gas used to murder millions of Jews during the Holocaust, was first produced. But Einstein rejected Haber's jingoistic fervour and his predictions were darker. For the Jews, said Einstein, no good would come of narrow German nationalism.

It was a captivating read. Stern positioned the two men not only as scientists but also as important figures in the intellectual–social life of twentieth-century Germany. Except when talking pure science, they traded strongly opposed views of the world: 'Haber in the service of his country and of science, Einstein in the service of often unpopular political-humanitarian causes'. This excited me. Here was a disputatious dialogue between two great minds, right at the centre of the grand irony of Jewish existence in Germany. Leading up to World War I, through the Weimar Republic and right up to the establishment of the Nazi regime, the Jews of Germany saw themselves as fortunate citizens of a state that in so many respects was the most liberal in the world regarding their hopes of full assimilation. They were achieving so much. Yet at the same time, the voice of anti-Semitism embedded deep in German and European society was growing louder.

This was exactly the story that people, not just in Germany but worldwide, wanted to hear and surely what our museum had been established to pursue. And the thesis Stern was exploring reeked of theatre. I set to work then and there on a dramatic structure and bullet-pointed script. It was hurried, incomplete and loose, undoubtedly full of inaccuracies and misconceptions, but it had a nice feel to it. In one performance, say no more than 12 minutes, I would interweave related events and people, issues and historic developments.

I stepped forward and populated my imagined stage with sets, props, screens, sound, light. In a street scene and coffee shop, Haber was on one side and Einstein on the other. They were writing to each other. A voice-over carried their exchange. Haber promoted the promise, but Einstein responded, 'Can't you see the gathering storm?' The words of Heinrich Heine rang out, 'Where they burn books, so too will they in the end burn human beings.' Others contributed in their own way, Kurt Weill perhaps via song. I even had the jagged Libeskind windows behind me delivering lightning flashes – perhaps in retrospect a little over the top. Movie and object, some animated, carried the images of scientific results, good and bad; Einstein's dilemma about the military uses of small-particle physics that eventually led to the atomic bomb but also to understandings of our universe. Other characters spoke of the issues of the day, the hope and eventually the hopelessness of this period of history. The action reached forward in time to three contemporary generations, grandmother, mother and child, born into different times with different personal histories, candidly questioning their beliefs and attitudes.

I finished. Surely my performance had convinced everyone.

'That's kitsch, Ken!'

Horst Olbricht was one of the researchers, a tall, gentle man but always good for an argument. His was the intervention I needed. He had supporters. They worried about the popularist nature of my piece of theatre. The terrible word 'Disney' was heard. Others questioned the ability of such an imagined presentation to maintain historical accuracy. In response I explained how the senior historian at Te Papa, Jock Phillips, had consulted many diaries to write a digital game in which the visitor, young or old, became captain of a nineteenth-century sailing ship bringing immigrants to New Zealand. Every incident in that game had happened and was part of the established historical record. Accuracy was certainly something to be worked at and Fritz Stern's book gave us the academic foundation. I disagreed, too, with the 'popularist' criticism. This was part of capturing the attention of our audience who were, by our own definition, intelligent people bursting to be informed and moved. They would, I suggested, instantly separate the device that transmitted knowledge from the core knowledge itself. I denied the 'kitsch' label in no uncertain manner. We would make sure it was a quality production; there need be nothing sentimental about this piece of theatre.

Others quite liked what they heard and challenged the detractors. It was a lively exchange, in which everybody felt they could get involved.

The Haber and Einstein theatre made it into the board paper as an example of the character of our new museum. It was never produced and for that I was both sorry and grateful. At the time of my presentation I would have sworn that this was a totally new idea, arising out of the performances by the theatre company attached to Waikato Museum decades before and the animated set-pieces we had achieved at Te Papa. But later in that year, 2000, I would discover that a Berlin coffee house with its cluster of tables had been a feature of the Museum of Tolerance at the Simon Wiesenthal Centre in Los Angeles for some time. Their topic was general, the descent into Nazism, but the stage was the same.

The Haber–Einstein relationship has been the subject of a play but it still awaits a museum treatment. It sits in my mind as one of those projects that deserves to be brought alive in a three-dimensional magical theatre. Now, with so many more technologies available, I could add much more activity. Around some central spectacular built core, interactive cells would allow the audience to investigate further and build their own performance. The whole circumstance of German Jews across the ages and into the contemporary world could be captured in this strange, even heartbreaking, relationship between two men of genius.

*

Now it was the turn of the staff. 'Tell me about an idea you have. Don't worry about the whole storyline. Just give me an idea. Where might it fit into our story and then we will see how it fits into my pace diagram.'

Thomas was the first to respond, describing something that had obviously been on his mind for some time. This was an alley of street signs loaded with the presence of the Jews. It was a good idea and he presented it in a nicely theatrical way, by movement through his imagined street as much as words. It would be included as part of the exhibits on opening day. Others followed, some good, others overly stern and worthy. Generally they were not fast paced. A historian's academic training puts great emphasis on balanced discourse told in steady and impartial tones, but I needed more drama.

Famously, Alfred Hitchcock once explained that if he had 13 'bumps', he had a film. Hitchcock was talking of the high-impact moments of action, excitement, emotion and sheer terror that we still remember from *Rear Window* and *Psycho*. The dramatic impact of these moments comes equally from the calm and even restful periods between. The more elegantly fabricated these are, the greater the force of the bumps. I contended that good museum visitor experience was in some ways structured like a good movie. The difference was that cinema-goers were captured in their seats for a prescribed length of time, whereas museum visitors were largely on their feet, moving about to build, piece by piece, their own production, based on prior knowledge supplemented by new information taken from the exhibitions. This was how great leisure-industry experiences worked: moments of high energy followed by long periods of rest, with lesser encounters and events, or time at the food stall, or just standing in a queue waiting to get into the four-minute-high of the *Back to the Future* ride at Universal Studios.

Horst's supporters continued their questioning. Surely this was dangerous territory. Might my approach not lead to a story being skewed for effect? They were right. The danger was real. But progress had been made.

My copy of *Einstein's German World* got passed around the museum. I forgot all about it until 30 months later, as I was about to leave Berlin, it was returned with the thanks of the librarian who, unbeknown to me, had been overseeing its circulation.

CHAPTER 15

THE ERA OF PROBLEMS

IN EARLY JUNE 2000, the board met. There was one item on the agenda: this would be the one time that they would consider and, we trusted, approve a full concept for the Jewish Museum Berlin. We would present to them the result of two months of hard work, our grand idea of a magical theatre that was the equal of Daniel Libeskind's extravagant yet elegant building. They expected a list of exhibitions. What they got was so much more – institutional culture, marketing and the logistics of getting to opening, such as timelines, a swathe of initial business plans and budgets important as evidence that we had taken control. We called this document 'The Book'.

The meeting took three hours. I indicated that we were finished. We waited. A corporate sigh and then suddenly they were vigorously rapping knuckles on the table. I had never experienced this before and was taken aback, only to then realise that their faces indicated that this was a gesture of approval. Later Cilly Kugelmann would explain. 'It's part of the academic world. We don't clap. That was a rousing acclamation.'

*

The meeting closed. Euphoria bubbled. Invention and progress lay ahead, the stuff that feeds the spirit. But, as I had warned everyone, we are also entering the Era of Problems. Someone had to face those problems, and they were in my job description. My means of capturing, confronting and resolving them was the Day One Management Team (D1MT).

No one was excluded from the D1MT. It brought together exhibition team leaders, production people and concept talent. Weekly, then twice weekly as the opening approached, up to 25 people crowded around a large table. Many of them were young and comparatively inexperienced but they were busting to learn. The meetings were cumbersome but effective. I chaired and wrote the minutes.

Every meeting minute, every presentation, started with a reminder of just how tight the timeframe was. In the very early days my first report to staff shouted '69 WEEKS TO OPENING'. That bold announcement counted down, and down, until we came to hate it.

Everyone soon understood that we would not be leaving the room until we had agreed on a solution or an action, if necessary thrown resources into a problem area. Body language spoke volumes. It might seem that we had reached a solution or that all relevant facts were on the table, but someone, if not me, would pick up a sign, a look, a fidget, the way shoulders were held, and more searching questions would uncover another difficulty or some unexpected consequence, and, frequently, a more elegant solution. Nothing was allowed to escape our attention.

'Look – we're making this up as we go along!' I would say as a new approach emerged, requiring some of, or all of us, to readjust.

Nigel and I were not immune. We knew about the process, but had limitations when it came to organising some of the exquisite administrative detail. Fortunately, after the euphoria of the board adopting our paper, we were brought up sharp by Oliver Bätz. At his dictatorial best, a manner that sometimes annoyed staff, he raised the issue of structured spreadsheets of objects, text, images and props. Along the base of that meeting minute I wrote 'Good work Oliver', and was very glad to do so. But generally, when it came to exhibitions it was enough for us to note that a team had successfully reached a particular stage. The D1MT was more about creating the whole operating institution.

A fairly typical D1MT minute, of the 8 January 2001 meeting, noted that we were '35 WEEKS TO OPENING'. It was cold but with new coats and boots we no longer feared the Berlin winter. Not minuted was my expectation that the Germanic gods would send snow for Christmas. Inka looked up meteorological records to tell us this would not happen, as snow always comes in January. But the evening before we closed down for Christmas, as I was preparing to leave the museum in the dark, it began to snow – a concentrated slow-moving whiteness in the still air. Outside my window the flakes drifted into the arc of the street lamps and adhered to the heroic sculptures fronting the Kollegienhaus. Trees were outlined, stark black and white. As I walked to the U-Bahn, flakes brushed my eyelids and in a moment disappeared. The roar of car tyres on tarmac had been replaced by a low squeaking of new snow squirted aside by creeping vehicles. A dead leaf chose a moment of absolute silence to detach. I heard the faintest snap and stood watching it slowly dip one way, then the other, until finally it came to rest at my feet, framed by shining whiteness.

Susan and I were elated. Far from the New Zealand summer, our new home was turning on a performance of delight that deepened our emotional attachment. My children gathered in Berlin, Conan from New Zealand and Susi and her husband Erwan from London. Snow built up around the bottles of wine on the balcony. We threw a Christmas dinner, inviting Nigel and Susanna and their young children. On Boxing Day we travelled to the Tierpark, across in the East. Conan and Erwan played apes, swinging from the S-Bahn carriage straps and hooting. It was a happy carriage and everyone laughed. The zoo animals that could take the cold stood stoically, wearing caps of white. The following day we met the Cox family at Volkspark Friedrichshain, with its snow-coated Brothers Grimm water garden and substantial hill, a huge, partially demolished concrete flak tower piled over with the rubble of a destroyed city. The children had a new toboggan. We lunched in the park restaurant, a relic of East Germany that gave cafeteria food a bad name: slabbed grey wiener schnitzel, puddled vegetables. But it was a time of good cheer, the glory of a cold European city at its very best.

Of that D1MT gathering a few days into the New Year I have no recollection whatsoever. It was just one of many, many meetings, all the same, that marked the path to opening day. A series of cryptic shorthand notes show that the 19 staff who gathered generally reported progress, and that there was a new item on the agenda. The Blindenwerkstatt, the Blind Workshop, was to be incorporated into the Jewish Museum Berlin. This was a wonderful story of Otto Weidt, a German who strove to save Jews from deportation by employing, and hiding, them in his small broom factory in Hackescher Markt. Students had researched and saved the place; now we would be run it. A group of us would meet to plan the launch. Perhaps the most threatening issue raised at the meeting was that the reconstruction contract was falling behind. We had signalled this to the board back in June. Now the danger was real.

*

The original visitor estimates had been far too low. The museum would attract a far greater number, for which the building was not designed. Substantial changes had to be made to air-conditioning capacity, circulation routes, doors, cloakrooms, ticketing, toilets and security. The list went on, and it cost many millions of Deutsche Marks. Time was short so I was not that surprised when, by decree, a Berlin city construction agency was given the job. This was one of the things I was learning about Germany. A city might have its own construction company, even a bank. Berlin's bank was just about to go belly-up, greatly accelerating the city's slide toward insolvency. That should have been warning enough, but for a while at least I believed that this city construction arm would work in a business-like manner with the best interests of the museum to the fore. But Oliver began to report constant prevarication, explaining that the agency was subject to all sorts of political pressures to work on more than one job at once: they might work for a day or two, then disappear to another job, leaving the site deserted. And we could not access the galleries to install exhibitions until the work was done. I called a crisis meeting with the contractors but, because I lacked political clout in the city administration, I got nowhere. Construction work lagged, passing from the status of uncomfortable to grave threat.

It was time to bring in Mike; together we visited the minister in charge. Mike was at his best. I understood little but sensed that the minister was being invited, via subtle threats, to join the team and not become the obstacle that stood in the way of achieving this critical national and international project. He was convinced. The necessary actions were signed off. I carry this image: the minister leans across his desk, bypasses all other pens and selects one to sign the document – in red ink. Was it true, or has my mind invented such a dramatic flourish?

The red, or black, signature done, the minister had a requirement of us. He was very proud that his ministry had just been given the task of restoring the old 1936 Olympic stadium for the 2006 Football World Cup. He would take us there and explain his plans. Our small fleet of black Mercedes parked on the stark surrounding apron. Above loomed the heavy geometric concrete forms of the stadium. We walked to the main entry, past what had once been a Nazi parade ground for many thousands but now was innocuous playing fields. Long since stripped of its swastikas and more obvious Nazi symbols, the arena still had a heavy authoritarian air. In those rows of seats the adoring Volk had saluted their Führer. I thought of Leni Riefenstahl's acclaimed yet duplicitous sporting film, *Triumph of the Will*.

As we stood high in the stadium, Mike recalled how, as a nine-year-old Jewish boy, not really knowing what was happening, he had cheered every victory of the champions of the Aryan master race. 'I used to know all of the gold-medal winners. I could probably quote them for you now.'

He paused. I was standing on Hitler's podium. We had expressed surprise at how unprepossessing it was, a small area of concrete slightly raised above the rest of the seating. Mike looked over at me. 'One of them was a New Zealander.' It was said almost as a question.

'Yes,' I replied.

One of them *was* a New Zealander: Jack Lovelock, winner of the 1500 metres. It had been a great moment in a little country's history.

Suddenly it was 1936 and I was Harold Abrahams, BBC commentator, Lovelock's friend and fellow athlete. Memory played the film I had seen so often in the course of planning a Te Papa exhibition. I saw Lovelock racing down the straight. In front of 100,000 vacant seats, a phantom full house, I called Lovelock home.

'Come on, Jack! Come on, Jack! … My God, he's done it! Lovelock wins!' I shouted it out across the years. 'My God, he's done it!'

I was aware that my eyes were full of tears. I had bowed my head but Mike noticed and said, 'That's nice', in an almost fatherly manner.

Those tears were born of complex emotions. In part they were for the New Zealander who had prevailed on that cinder track below and died in front of a New York subway train some years later. But more it was the emotion of connection, with new friends and the staff back at the museum who were part of building a new moral landscape out of histories that included much darkness, and with the country that was reforming me.

*

I had concerns about the now well-entrenched sequence of exhibitions. The Mike and Shaike Weinberg scheme was a very fulsome step-by-step coverage of 2000 years of German-Jewish history. It was easy to see how they were drawn to this approach. On the surface at least, a year-by-year and century-by-century chronology of episodes and events offers an ordered structure that everyone understands. Mike had used this approach to trace his family's history from his earliest ancestor right up to his father and himself. Shaike, the ultimate museum storyteller, had structured the Museum of the Diaspora in Tel Aviv, today the Museum of the Jewish People at Beit Hatfutsot, and the Holocaust Memorial Museum, along not dissimilar lines: segments of the relentless march of time coupled with the exploration of themes relevant to each era.

The story would go something like this. The disputatious tribes of ancient Israel and Judah were finally dispersed and their temple destroyed. The Jews became the people of the diaspora. But through their religious beliefs and practices they retained a strong sense of self. They were valued for their skills and loyalty to the states they lived in. As literate traders, linguists and craftspeople, and even as slaves and soldiers, Jews settled around the Mediterranean and accompanied the Roman army throughout Europe. By AD 321 they were living in the city of Cologne, in the Germanic province of the Roman Empire, as is evidenced by an entry in the *Codex Theodosianus* which, in essence, allowed the resident Jews to be taxed to the hilt.

I delighted in the story of Isaak, a Jewish trader with the necessary knowledge of geography and languages, whom Charlemagne charged to guide a Christian delegation to the court of the Caliph Harun al-Rashid in Baghdad. The Christians died, but five years on Isaak returned leading a gift from the Caliph, the elephant Abulabaz, complete with a glorious tapestry cloak. Charlemagne loved the huge animal and chose to be buried wrapped in its cloak.

But in a growing Christian world the priests of the Christian religion were portraying the Jews as the despised killers of Christ. The Crusaders turned on their local Jews. Why go all the way to Palestine when the enemy is at hand? In 1492 the vilified Sephardi Jews of Spain were told to convert to Catholicism or leave or be slain. The Jews were available as the cause of any catastrophe that might occur, such as the Black Death. Shunned and limited in what they could do and what positions they could hold, they became a very poor minority, able only to make the most of occupations Gentiles would not, or could not, follow. In some cases they prospered as bankers and traders. Glikl bas Judah Leib was a talented and independent woman of the seventeenth and eighteenth centuries who had travelled widely through Europe. She was unusual in being a female in the merchant trading business. Her writings offered remarkable insight into everyday Jewish life, including 'marriage-politics', that is ensuring the security of all her very many children. Glikl deservedly would have an exhibition segment of her own.

But Europe was changing and, even in the controlled intolerance of Germany, the influences of the Enlightenment were felt. In the mid-eighteenth century scholar Moses Mendelssohn brought secular culture and the importance of the individual to the Ashkenazim (German) Jewish community. A man of great intellect, he published widely and translated part of the Hebrew Bible into German. Not long after came the French Revolution, in 1789, and the conquering Napoleon held out the promise that Jews would become part of European civilisation. The long-held dream of full assimilation into German society seemed at hand. In World War I the Jews gladly fought for their Kaiser.

At the same time modern anti-Semitism was on the rise. The Jews, never more than one percent of the population, were represented as a degenerate race and the source of all wrong. The ground was prepared, and prepared well, for the rise of Hitler. The 12-year Nazi regime followed, the destruction of World War II and the horror of the Holocaust. Our 2000 years of history would finish with the Jews in Germany after the war and in contemporary German society.

I had two immediate and major concerns. First, the museum was overfull. Negotiations among the historians before my arrival had translated the story of the German Jews into 15 or so chapters and there seemed to be territorial claims for every square centimetre of floor space. Daniel's building was in danger of being overshadowed by a clutter of exhibitions. Second, at both Waikato Museum and Te Papa I had overseen exhibition experiences driven by larger recurring themes and issues and not by the relentless tread of time. Historical chronology had played but a small part and in fact that lack of sequence as structure passed unnoticed, or was embraced by visitors. Now, in Berlin, I found a long and convoluted history that would be understood by at least some academics but would, I believed, be difficult for visitors. What of those recurring themes? Deprivation and prosperity, family life as continuity and as change, inclusion and expulsion, assimilation and anti-Semitism, particularly the latter. Might these be lost in the confusion of a detailed history of which few had any prior knowledge?

I put my concerns to Mike. 'I would like to introduce more pauses, actually cull out a few segments and combine others. I would like to bring forward a number of themes. Currently all I have at my fingertips is anti-Semitism and the changing family through the ages. These themes, and perhaps others, require commanding and dramatic segments that concentrate attention, that shout out, "This is important!"'

His face signalled annoyance and I was dismissed with a wave of the hand. There would be no change. I had expected as much but had to try.

After we opened, a number of thoughtful critiques of the museum would pick up on these concerns, pointing out that the museum's approach had not done justice to anti-Semitism, and had swept the whole subject under the rug. Others would comment on an overfull museum. I felt justified but there was no pleasure in it.

*

Germany has a long-established critical media that early expressed a keen interest in the museum. In most cases their questioning had been a positive experience, to be learnt from and even enjoyed. But a number of commentators, those of the raised-voice headline-grabbing variety, were prepared to predict the early demise of the Jewish Museum Berlin. The Kiwi and his links to theme-park Te Papa made the outcome inevitable. Some of the more outlandish contributions held that the purity of German museums risked infection. I had expected this. Over the decades new museum developments have been labelled and dismissed for Tivolisation (referencing the creation of Copenhagen's Tivoli Gardens in 1835), and for being too much like Coney Island, expos, shopping malls and Disneyland. In the first year of the new millennium and long before the opening, one critic would actually title his book on the Jewish Museum Berlin *Jewrassic Park*. We were all embarrassed, Germans and Kiwis.

Mike knew these critics lacked substance but it was clear, from his occasional concerned comment, that they were unsettling. I did not discount what was being said: experience had shown me that such criticisms can grow to become a rallying point for a highly concentrated public campaign. I was aware that many museums, Te Papa included, but particularly some in the United States, had suffered in culture wars led by such critics, the worst of whom cast themselves as patriotic defenders of great nationalistic myths under threat from revisionists.

Not so many years before, an American national museum director had lost his job in the face of the rage generated among war veteran groups by his team asking a pertinent, but in retrospect exceedingly provocative, question: Was there a need to drop those two atomic bombs on Japan at the end of World War II? And here we were about to engage with Jewish culture, a tribe of powerful lobbyists, in a nation whose history was so much defined by what Germans did to the Jews.

To reassure himself, Mike formed a plan. 'The two of us will go to Te Papa and I will show you what I do *not* want!' he announced.

I could ill afford the time but this would be my chance to show him Te Papa, to let Mike experience Te Papa's visitor-oriented culture. Look, Mike, although we have learnt much from the leisure industry, Te Papa is not a theme park. I would make sure that he got the full Te Papa treatment. As befitted an international figure, he would be welcomed in Cliff Whiting's spectacular Māori hall, Rongomaraeroa. Protocol would demand a series of speeches and waiata (songs) and we would have to respond with our own (German) waiata. What would it be? I worried about language and my failings in this area. The Goethe Institute might act as our supporting chorus? We would also do a side trip to Canberra, where my colleague Dawn Casey was completing the new National Museum of Australia as some politicians railed against her attempts to deal with Indigenous in a balanced way. At Mike's suggestion, I would visit the yet to be built Jewish Museum San Francisco, the Wiesenthal Centre in Los Angeles and New York's Jewish Museum.

'Shall I get the museum to book your tickets, Mike?'

'No,' he responded. 'Marie will do that.' Marie was his Princeton PA.

He then alluded to the fact that, since planes do fall out of the sky, it was important that we travel on different aircraft. The real reason, I suspected, was that Mike travelled first class and he was not having me accompany him at that level of luxury. Old bugger.

Then, over the weeks, his messages began to change. He seemed less certain about the trip. His wife was telling him that he travelled too much. But there was more in his voice and manner. Was he perhaps developing a greater confidence in what we were doing? He was seeing progress. Despite what a small group was saying, the critics were treating us well. A design was emerging that Mike approved of and liked. He seemed to be visiting Berlin less often and, when he did, had other things to do.

For whatever reason, he delayed booking his flight to New Zealand and then found that every plane was fully booked with people heading to the Olympic Games in Sydney in September and October 2000. He broached this problem during one of our long-distance conversations.

'Who do you know on the Qantas board, Ken?'

If we had been in his office my face would have betrayed me. I checked my immediate memory. He had not said, 'Do you know anyone on the Qantas board?' Mike had assumed that I, too, would know board members of huge corporations. Sometimes the fates work in your favour. The very next morning I would be showing Alexander Downer, the Australian minister for foreign affairs, through the still empty museum. He would be accompanied by the Australian ambassador, an engaging fellow with whom I had become acquainted at official functions.

Secretly pleased, I was able to say, 'Mike, what I can do is slip a letter to the ambassador when he visits with Alexander Downer tomorrow. Perhaps he can free up a diplomatic seat.'

The letter was written and delivered. To no avail. Every seat on every flight was taken by Olympic dignitaries. Mike pulled out of the trip. I went, to fulfil appointment obligations, including meetings with German-Jewish refugees along the way. Susan had gone ahead to see her 90-year-old mother and we met up for a weekend at deserted winter-storm-swept Pekapeka Beach. On one of our long walks I spied a stone, quite out of character with this endless stretch of sand. It was round, the size and shape of a cricket ball, and I was back in the game of my youth. I picked it up and raced down the beach to deliver my fastest and nastiest, albeit innocuous, delivery. Not clever. Every muscle, every joint, in my aging body cried out in complaint and remained sore for several weeks. At that moment I passed from one age, marked by a belief that the body can do what the mind commands, to another in which physical frailties must be accorded due respect.

I returned to Berlin and the museum sore, but with the feeling that the problem of uninformed criticism upsetting the project no longer loomed as large. The growing trust between Mike and me was most encouraging.

CHAPTER 16

MAKING PROGRESS

EVERY SIX WEEKS OR SO Mike would descend on Berlin. We would all know he was coming and there would be a change in mood and style. The women, and the men, would dress a lot more smartly. Even Nigel's faded T-shirt was set aside for newer gear come Blumenthal week. I would hear Mike arrive before I saw him. The thump of closing lift doors and a scurry of the multiple footfalls of his guardians.

'Good morning. Can I see you in an hour's time,' would be thrown through my always open office door.

We would settle at the table in his office and get down to business. First Mike would give me a rundown of what he planned for the week. Then he would want the true state of progress. There should be 'no surprises', he demanded. When he was at Unisys he would travel around the many divisions at quarterly reporting time, asking the same of his staff. The museum was no different. He would temper his interventions and explorations according to the comfort he felt regarding progress. In the first months, as spring and then summer came to Berlin, we had much to discuss.

Then change was evident. The project was less exciting. My every action was to forestall excitement, at least that generated by pieces of work going off the rails. I was reporting the ordinary, the effort, sometimes the pain, of steady progress. This bred greater confidence and led to fewer questions and interventions.

At our June 2000 board meeting we had both signalled significant intentions. With Mike it was an academic review. He was concerned about the historical accuracy of the exhibitions and wanted peers, well established in the scholastic world of German-Jewish history, to anoint the museum. I had to get the design work up and running.

*

Mike held a dinner in his apartment for the gathered professors. He threw rather formal parties; he liked them to have a focus, something that could be discussed, seriously. This time it would be the academic peer review.

The food was always excellent. Two waiters hovered. But of greatest interest to me was the overseeing maître d'. She was a tall and handsome woman: short-cropped upward-styled hair; a striking suit, straight cut, black, tailored. If a gender-reversed *Cabaret* was ever to be played in an upmarket Weimar restaurant, she would be the Emcee.

Mike asked each of his guests to outline their expectations of the two-day review.

I said my piece: 'You tell us everything we need to know about the current state of German-Jewish scholarship. All I ask is that you take on board everything I tell you about the modern visitor-oriented museum.' In particular I needed to communicate with an audience whose level of understanding would be nowhere near that of our scholars. This brought a small complaint from Fritz Stern: 'We historians are into complexity.'

I could not disagree but had to explain that the people attending our exhibitions were not the same as those who would read his research publications. 'The public does not have your background knowledge. We need your scholarship to make sure that the messages we write in our everyday language are fundamentally correct. But you need us to communicate your knowledge.'

Each of the other professors had their say. It was a powerful group. Next day they settled to their task of testing the intellectual rigour of the exhibition concept. We started with all discussion in English so that I was able to assert myself, at least to begin with. Then a switch to German and I retired. There was some tinkering with content and they would return in September for another review. We set up a system whereby texts could be checked by the scholars as work proceeded. Of equal importance for me was the fact that we now had the best brains in the business of German-Jewish history owning the museum's exhibitions. We could refer to them when anyone challenged some element of the museum as historically debatable or even inaccurate.

*

For reasons that I was never able to determine, a small city-operated research and design group had been contracted to do the exhibitions for the new museum. After their uninspiring treatment of that solitary exhibition for the October 1999 review, during my November visit that year I had staged a design work session to test capabilities, driving the team into the late evening. This caused consternation, also difficulties for at least one who had a child to pick up. But I was playing the bastard and on we ploughed. Finally, I took them all to a restaurant of their choosing as a reward and for the purposes of bonding.

The whole experience had confirmed my first impression: this team could not be part of a successful museum project. Later that week I told Mike that one of the conditions of my appointment would be the termination of their contract so that we could employ a major firm with a proven record of achievement in both design and building exhibitions. The search began immediately.

I resolved to place myself on the side of the angels: the Jewish Museum Berlin exhibitions would be designed by Germans. This was undoubtedly a nod to my uneasiness at being the foreigner in charge. We arranged a schedule of interviews. Newly appointed project managers Stephanie Kluth and Doreen Tesche acted as translators and cultural commentators. Given my love of trains, it was appropriate that it was a sleek ICE (Inter-City Express) that took us to Hanover, site of Expo 2000, where we met a team of young designers. Another 250-kilometres-an-hour glide through the German countryside and a talk-fest from designer as super-design-ego. In the taxi he was red-pencilled.

We flew to our final appointment. When we were travelling by van to Seefeld, outside Munich, a road sign hit me with a jolt. Dachau. It pointed to a town where ordinary Germans lived, but for us it represented a concentration camp, the place where our Wellington friend Paul Seideman was finally freed after long years of incarceration and a deadly march from Auschwitz.

Klaus Würth and Petra Winderoll ticked all the boxes for design and construction. Perhaps most important, they understood, and had used, visitor research to good effect. They spoke the language of the visitor-oriented exhibition. We had our designers.

*

The exhibitions were going to cost a lot, perhaps around DM 15 million. The figure was uncertain because of the state of the museum's accounts, which hovered at the dismal end of terrible. I had done a budget for the two years covering the opening and the first year of operation, but it was an exercise of limited worth until it could be tied to the realities of what was actually in the kitty, what was coming to the project and how the cash could be made available over the next 24 months. Mike called it a wish list. He might have been more sympathetic.

In normal circumstances the exhibition task would be very achievable. It was of medium size, around 3000 square metres of main gallery exhibitions plus the dressing of a swathe of circulation and public areas. But what threatened everything was the timeframe. It was now early July 2000 and we were to open in September 2001; at 14½ months, this was extremely tight. The comparable time for Te Papa, albeit a bigger task, was 44 months. Unforgiving time pressure would plague us until opening day.

I needed more than just a solid design contract; I also had to have a culture of trust between designers and staff. I had already heard one of my staff describe the natural relationship with designers as simmering insurrection followed, after opening, by all parties automatically suing each another.

It was time to bring in the expert, my former Te Papa colleague Sean Sweeney. Sean knew everything there was to know about delivery contracts and design processes. He would lead an intensive workshop to close the contract and build a special relationship between the museum and our newly acquired designers.

A dinner party, like Mike's for the academics, was never going to fly. Not my style; nor did I feel I could use money in this way. But the Libeskinds would, unknowingly, provide the social occasion. Three weeks after the June board meeting I picked Sean up at Tegel airport. It was one of those pleasant summer evenings when Berlin was glorious in its surprising greenness. Sean just wanted rest after his long haul from Australia, but I would have none of that. What better way to introduce him to my new city than take him straight to a Daniel and Nina Libeskind party in their new apartment.

'You can't miss this. It's like a Hemingway novel,' I explained.

Indeed it was: intellectuals, performers, artists, writers and architects with a fair sprinkling of mysterious unknowns. Sean was impressed and put aside his exhaustion. We stayed quite a while. He even tried to contract a bit of business. For Sean and I had, in our roles on different sides of the world, struggled with a problem of infringed intellectual property rights, plus not a little inflamed ego.

The architect of the new National Museum of Australia in Canberra had used, measure for measure, zig for zag, Daniel's Jewish Museum Berlin floor plan as a symbol to indicate that the Indigenous section of that museum represented genocide, Australia's Holocaust. For me this was just an annoying misreading of our institution as another twentieth-century atrocity museum, but Daniel and Nina were infuriated, incensed at the exactness of the replication, and at having their main design element stolen in this way. They came to me for advice. I advised against their first option, suing. There was no way Daniel could claim copyright over such a generic design, especially as he had borrowed other emblems as part of his design. Also, I knew that Dawn Casey was having her own political problem at that time and could do without this particular distraction. I had drafted a letter to go to Dawn from Daniel. Perhaps Daniel and Sean, who was now working with Dawn, could discuss this matter, even resolve the issue. At the right moment I introduced Sean and Daniel. It was a slightly distant meeting, albeit civil and brief. They talked. Contact had been made, perhaps softening what might have become a vexing hindrance to progress. Over the next year the disagreement would die away.

In the week that followed Sean asked us all, staff and designers, to burrow deep into our innermost souls.

'Do the pain and angst now and not in the months to come,' he advised us. In some detail he sought answers to the questions of who was responsible for what and how would we work together.

By the last day we had a list of work to be done. Suddenly – it surprised even me – I chose to do something I had not done before. Perhaps it was the way we were seated, staff grouped at one end of the boardroom table. I just seemed to sense the need for us all to acknowledge the scale of the project to be achieved over the short months ahead. We would make a pledge with a grand, even melodramatic, gesture. I called for attention. Klaus and Petra looked a little perplexed but this was aimed at my new staff.

'You see what's in front of us, the complexity of it all. Are you with me in creating a great museum?'

Nigel saw what was needed and jumped straight in.

'Yes, Ken, I'm with you!', and he went on for just the right number of words, reinforcing the importance of the task and the opportunity. Others chimed in with their support, perhaps not fully comprehending what they were committing themselves to.

One may well have:

'I'm with you, Ken. I think we have a 40 percent chance of making it. But I'm with you.'

This response was at least honest, but would also cover him when, as he was expecting, opening day had arrived and the museum was a failure.

I really could have done without it.

*

Nigel and I were thrilled when Cilly Kugelmann joined the museum. She had a sharp mind and was a conceiver of exceptional ideas. The three of us made a great team.

Nigel and I visited her more than she came to us. This was a response to the Beijing-level air pollution that I will always associate with Cilly. Better, we reasoned, that the toxic atmosphere be confined to her office and not sully our environs. Now, more than a decade later, she is a smoke-free zone.

Cilly acted as our tutor. I would take ideas, ill defined and still forming, to Cilly and always get a knowledgeable comment, sometimes after a few days of research.

'Tell me of the origins of Jewish humour.' I was testing appropriateness. 'What are these Holocaust jokes and do they have any place in the museum?'

Cilly gave me an example from her seeming endless stock. It was really tasteless. 'But that's a neo-Nazi joke,' she said.

Some years later I would glean from one of Susan's academic studies on humour that this was not absolutely so. The joke had been collected in Mainz in 1982. It spanned a number of cultural and political divides and was available to be used by stand-up comics as well as skinheads. The important thing was that, as the comedian of the time had said with heavy irony, 'Not everything that happened in the Holocaust was funny.' A decision was made. There would be no attempts at Holocaust humour in the museum. But the humour that spoke of Jewish culture and existence, acceptance that the tribe's place in the world joked about today might become tomorrow's reality, had to form part of the voice that visitors would hear.

One theme explored was Holocaust symbols: railway tracks, barbed wire, suitcases, bales of human hair, scattered shoes and other personal items. With this came a discussion of the line beyond which symbol becomes cliché. Both Cilly and Inka Bertz would draw fine distinctions in the ways that words and phrases might be used: a shift, an inflection, an ordering and the innocuous could become Nazi. Cilly plied Nigel and me with esoteric and hard-to-locate articles. I have them still.

In short time Cilly became our conceptual leader, but her considerable intellect tended to dominate meetings, which she barely tolerated, and the disciplines attached to them did not necessarily come naturally to her. This was something I had to step around with care, for at every opportunity I taught teamwork and meeting procedures as a way of opening new and unexpected horizons among talented people. For some, meetings were maligned creatures, the butt of frequent jokes and derision, dismissed as the antithesis of making progress, evidence of procrastination and a sly means of spreading or transferring the blame in the event of failure. I could never see them like this and was prepared to invest the time to make them part of our evolving culture.

Cilly may have lacked the required patience, but she did have a sometimes useful ability to curtail unproductive discussion, particularly when it was in German. A quick, often cutting, comment would be enough, sometimes accompanied by a humourless laugh and a toss of her blonde hair. At other times a shiver of her shoulders and stern face would carry wordless disapproval and indicate that it was time to move on.

*

The exhibitions were taking form. Petra and Klaus, and the Würth & Winderoll team, completed an overall design concept that laid out all segments and identified major features. We gathered in the boardroom, according to my timeline at midday on Monday 18 September 2000. A huge plan covered one wall and what we saw was good. I gave my official approval. The board could see it sometime but I did not need anything from them. From here all effort was detailed content and design, then into production.

Cilly and Nigel, with Christiane Birkert, the new market-research staffer, acted as my approval team. At defined steps along the way they would go over each exhibition in detail, ending up in my office with a final report of work well done, of crushingly boring ideas eliminated, of more engrossing directions signalled and, in particular, evidence that our key audience would be interested in what was planned. Only then would I sign off the exhibition to go into the next stage.

The best of times were outside this structured, rather arid, sign-off process, when beaming faces at my door would announce something. How to explain the Talmud? An ever-expanding text of great complexity, each page was full of confusing blocks of commentary and explanation. The solution was beautifully restrained, even poetic. A brief discussion at my office – we did not even sit down – and young and talented digital design practice Art+Com, now world leaders in their field, joined the team. The visitor's breath would appear to release successive parts of the Talmud onto a blank page. It was almost as if blocks of words tumbled forth from that breath, followed by another, and another. The secret was breath-sensitive triggers and a projection unit hung overhead. The effect was wonderful.

Another high was the day Nigel announced he had the story that would suit being transformed into a game, one that could carry that most human of qualities, humour. It would revolve about the travels of merchant Glikl bas Judah Leib. Visitors would help Glikl pack her bags, selecting from a display of likely and unlikely items, including her mobile phone. It proved to be a marvellous intervention. People queued so that they could put the phone into Glikl's seventeenth-century travel kit and be gently chided for such an obvious mistake. It was so popular that after opening we had to install a second unit. The point of it all? To reinforce in a memorable way some of the key messages of this segment, such as the role and personality of this independent, astute woman, and bringing women out of the silence in which history so often cloaks them. Also, the game demonstrated that this museum would not hold people at arm's length but would encourage everyone to have fun.

A Christmas tree appeared in a Jewish museum, exemplifying the acculturation of the liberal Jewish community, who would blend their ritual of Hanukkah with the mainstream German celebration of Christmas so they could share the trappings of their neighbours' celebrations. That received quite a number of complaints from devout Jews.

Cilly's depth of knowledge of both history and cultural understanding was invaluable. It was she who decreed that the large photo mural at the end of the Nazi segment and the beginning of the post-1945 era should be a somewhat enigmatic image of double meaning. It looked like a concentration camp but it talked of continuity, for the image actually marked that crossover between war and peace. It was a displaced persons' camp. 'I was conceived in one,' she explained. Her survivor parents had met in such a camp.

Cilly and Nigel also brought to me the question of the appropriateness of photos of Hitler appearing in the museum. This had arisen in exhibition team discussions. It seemed inconceivable that there should not be such an image. The question was its nature and what it said. They suggested there should only be one photo of Hitler in the whole exhibition. It would show him as a small figure addressing a gathering of the Reichstag. I readily agreed.

Another memorable photo incident became political. We had appointed Signe Rossbach as publisher. Her main task was to complete our opening catalogue. After we reviewed likely cover photos, two suggested themselves strongly to the joint Cilly/Nigel/Ken sensibility. Both could be read in a number of ways. They needed to be looked at twice, and thought about. Therein was our downfall. The one finally selected was of the proud kosher butcher showing off line upon line of cooking sausages, the first to be produced in Berlin after World War II. Signe knew Minister Naumann well and at dinner one night proudly showed off the finished design. He was horrified at our choice and explained in no uncertain terms that the lines of sizzling meat and Holocaust imagery were just too closely aligned. The image was changed the next day to three happy young adults looking out a carriage window before escaping to a new life.

Projects are full of mistakes made and recovered from. Anyone who says otherwise has not actually completed a large cultural project.

*

I was not satisfied with the current museum logo and publication design. Its cold blue-grey and knife-like edges had a jarring feel. We needed to start afresh and Mike was keen. He and Eva Söderman, manager of all public relations, were about to announce the opening, now about a year away, and they needed letterhead at the very least. Brand was new territory for the staff but their interest increased every time the subject arose.

I stopped procrastinating and arranged the long-promised branding exercise. We had a perception problem: the public was already talking of the museum as a Holocaust memorial.

With a flood of papers, I prepared the ground. A set of these went to Mike in Princeton. His reaction was immediate. 'Recall all those papers – I want none of this out in the public domain.' In the next phone call, it became obvious that he feared that we would be accused of some sort of enforced social engineering.

I tried to calm his worries. 'Mike, it's just good business practice. At the very least we have to influence the behaviour of our staff so that the JMB can carry this difficult story in a manner that's not threatening to our public.'

We agreed to proceed. It was an enthusiastic bunch that gathered on 7 September 2000. We had come a long way in the preceding 11 months. The earlier disdain for philosophical positioning had long passed. We were now better able to talk about the values that underpinned everything we did, right down to the last decision on the finest point in an exhibition concept.

'It's like an iceberg,' I explained, 'with title and corporate imagery above the surface supported by those fundamental values beneath the waterline. Let's try to find a statement that expresses our core beliefs.'

It took a surprisingly short time. We had been there before. The museum was to be about tolerance and for families. It was to be safe and trustworthy: a lively place of colour and engagement. We soon agreed that the principal theme of our museum was life.

'Are we all happy with that? Okay, Mike's here. Nigel and I will put it to him now. Wait here.'

We strode along the corridor. Mike took our piece of paper and, in one of those interventions he was so good at, scrawled after 'Life' '– not just death'. It was perfect.

The workshop continued with marketing messages and staff behaviour. A brief for a redesigned logo emerged. Cilly had written and distributed 'The Duffer's Guide to the Pomegranate', about this fruit as an important Jewish symbol. It had a warm, life-affirming ruby colour. I wanted the Libeskind-Bau zigzag because it was part of our appeal and already well embedded in people's consciousness. Marion Meyer did the design and it was adopted by Mike and Minister Naumann and endorsed by the Libeskinds.

I suggested to Mike that the first use of the new logo and letterhead should be our 'save the date' letter to go out to principal guests for the opening. We discussed the progress made at the brand workshop and my next task, to bring together a statement of fundamental philosophy. 'Leave this with me,' he said as he departed the building that night.

Next morning he brought to me a perfect encapsulation of everything we were trying to embed in the exhibitions. He had written:

> Our mission is to focus on the history and culture of the Jews in, and originating from, German-speaking lands. The museum does this so as
>
> - to make the two millennia of German-Jewish experience relevant for the present and future populations of Germany;
> - to emphasize the benefits of harmonious interaction between various ethnic, cultural, religious or linguistic groups; and
> - to call attention to the high cost to all of intolerance.

All in all it was a great outcome. The logo now headed everything we did, particularly Eva's work with the media.

Opening hours became a brand-driven discussion. German museums were always closed on Monday or Tuesday, and open 10am to 4.30pm, but now I could insist that we would be open seven days a week, and for extended hours. I did lose one battle. 'This is a Jewish museum,' I said. 'We'll be open on Christmas Day!' However, the German bureaucracy could not encompass such a thought.

The new brand was at the forefront when recruiting front-of-house staff. Our people would put visitors at their ease, greeting and conversing with them, anticipating their needs. They would show that this was the friendliest museum in Germany. They would all be bilingual and I wanted cultural and ethnic diversity. My hope for a cluster of second-generation Turks did not come to fruition, but a delightful older Indian couple became one of the high points of any walk through the galleries, with their bright smiles and joyful greeting of a little bow, hands pressed together.

There would be no overpowering and militaristic uniform. Cilly, Nigel and I all hated blazers with a passion. Instead we settled on a scarf, red with the museum logo in yellow, that we would encourage the hosts to wear in any way comfortable to them, draped over shoulders, tied about the waist or as a head covering. It became yet another distinctive marker of our museum.

*

Part of the project director's life was acting as spokesperson for the museum. Being a Kiwi seemed to make me an almost exotic figure. There were Australians all over the city and every second travel poster featured a kangaroo or the red bulk of Uluru. But New Zealand was different, not just Downunder but a whole leap of mystical proportions to the true far side. I was plied with invitations, requests to be part of some event, to address some gathering and many moments before the press. If I am honest, I quite enjoyed the attention.

Eva set up interviews and for each, despite her strong controlling hand, I would try to be or do something different. A paper was doing a series on the recent migrants visible on the streets of Berlin. There were people bringing exotic Asian food to the city, and others in interesting jobs. I saw an opportunity. The Jewish Museum Berlin stood for tolerance among all peoples: I would bring together the flags that represented the city's many cultures. To do this I had to overcome my aversion to the New Zealand flag. With the British Union Jack to the fore, it reeks of a tainted colonial past – and is only a star or two removed from Australia's. At one level this was good, as I was a bit of a federalist. To me Australia and New Zealand are so similar culturally and economically that I can think of them only as part of the same nation. When a sea of flags stretched across the grounds with the Libeskind building behind, at the front were those of Australia and New Zealand, and it was with them that I stood to have my photo taken.

Other duties took me into new territory. I was asked to front the main press conference for the Berlin-wide exhibition of the works of American neo-conceptual artist Jenny Holzer. She had come to the museum late one cold winter's night and projected huge images of official Nazi documents through the leafless trees onto the industrial cladding of the Libeskind building. It was a haunting moment. The main elements of her exhibition, however, were in the New National Gallery. The work captured Susan and me, and we spent a long time watching the lines of Holzer's words, orange and bright, streaming across the tall ceilings of architect Mies van der Rohe's glass-walled gallery building. What was I to say before a very large gathering of cultural commentators? Eva had written me a speech but it was not what was required. After a few sentences I cast the notes aside and turned to Jenny. The work, I told her, brings me that much closer to my adopted city. The lines of words adhere to channels of light above the viewer yet they refuse to be contained. The ceiling becomes sky and as reflection on the glass walls the words burst out into the night. Like those lines, I raced on, one dominant image in my mind: an extension of the U-Bahn, the orange metro that, in its elevated sections, ran above us with the same sense of urgency. The speech did not take long but it was heartfelt. At the end of the questions Jenny expressed some pleasure at my take on her work and asked for my notes. I had to admit I had none. Mine had been a reaction straight from the heart, a stab at the meaning of lines of speeding words.

I hosted dignitaries from the political and cultural world. Prime Minister Helen Clark visited. Leaders of the liberal democracies, including Bill Clinton, were in town, and all week vast thundering flotillas of motorcycle police, sometimes as many as 60 accompanying official cars, had closed the streets of Berlin. But when New Zealand's leader came to the museum, two silver Mercedes and six motorcycles did a restrained sweep to the door.

An intelligent and affable woman, she ambled with me through the empty building, discussing what was planned. Nigel gave her a copy of his latest novel. She then went to an informal conference in the grounds with the world press. When I went back to the front door to await the PM, I found that one of her silver cars was standing directly in front of the panelling of the Libeskind building. There I also found a photographer from the *Süddeutsche Zeitung*. This man was an artist. I think of a great photograph as concentrating attention on a subject in the midst of the action. The PM finally arrived and was farewelled. For a brief moment she was alone in the car, looking back at us lesser actors who had retired out of frame, and the photographer, from an elevated position 25 metres away, had his shot. It appeared the next morning. There was no sky, no evidence of a natural environment. The larger frame of the photo was machine-age, the texture of the building's silver metal façade. Then came the car, set low in the picture. It looked much smaller than it was and its silveriness gave the impression that it had been specially selected to either go with, or be camouflaged against, the building. Next the photo forced the viewer to focus on that rear window where the PM leant forward to look out. She was a small part of the whole yet the entire focus of the composition. It was a brilliant piece of the photographer's art.

*

Barely six months into our residence in Germany, the mayor of Ahlen phoned. He knew of me from the national news media as a strange import from down under – even further removed than Queensland, as one woman had said with amazement. Would I talk at the town's Kristallnacht commemoration this coming November? I demurred but he insisted.

'It's important to us.'

'Why is that?' I asked.

'Because every year, at this time, we acknowledge a terrible thing. We were the first town that with pride announced to Hitler that we were Judenrein – cleansed of the Jews. We still carry that guilt.'

It was a compelling statement and I could not refuse. But to say something of value would require thought. It was not for me to chastise these later generations of this small town, the children and grandchildren. More could be gained by stepping down off the victor nation's soapbox and drawing parallels from opposite sides of the world to explore that capability we all have to commit terrible deeds and then, the deed done, to forget. I would take my text from my own country's history. It was to be a memorable night in so many ways.

Perhaps 400 people gathered in the street, muffled against the cold. My message was simple. Germany has sought to come to terms with a shameful recent past. New Zealand, too, has a history that is tainted by wrongs done to Māori in the name of government, nationhood and greed. All too often from 1840 the European arrivals plied the language of hate. Māori were not worthy, denying the new settlers access to the land they craved for their new farms and settlements. There were those, mainly from the religious orders, who spoke against this outpouring of greed; they achieved little and were hated for their stance.

How can we all recover a new and higher sense of moral being? I answered my rhetorical questions with reference to Te Papa, to Germany and to our plans for the Jewish Museum Berlin. New Zealand, like Germany, has begun to find ways of securing and strengthening its future and establishing a truer sense of moral order. We are in this together.

I have no idea how my speech was received for the townsfolk dispersed quickly. We were taken on a short walking tour of the town.

'There, see that room. That's where Jews were processed before being shipped off to their death.'

We had to visit the jeweller, who had accumulated a collection of Jewish religious artefacts, and along the way were introduced to citizens. Everything that evening was part of an act of contrition and restitution. We had a meal before Susan and I were rushed to the train. Then a mishap caused a long delay. We arrived home in the early morning Berlin light. I showered and went to work.

CHAPTER 17

THE GALLERY OF THE MISSING

AS A PERSON NEW TO THE MUSEUM PROFESSION, in the very early 1970s I had read anything I could get my hands on. The question soon arose: Why did so many of these texts talk of the failure of institutions in crisis? Had I made a bad career choice? No; it was soon evident that I was encountering a debate that was at the very core of our institutional being. Were museums socially responsible agents of change or collectors of stuff? It was the revolutionaries versus the hoarders.

That debate rages still, with the same questions being asked. A painting by Australian artist Joan Ross, which depicts an ancient museum with the 'butterfly murderer' standing to one side, accuses: 'oh History you lied to me'. The accompanying manifesto speaks of museums harbouring 'the ongoing disease of the collecting mentality', responsible for 'the damage [of] infinite collecting'.

I understand this complaint, that museums are focused solely on inanimate objects to the point where they turn their backs on people, particularly those who have cultural ownership of those collections. There are still arrogant museums driven by aging museological mythologies, not too far removed from the attitudes that created the eighteenth-century catacomb of curiosities. A long time before Nigel and I came to Berlin I had joined the revolutionaries pursuing people's stories, and the contexts in which these were remembered, in order to make of museums places of social wealth and conscience.

The object, the thing that has form and can be touched – even if only by museum workers in their privileged position – might well be embedded in that storytelling. But in the magical theatre, a collection item becomes part of the drama, to be considered, understood and treated in different ways. It might have multiple meanings, be subject to manipulation, augmentation and even reinvention.

Now in Berlin my staff's experience was European academic. Multiple cultural points of view were not their intellectual bread and butter. Take, for example, the one valuable painting we pursued. For some the right place for such a painting was on a white gallery wall. I had other ideas.

From time to time Inka, a firm believer in the idea of museums as places that accumulate treasures, would bring the current catalogue to me, extolling the worth of some painting or sculpture on offer. Her argument was always the same and well rehearsed: the artist had a German-Jewish background. With each approach I would consider the object in the context of our wider narrative and ask if it added strength to the story we were telling. Despite her entreaties I was rarely convinced.

But this painting was different. It stood at the core of what we were about, intolerance, and I was prepared to throw my weight behind this proposal. The money required was going to be significant so Cilly and I took this one upstairs – that is, along the corridor to Mike's office.

In the 1920s and into the early 1930s, Felix Nussbaum produced pleasant landscapes and portraits. Then a flick of legislative decree and German artist became German Jew, a degenerate marked for annihilation. Fear showed in his paintings. They became agonised revelations of his new status as hunted fugitive.

At the auction house I stood in front of the work. Just a face and shoulders, human-sized, a bit of harsh background. The artist looked out at me and our eyes met. For a moment we engaged in our own silent, haunted conversation. His face said, 'I know I am facing death.' He was: eventually he was betrayed and murdered in Auschwitz.

We had not discussed tactics but when we arrived Mike marched straight up to the painting.

'We want that,' he announced to the owner. His manner said, 'We're not here to discuss price. We require the Nussbaum to be gifted to the museum.'

The owner knew this was coming. He was sympathetic but the Nussbaum was the prize piece of the auction. He was not about to give it away. In the preceding weeks, the rumour mill had been full of authoritative statements that we had DM 1 million of government money to claim the work. But actually we had nothing, and the portrait would go to a new home for close to the sum we were supposed to have. The silent conversation I had with this condemned man was now overlaid by another piece of history. The marketplace had put a price on his suffering. It would likely hang on white walls alongside others – Ernst Ludwig Kirchner, Max Beckmann, Otto Dix, Rudolf Belling, George Grosz – and contribute to a history of art in the period.

That was not what I had had in my head for the Nussbaum. Some might say I planned a manipulation of a work of art but I could only see another arresting context. It had arisen the first day we had met Daniel and Nina Libeskind, some months before the Nussbaum appeared on the market. As Daniel explained, the concrete Voids in the museum building spoke of erased Jewish culture. The Nussbaum self-portrait was a single person facing that same cruel void. What about a juxtaposition of a solitary painting of torment intensified by the emptiness of Libeskind's black Void walls? The painting would be high, at eye level, slight cyphers of context, blackness behind. Gone would be the supposed neutrality of the white cube gallery. Rather the painting would become part of a fuller statement. Two men, Felix and Daniel, standing 60 years apart yet speaking across the decades, the painter certain of his dismal fate and the architect pouring his survivor family's and tribe's history into this building. The visitor would join this silent discussion.

But it was not to be. Instead the self-portrait came to be defined, in part at least, by possession and price, and we lost what could have been a striking contributor to the raw and powerful narratives of a great identity museum.

*

In normal circumstances I was not involved in collecting objects. That was a task for curators and the exhibition teams. They knew where to search. It was best that I stayed away, except when a management concern arose. That was how I came to spend time with Dr Vera Bendt.

A scholar, Vera had a fine, trained mind, able to undertake deep research and hatch new ideas. Before my arrival, the museum had got itself into a spot of bother. They had tried to move her into retirement, only to find that she had an employment status born of years of service that made any such moves quite inappropriate. I therefore inherited a risk born of existing internal disagreement, and the last thing I needed was for that to grow and spread.

A functioning team is a beautiful thing, but by the accounts reaching me, teamwork would sorely test Vera's reserves of patience and ability to respect other, frequently conflicting, views. In a group she would be an unacceptable risk. I made her responsible to me. We were to meet every Friday morning.

'Tell me, Vera, what work are you doing at the moment?'

So began exchanges that would take me back into my curatorial days decades before, back into the nature of objects with meaning beyond ordinary function. Vera and I, a couple of anthropologists, would engage in intensive tutorials on the fundamental elements of the identity museum: memory, story, myth, practice, ritual, virtue, community values and, above all, morality. We would exchange historical insights and argue philosophical positions that tested and extended our beliefs and understandings. What was the nature of value, especially in this nation with its self-inflicted traumatic wound? Was the worth of the Nussbaum portrait a thousand, or even a million, times greater than some abandoned textiles, or a small and very ordinary hand towel, or nothingness – the ghostly manifestation of loss?

'Currently I am working on some textiles – Kristallnacht, November 1938 …'

Then followed a tale of a Jewish community rent asunder in the terror of the Nazi era. Most perished but a few would survive and return from the camps.

Vera continued. Probably she used the term 'Reichspogromnacht', and not 'Kristallnacht'. This was an ongoing topic of conversation between Nigel and me and the staff. 'Kristallnacht' was wrong, the historians said. The correct term was 'Reichspogromnacht'. Nigel and I would argue that in this case the 'correct' terminology was probably too obscure for the visiting public. Kristallnacht, the Night of Broken Glass, the broken windows and ransacked contents of Jewish shops and apartments strewn across the streets, was evocative of an organised spasm of vandalism, planned to inflict humiliation and bring destruction, injury and even death upon the Jews of Germany.

'The synagogue at Mannheim was destroyed. The religious and revered objects, crafted silver objects, Torah and textiles, including two Torah curtains, were brought to Berlin.' My notes record Vera's use of the evocative word 'flight'.

'They were taken to the partially destroyed Synagogue Kottbusser Ufer, where a community, increasingly aware of the fate that awaited them, walled up the treasures in part of the ruined cellar. The Jews of Berlin and Germany were transported, along with so many others of Europe. The collection lay undiscovered – hidden from plunder.'

I noticed that not only was Vera's English excellent, but she had a way of summarising what had just been said with a flash of poetic language. This was something I relished; she was a storyteller.

'After the war survivors, one of them from Auschwitz, returned to the synagogue, broke down the wall and recovered the hidden ceremonial items. Most of these were put back into use among Jewish communities in Israel and the United States. The textiles were not so valued and these objects were stored in the attic of Fränkelufer Synagogue and forgotten.'

We talked of the perception that intricate woven objects were from the feminine side of our nature and seemed to have a lesser value than more manly metallic stuff.

'Eventually the textiles were rediscovered in the mid-1980s.' In her always effective summary, 'lost and found again'.

Fifty-two pieces were brought to the museum in 1985, where they were conserved and treated and my research began. It is my aim to link the Mannheim community with their treasures once again.

Vera wanted the community to use the textiles in their religious ceremonies. The museum would not acquire the collection to go into our storerooms. Rather we would act as cultural facilitator – 'brought to life'.

The story was too powerful not to be told. So Vera and I would frame a temporary exhibition about the value placed in these small treasures, the threat, flight, hiding from plundering, recovery, purpose and function, lost again and found again, reunion and re-establishment of contact. We would point out that, despite so much destruction, the Nazis had not won. The Jewish communities in Germany, increased by an influx of Jews from Russia, were alive and growing. At the end of the exhibition, all the objects would go back to them.

I liked the elements of mystery and intrigue in the story. By this stage I was on my second reading of Art Spiegelman's *Maus*, an acclaimed graphic novel that recorded both the father's story of Holocaust survival and their fraught father–son relationship. It gave me the idea of bringing the exhibition alive by using the comic. A series of wall-sized, starkly black-and-white cartoons would show the actions and capture the drama in each segment. The text and objects would rest in the gutter between each large cartoon. Some things we would not emulate. In *Maus* the Jews were depicted as mice, the Germans as cats.

'This tradition of large "hero" features in an exhibition to capture the attention of a wider public is very well established,' I told Vera. 'We might even use Spiegelman to do the cartoons.'

I thought this might convince her, but I could see her discomfort. 'Your approach would have to be agreed on by the Jewish community.'

*

In the spring of 2000, with sun streaming into the museum lecture room, the collection staff put on a show and tell, with an English commentary for the three Kiwis in the audience. News of this Jewish museum was out and people of the German-Jewish diaspora throughout the world had started sending their memories, and accompanying items, back to Berlin. Those who had left early in the Nazi regime and been able to relocate to a welcoming part of the world had taken with them crates of belongings. But as the administrative weaponry of the Third Reich pressed in upon the Jews of Germany, and as the world's nations became less willing to accept these targeted peoples, they escaped as and to where they could, carrying almost nothing. It was that 'almost nothing' that now returned to Berlin in slight packages.

The collection managers held up a couple of old photographs and a folded hand towel and told a story that has never left me. It was of a Kindertransporte boy, Paul Kuttner. After the November 1938 Night of Broken Glass, Britain agreed to accept 10,000 children. They would travel to their refuge by trains, the Kindertransporte. A package had arrived at the museum from a now very old Paul with a letter of explanation. The story went like this: *In February 1939 my parents arranged for me to be evacuated. On the station platform, standing before my train, mother gave to me this hand towel, monogrammed M.K. for Margarete Kuttner. She told me that I must always wash and keep clean. The towel was to be used to dry myself. But I never saw my mother again, nor did I unfold that towel. The towel was evidence of mother and the few and incomplete memories I have of her. Later I would find that my older sister, Annemarie, survived by going underground in Berlin. From her comes the photo of my sister and mother taken at the time mother was deciding that she could not take upon herself the constant stress and danger of being a fugitive. Mother was swept away in the Holocaust, dying in Auschwitz in 1944.*

There was hardly a dry eye in the house. Other items were shown that day but I remember only the hand towel and photos.

Paul Kuttner's towel was a given for opening day. The story found its natural home in one of the eccentric display cabinets that Daniel Libeskind had embedded in the walls along the underground Axis of the Holocaust. I asked the designers for some form of heightened view. Strong and harsh light was out of the question, since it would quickly fade photos and objects made of cloth and paper. The designers' response was to darken the glass around the edges of the case, creating a lens effect that directed attention inwards to these small objects.

Paul's story became known through our media campaign and every day, as soon as the museum opened its doors, people would cluster before the showcase, five, eight, frequently more, quietly manoeuvring to reach the small display window. It was as though the hand towel were a masterpiece of great art. But this was never the pressing and frenzied activity, the milling international tourists on tight timetables, in front of the *Mona Lisa*. This was a more respectful group of ordinary people empathetic to the loss and sorrows of a small boy. Before them they found a story stating at the simplest level what had been done in the name of genocide. The towel had passed the scrutiny of the overseeing German officials who moved through the Kindertransporte carriages, bent on making sure that these small children were not committing the heinous criminal act of carrying anything of value. In their eyes the towel was worthless, probably getting no more than a fleeting glance. Certainly, no curator would have confiscated this piece for their museum's collection, as they would do with finely crafted silver pieces after each round-up of the Jews. Its worth rested solely in a small boy's bond with his mother. It was very different to the Felix Nussbaum portrait but of equal value.

*

These slight objects not only moved visitors; they could also take an emotional toll on the guardians. Most of us had learnt to place a carapace around our emotions. The books and texts we read, and the personal items we handled, could inflict personal injury. Protective behaviour allowed us to live normally, to tell jokes and laugh still. Most of us. But some could not. Once I noticed Leonore Maier at her desk quietly sobbing over a letter and a few scattered items. Shocked that our work could put such a burden on a gentle young woman, I marched down the corridor to Inka, her boss.

'Inka! Leonore is to go on holiday now. Organise it and report back to me.' I was upset and had become all officious. Inka came to me a few hours later. It had been arranged and it would happen soon.

*

Vera and I owed no allegiance to academic disciplines and museological traditions. We could not accept that collections grown as a consequence of curatorial fashion and random opportunity could not be the main elements of a proper and logical treatment of a 2000-year history. She pointed me in the direction of a local museum. I visited and took home their catalogue. This stated, with great honesty, that any idea of a comprehensive coverage of the history of Berlin had been abandoned. Instead the exhibitions were a series of historical snippets, remote from each other, that emerged from the collections. Herein lay a problem. Over the decades curators had worked within the formal dictates and unofficial pressures of successive regimes to build collections that reflected the political ideologies of the day. As a result, the collection was full of gaps. The Nazis, represented by the propaganda of nationalism, seemed a quite benign organisation. What had happened to the museum's Jewish patrons was not addressed because the collections told little of genocide. Similarly, in the communist East, a director 'faithful to the regime' represented life in this grey nation through workers' movements and socialist realism. Of the fall of the Berlin Wall and reunification there seemed little, at least that I could find.

The formula was simple: 'It's the collections, stupid.' If the artefacts did not exist, it was better to leave dark yawning gaps. It was as though the museum's collections might in some way be offended should those holes in history be illuminated by the narrative of research. At best this was a history of a museum fractured by political realities. At worst it demonstrated an inability to deal with the great issues confronted by Germans living in modern Berlin.

This was not the position of the Jewish Museum Berlin. Our narrative of the German-speaking Jewish people did not depend on which collection items might or might not remain after campaigns of annihilation. The perpetrators, of course, had looted the persecuted of their possessions for the good of the nation's museums, as redefined and operated according to racist Aryan principles. When an Aktion against the Jews became known, museum directors from Berlin, Hamburg and other German cities would rush to the warehouse where the current transported group's stolen property was gathered, to trawl through the silverware and pick out the best for their collections. (Immediately after the war one of these collections was in turn looted by soldiers.) Then, and only then, was the rest melted down into bullion by the Degussa company to enrich Nazi coffers. The remaining ghostly museum catalogue cards of lost items are like blood on the hands of our profession.

In a short time, at our Friday meetings Vera and I tackled 'missingness' and the stories that attended absence. It was an important shift in perspective. Museums have a strong institutional mindset to collect and preserve objects and not to deal with histories that do not have accompanying materials. It takes an effort to shift towards a view that does not depend on collections. Objects have physical presence and cry out for attention and space. Also, they are nice to handle and to possess. Within the Jewish Museum Berlin we created the Gallery of the Missing, to focus on the silence that had fallen over the remnants of a former Jewish presence, to identify and bring to the museum knowing attempts on the part of perpetrators to eliminate all memory of a Jewish presence, and to give an elevated status to cultural property that had been destroyed.

I tried it out on Daniel. He liked the name and suggested we visit the old Jewish cemetery at Weissensee, a vast and now overgrown wilderness where the Jewish of Berlin buried their dead until suddenly forbidden to do so in the 1930s. He described it as a dead cemetery, a place that raised the hairs on the back of even the toughest necks.

Vera confirmed that the Weissensee cemetery was chilling, marked not so much by what existed – this was a place of gravestones – as by what was denied and missing. It became for me the first item for our gallery. We would promulgate our idea to senior and research staff and invite their thoughts. Nineteen responded with instances where, despite the Nazis' best intentions, surviving stories and values had proved resilient. Inka, for example, contributed a statue of Heinrich Heine, melted down by the National Socialist city administration for weapons.

The staff trip to Weissensee took place on an appropriately cold and misty day. We trailed through a forest of spindly trees and thick, progress-inhibiting creepers to find a grandmother's grave here, a famous person there, and to look up into the narrow ceiling ledge of a large classic temple tomb where a number of Jews, U-boats, would huddle in the cold of night to escape capture and transport to the camps and death.

I wrote the entry on Weissensee. Here, from 1880, the affluent Jewish bourgeoisie had built tombs that were architectural monuments, statements of growing social and economic confidence made by people who regarded themselves as an accepted part of German culture and who took pride in being German. Some were 'complete', the inscribed surfaces recording lives lived to a natural end. I included in this category the area set aside for those German-Jewish soldiers who died in World War I. But some of the most poignant places in the cemetery were those family monuments where blank polished stone faces seem still to await the family members who, in the 1930s and 1940s, either fled overseas or were murdered. Occasionally survivors had added simple references to those who had died in the camps or overseas. Some of these were quite crudely executed. 'Umgekommen in Auschwitz,' said one, or 'Erschossen 1942 Buchenwald' – much the same thing, perished, shot. A small chiselled inscription recorded that Betty and Erich had died in Sydney in 1946 and 1965.

One of the most evocative suggestions for the Gallery of the Missing was also problematical in that it was an oral account, that is, not far removed from gossip. The headstones of Jewish soldiers killed in World War I bore the Star of David. The story claimed that, following the German occupation of France in 1940, Jewish headstones at Romagne, near Verdun, were replaced by headstones bearing the inscription 'Unknown German Soldier'. It was a powerful thought: patriotic Germans who had paid the ultimate price were to be eliminated from the record. Conversely, did not this convoluted Nazi logic admit these young men to 'full' German citizenship, albeit in the afterworld and without name? Despite more research, the evidence was not strong enough and we had to drop that one from the list.

A submission raised *Degenerate Art*, Hitler's exhibitions of modernist painting and sculpture, as a possible candidate for the gallery. Modern art, with its experimentations and rejection of traditional form, was an easy target. It could be portrayed as evidence of everything non-Aryan, everything that corrupted proper German values. Harshly lit from below to accentuate its angular features, the sculpture *The New Man* by Otto Freundlich achieved the worst kind of fame as the front-cover illustration of one of the exhibition's catalogues. It was described in the sickest of racist terms: 'primitive', 'Negro-art', 'degenerate', and ultimately an example of 'typical Jewish physiognomy'. The sculpture was then lost, probably destroyed, as was Freundlich, deported to be murdered in the Majdanek death camp. The staffer who proposed *The New Man* thought it might be replicated.

How, though, could we give some experiential form to missingness? Ever since the day that Susan and I had met Nina and Daniel Libeskind I had carried an image in my mind of the work of a New Zealand artist I greatly admire. Denis O'Connor would take elements of his history and the harbour environment he loved so much and blend these into ceramic or stone sculptures suggestive of a form, while never quite being that form. I saw such reinvented forms sitting against the dark walls of the Void. I described them to Daniel and he thought the idea a good one. The Gallery of the Missing would be a contemporary artwork. But who should be our artist? It was Inka who came up with Rachel Whiteread. I had to admit I had never heard of her. Later I would see her Holocaust Memorial in Vienna and her massed boxes in the

Tate Modern, but for now I had to rely on the photos Inka plied me with. Her way of turning negative space into a positive form seemed ideal.

But Rachel was a world-famous artist, booked solidly some years ahead. So we turned to Via Lewandowsky. His response to the commission was an enigmatic glistening dark glass stele, a sound sculpture that quietly told stories of the missing.

*

I was determined to build further on the missing idea. It was agreed we would do a temporary exhibition, *Exil*, about those exiled in haste by the Nazis, carrying little, to all corners of the earth. I already had one idea in mind. Perhaps an artist or artisan could recreate the meaning and context of what had been lost in this exile. My first take on this idea revolved around Oscar-winning film designer Ken Adam.

I knew of Ken because his brother Denis had come to New Zealand, prospered and become a well-known patron of the arts. As boys they had escaped the Nazis to reach England and then, as young men, flown with distinction as fighter pilots in the RAF. I had this fond idea that Ken's dark film sets had arisen from his history as a Jewish boy growing up under the rise of the demonic Nazis. I would have built a model of one of his greatest sets, the vast underground war room from *Dr Strangelove or: How I Learned to Stop Worrying and Love the Bomb*. It was here that Peter Sellers famously said, 'Gentlemen! You can't fight in here! This is the war room.' The model would demonstrate my thesis, and then perhaps become part of the collection, though I would favour it being sold on.

I interviewed Ken in London. The house was easy to find: it was the one with the white Rolls parked outside. Brother Denis also had a Rolls – sibling rivalry? We settled into Ken's office, surrounded by a clutter of awards, including two Oscars. It took just a few questions to destroy my bright idea. Although the creative mind of this bright octogenarian could conjure up unrealistic flights of modernist fancy that cinema goers fell for every time, as Bond, James Bond, overcame an evil maestro, his fantastical designs were not, he informed me, a deep reaction to the destructive power of the Nazis. His work had been influenced by his family and broad life experience, perhaps by the expressionistic sets of the German cinema company, UFA. At least I was not the first to raise the idea with him.

I had a second idea to fall back on. This concerned the Wolf family. Unlike most of the German Jews who escaped in the 1930s, they did not head for the promised lands of the West. No. Good communist that Father was, they joined the 1600 or so who moved east into the Soviet Union. The family survived Stalin's purges and came back into Germany, Konrad as a soldier, Markus as a propaganda officer. Both had prospered within the DDR regime. Konrad became a maker of highly acclaimed films and rose to be president of the Academy of Arts; Markus was an international Stasi spy chief. It was a wonderful story full of convoluted relationships, a commitment to Stalin's brand of communism and not a little determined careerism.

But when I took it to Mike and Cilly both were dismissive, saying in effect that the family's Jewish origins were not important, that in some way being communist meant they could not be considered for the museum. To dismiss them on the basis of a simple one-word designation, I argued, was dangerous ground. In a museum about tolerance surely we needed to look to the whole human relationship, east and west, and who better to do this with than the Wolfs. They lived in Primo Levi's grey zone, much closer to the dark of deep corruption than the light of moral purity. I was disappointed, probably more than I admitted at the time, that their escape and return could not form some part of the stories of success and failure told in *Exil*. By the time the museum was being planned Konrad was dead and Markus was in disgrace, but I would have liked them to be called to account by history, to offer our scholars the opportunity to speak for them. In striving for a greater good under communism, they had a string of cruel actions and failures to explain. Had we included them we might have talked of the East, not just as the stage on which German armies had strutted about doing terrible things, but as a part of the world in which people lived their lives as best they could, given circumstance and situation. For me, to exclude them because of politics, because they were communists, because they were 'other', was not reason enough.

Although this proposal did not succeed, it enabled me to develop another collection, or anti-collection, idea. Consider the following, I would tell anyone who would listen. Konrad had created wonderful films, despite his struggle with censorship. The regime required nothing more than propaganda pamphlets but Konrad, the artist, demanded more of his work. *I Was Nineteen*, his portrayal of his younger self as a soldier in the battle for Berlin, was a masterful rendering of cruel conflict full of powerful images. His brother had lived a life glimpsed but never truly seen, except when, so the probably apocryphal story goes, John le Carré used him as the model for that great Soviet spy Karla, George Smiley's nemesis. I saw this as story-as-collection-item constructed imaginatively within a scholastic framework but employing all the talents of the novelist, film director, artist and experience creator.

Approximately a hundred great ideas have to be tested before one is found that passes the tests of worth, achievability and timing. So far, I had not achieved much with two ideas, but I did have a third. What of the other survivors from among those committed Jewish communists who came back to Germany from the East? What might their roles have been? I felt it was a story worth investigating and telling in the Jewish Museum Berlin. But how?

A lawyer was doing personnel contract work for the museum. I told him about some of the more intriguing stories that were emerging as we researched the Gallery of the Missing. He too had a story, though he did not know if it fitted. He was president of a professional club and recently had been contacted by the agency sorting out ownership of the chattels of the DDR. They had a painting, old and beautifully framed, of his club's founder. At the end of World War II the painting was in the Russian zone and was offered to a literary society. The members had no need for this particular venerable gentleman so the canvas was turned around, and upside-down, in the frame, allowing a new portrait, of Goethe, to be painted on the other side. The club had reinherited their founder, but history had given them choice, to hang him or the national literary hero. Our lawyer was off to pick it up from the official repository, a DDR warehouse, and he gave me the address. Perhaps here we might find evidence of one of those German-Jews who went east.

Early morning, full of the promise of a sunny summer's day. Cilly, Inka, Susan, Nigel and I met at the rental-car office. Inka knew the way and she drove. Our final destination would be Eisenhüttenstadt, but first we would visit the small town of Beeskow, crumbling and not prospering. We found the three-storey warehouse but the curator was nowhere to be seen. When she finally arrived after some telephone calls, we soon realised that she was not enjoying the prospect of yet another group from the West with their condescending language. We went out of our way to put her at ease and praise the work she was doing.

It was a fascinating few hours moving among the paintings, wall hangings, plaques, sculpture, pottery and other paraphernalia that had decorated official venues, clubs, holiday camps, offices and the houses of the leadership.

This was art to order, and the clients, various government agencies, required a commitment to the regime.

There was stack upon stack and shelf after shelf. Cilly and Inka pointed out to Susan, Nigel and me the officially established and approved artistic symbols that had to be incorporated in all art. Industrial smoke on the horizon was a required indicator of modernity and progress. Our two guides also identified the contrivances that artists had used as subtle reactions to the oversight of the official censors. 'The trouble for the government officials,' noted Cilly, 'was that the artists were always more intelligent.'

A group of young bathers, reminiscent of a Max Beckmann painting, frolicked among the waves. The group included the necessary global citizen, indicated by the dark-skinned African. But on closer examination there was a separation between these friends. Each avoided eye contact and seemed to be involved in their own solitary game. The mood depicted was not fun in the socialist paradise, but isolation.

A cluster of weekend huts in a clearing in the idyllic forest portrayed the DDR citizen at rest. Well-earned recreation and respite, said the official version, with the smoke on the horizon marking their workplace. But the painting was strangely angular and bereft of people at play. The dominant message was that in a society held to be free and classless, each hut was a symbol of rank, management to worker, in a setting not far removed from a prison camp. Not all, but some of what we saw that day could only be described as coded subversion.

But the strangest of the many works we rifled through defied categorisation. At one level it could only be a deeply religious painting. A pantheon of communist saints, every one a male, in two wings (angelic?) of serried ranks climbed either side of the very large panel. The Stalinist-era Moscow University skyscraper stood between, while above was a framed insert carrying a hammer and sickle and two workers, one male and one female. Each saint was suited and bemedalled, each head encircled by a halo of red. Some looked to the side, some to the front. The two tiers of saints were united by Stalin standing central and a head taller, with a halo of deepest red. Only he looked up in a way that bespoke thoughtful leadership; only he knew what the future held. What in hell's name was this? It may have been a parade banner, but it was too heavy and was framed as a work of art. Certainly, it carried the iconography of the beneficent patron nation, the Soviet Union. All I could think was, 'Who needs God and his saints when you have Stalin and his crew?'

Idea number three went nowhere but the exploration was a time of thrilling discovery.

*

How torn we heritage people are. We have absorbed a love of things. That includes me; I marvel at the splendour of treasures in the gorgeous art museums, am engrossed in the great reconstructed dinosaurs, challenged by contemporary art offerings and surprised by the Matisse dancers at the Hermitage, race through the museum just before closing to stand in front of the palaeolithic Venus of Willendorf, the smallest of objects but with such enormous scale and depth of unknowable history. I acknowledge the critical role of collections of record, such as natural history databases and archives. They support the maintenance of our democracy and, in the case of biosystematic collections, explorations of the state of our planet in the face of human degradation and climate change.

However, it is good to remind ourselves that such views are not universally held. The differing cultural attitudes to heritage items, the political implications of what is collected and preserved and the problems of sustainability came together for me as I sat in an office in central Tokyo. It was 16 October 1981 and voices outside shouted defiance from truck-borne loudspeakers. The gentleman from the Agency for the Protection of Cultural Property paused to apologise. 'They are right-wing party activists. I'm not sure their shouting does any good. They're so noisy.'

Mika Iba translated. I was totally reliant on this bright young woman's considerable English-language skills, but in this case the man's face said all that was needed. This was my second briefing. We were onto the agency's mandating act of Parliament, procedures and budgets. My visits to historic sites, temples and artists' studios had revealed the exhaustive nature of the process that resulted in only 20 or 30 or 40 new designations a year within the National Treasures system.

When I asked how such a serious procedure could result in such a small number in such a culturally rich nation, the officials responded. 'We extend financial assistance to the conservation of important cultural properties, and make compensation payments. With each new listing we must take into account just what that means in terms of the budget we have to allocate to each new entry on the list, from the largest temple complex to the smallest portable item. Our budget limits the number of designations the agency can make.'

It was a moment of enlightenment. Part of determining the significance of cultural property must be an assessment of the economic consequence of applying some higher worth. The message was clear: if you cannot support the act of preserving into the foreseeable future do not bother raising expectations by giving that item treasure status. Heritage advocates will argue value but managers are obliged to ask, 'Where's the money?' Or the even harder question: if circumstance and budget require it, what existing collection item will be removed, perhaps sold (deaccessioned is the official term) to make way for the newly blessed? In Berlin, some 20 years later, it was part of my job to balance a budget dependent on very high levels of tax-revenue subsidies with the pleading of my heritage-trained colleagues.

I travelled to other museums and heard of their struggles.

'We have huge collections of art and historical pieces in store but supporting these has meant I have no budget left to achieve what I was appointed to do,' said a European director caught between a board's desire for a new public face and tradition-bound deference to the collections-defined museum.

I learnt of decisions already made where the collection had been swamped by lack of money. 'See that building there,' a friend pointed to a large older structure. 'It was an archive but now the state government have closed it. They can't afford to keep it open.' We have a term for this, 'cocooned' – the process whereby a collection, perhaps many decades in creation, is quietly locked away and forsaken as budget and staff are either cut or allocated elsewhere.

The Association of Independent Museums of Great Britain sponsored research on museums into the twenty-first century. They were aware that big money would come available for new millennium celebrations and wanted their piece. What struck me, though, was the table of museums that had opened and closed in Britain over the previous decade. They almost balanced each other and matters were to get worse as 'millennium madness' opened, then closed, a rash of new museums all based on starry-eyed, but false, marketing plans. Shortly thereafter we would face the devastation of the global financial crisis. It seemed that the only positive headlines about new museums welcomed a billionaire's vanity project, far removed from community-owned places.

The professional discussion rages on. Do we collect through force of habit rather than in pursuit of a well-defined mission? Do the politicians we are inclined to deride have a point when they question the worth of 'hoards of stuff' that seem buried with no use? Many say 'yes'. A number of museum industry leaders have asked whether museums, as large pieces of costly capital plant with their energy-consuming air-conditioning, are contributing to the problem of climate change. How often do collections, tangible representations of the past, cause us to create nostalgic set-pieces that exist in our imaginations but not in reality? Do collections reinforce conservative attitudes?

It is possible to despair. So many museums are lamentable experiences that damage the idea of the lively cultural facility in service of its community. But equally so many are desperately trying to become more like the modern library, a welcoming and even joyful place. Yet at the same time we seem trapped by our history of collecting. Consider New Zealand scholar Professor Pare Keiha, of Māori descent and versed in the worlds of science, economics and business development. Some years after Berlin I listened as he complained about taonga disappearing into a New Zealand museum, one that really was trying to rise above its history. For him this museum was presiding over the death of collections, burying them in storerooms cut off from their roots and any consideration of continuing cultural association and fresh stories. One such collection consisted of many hundreds of hei tiki, small jade ceremonial figures, each of which would have once had great spiritual importance to a tribal group.

'The collection was dead,' he later wrote to me. 'The experience left me disturbed. There they were alone and cold. The museum was presiding over their death, and not the salvation and preservation of these objects. What is the point of owning them? Surely, they should be sent back to tribal groups and families, be returned to a warm and human state where they would be enriched by the telling of new stories and the forming of new associations as they grew back into Māori contemporary culture.' More than that, Pare the economist had no qualms in advocating that some collections be returned to the market to begin a new and probably unexpected history in private ownership.

Of course, there are some treasure-based/collection-saturated museums that have, and display, wonderfully rich holdings, but these are surprisingly few in number. Perhaps that is a good thing, for in the main they reinforce wealth and privilege. They contribute, of course, even if only by dragging in the tourists.

But for some decades now leaders in museum thinking have had the courage to suggest a change of tack and act accordingly. Our storerooms are already overfull, our budgets limited. Surely it would be more useful to severely limit the items accepted into the community-financed collection, and instead place greater emphasis on contributing to community discussions about the fate of significant cultural property, be it an ancient artefact, old building, painting or family papers. Museums would become cultural facilitators and adjudicators, not holding places, helping to make hard decisions that might mean an object was held in an agency or by a family outside the museum, or preserved within a private collection; it might even be given appropriate and respectful demise.

CHAPTER 18

TRIUMPH, 9/11 AND DESPAIR

ON TUESDAY 11 SEPTEMBER 2001 we gathered in Mike's office. We were a happy bunch. The official grand opening, a concert and dinner for 600, had gone well. Now all the invited donors were out there in the galleries. Praise was high. A few critics had voiced the expected negatives, but nothing that surprised or worried us. In my euphoric state I would typify and dismiss it as the usual spiel. Everyone was agreed that this was a museum, not some aberration, though for some the *idea* of a museum had been challenged. We had made it and were on our way, open to the world.

A little over 55 hours earlier, the morning of the grand opening, I had come into the museum. It was still a construction zone. Mine was the usual early start but the Würth & Winderoll installation team had worked through the night. My role was only to encourage, suggest that this area might now be cleaned. I wanted to see some parts of the floor done to indicate to all the workers that we were almost there. I marched about. On one occasion I roused a drowsing woman: 'You can sleep soon, but not yet.'

I had divided the day with Nigel, who would cover the afternoon, and final, shift. The big problems were at the end of the digital delivery system. Some bits refused to work but I was not that concerned. The key objective was to get the walk-through environment completed so that the official parties could, well, walk through. It was that sense of three-dimensional space that we needed for the big night. It was 23 months from the October 1999 review, 20 months since my official appointment and 14½ months since the board meeting. Now the ultimate achievement was within our grasp.

Back in the apartment we dressed in our finery. Susan had a present for me, a Versace bow-tie purchased at great expense from one of the brand stores on the Kudamm. I wear it still and at the end of my days will pass it to my son Conan. A taxi took us to the Philharmonie, Berlin's principal concert venue. Mike had worked hard on the opening and had convinced Daniel Barenboim to divert the Chicago Symphony Orchestra, then touring in England, to Berlin. I now knew the cost of getting an orchestra to Berlin and a conductor's fee for the night. Neither was small change, though Daniel Barenboim had waived his fee.

We sat with Marylea and Gianni van Daalen. Gianni was an expert in managing underperforming hotels. His current challenge was the grand old Adlon Hotel on Unter den Linden. We had got to know Marylea at opera nights that she organised. Soon we had an arrangement whereby she would send special guests my way to get a personal Berlin experience in this new museum, something unique and in keeping with the Adlon brand. We would catch up again when they were doing something similar with the Hotel Baltschug Kempinski in Moscow.

The music began, Mahler's Seventh Symphony. Those clear plaintive brass notes over strings reached me and the tensions and stresses of the last two years began to ebb away. I felt lighter. Even now, when our national orchestra plays this music, I am no longer in the Michael Fowler Centre, Wellington, but far away in the Berlin Philharmonie, experiencing again that sense of lightness, the thought that life really is worthwhile.

The music was done and the applause sounded. Mike and his wife Barbara immediately hurried out. That was our signal to follow. In the foyer each group of main actors was led by a tall and beautiful woman to a swanky car. It was raining heavily.

The museum was ablaze with light and with the prestigious guests who had arrived from around the world to see this new thing that had come to pass in Germany's capital. First, however, I was captured for a radio interview and then we raced after the official party. The dust and disorder of the morning had been swept away and Daniel's interior shone. Mike busied about explaining the exhibits to Chancellor Gerhard Schröder and the other dignitaries in our party. He was so proud. This was his moment. He had delivered to the German government and people what he had promised, a great museum. Nigel brushed past me and offered a small discreet piece of paper. It said something like, 'Steer away from these – they are not working.' That I already knew. The Learning Centre, a separate system, was functioning. The chancellor was invited to investigate. Oliver's explanation was too drawn-out and Mike interrupted. We were on a tight timetable. Toward the end of the tour Mike called Susan and me forward and introduced us to Schröder, and his wife, with much praise.

It did not stop there. The meal was sumptuous. Mike and Peter Sauerbaum had done a great job. In the midst of his speech Mike paused and broke into

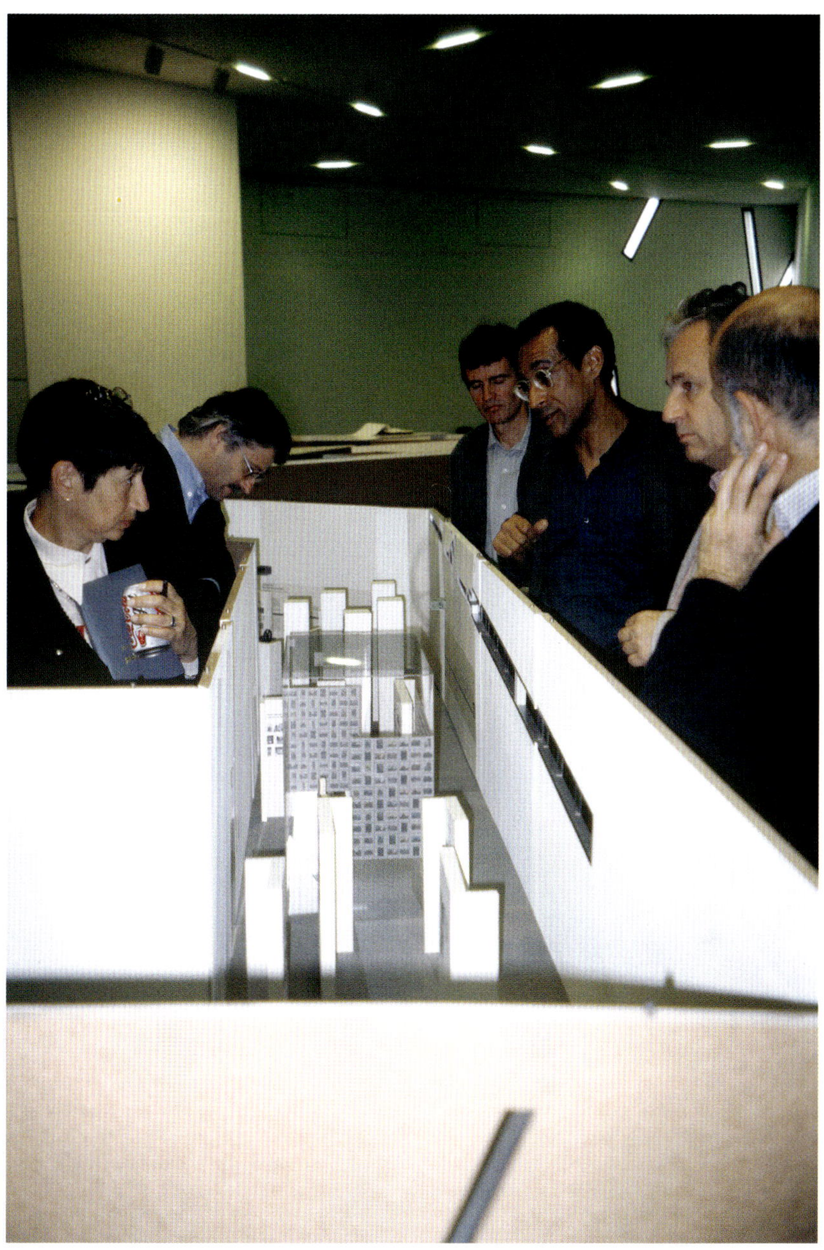

ABOVE: The review of the Jewish Museum Berlin, October 1999. This, the first of three photos I took, shows Elaine Gurian (left) doubting what she is being told about the one lonely exhibition produced by the team.

Photo Ken Gorbey

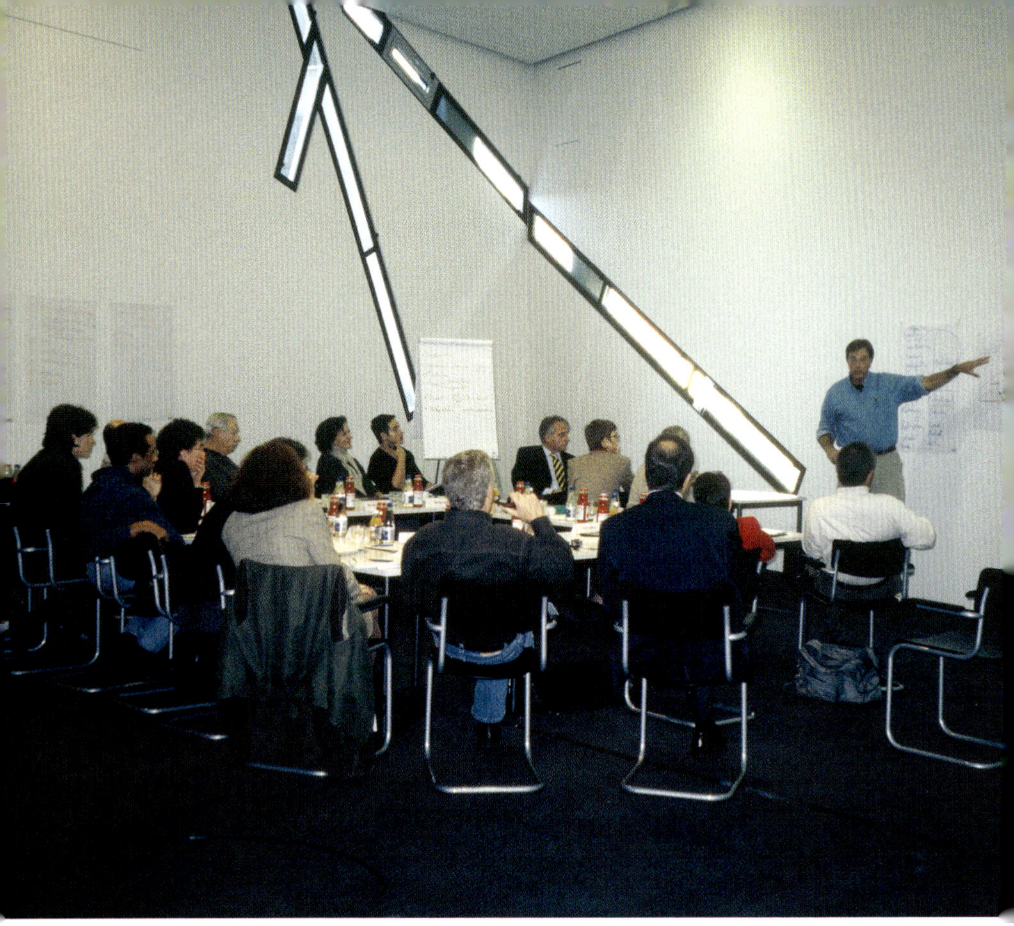

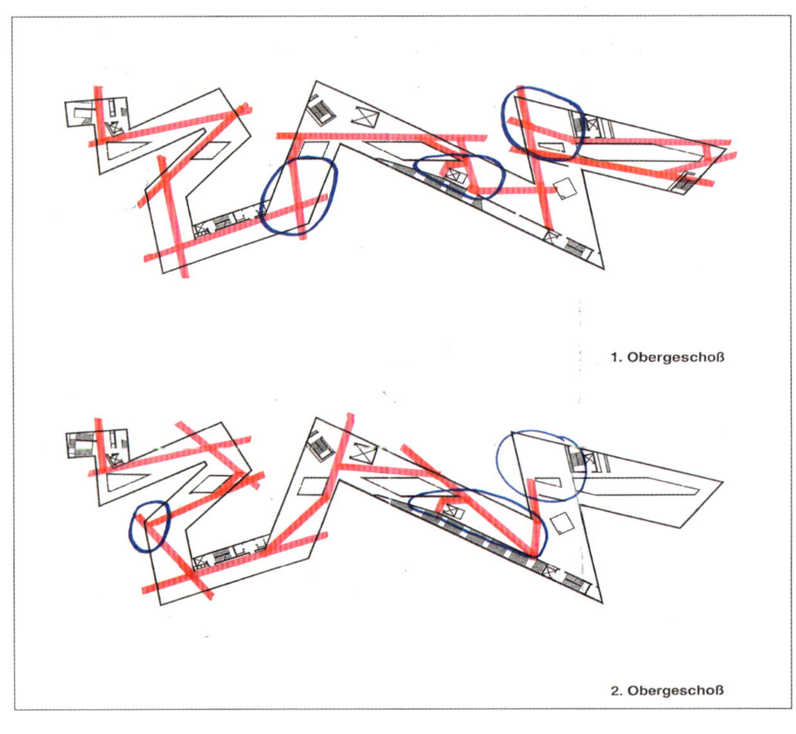
1. Obergeschoß
2. Obergeschoß

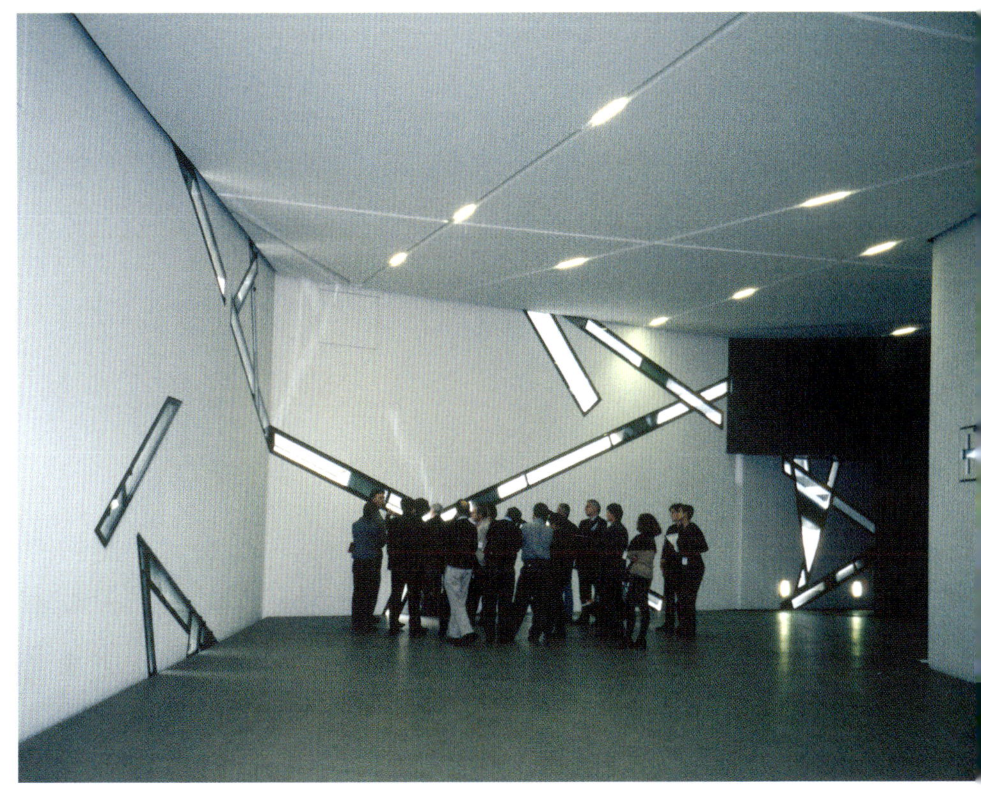

OPPOSITE, TOP: At the second click of the shutter we have moved into project workshop mode. Jim Volkert (standing) talks circulation. Mike Blumenthal (at back, towards the left, with grey hair) and Martin Roth (centre back, wearing a tie) watch intently.

ABOVE: In this, the third October 1999 photo, the review group clusters before the drama of one of Daniel Libeskind's powerful interiors. Some weeks later, and late one night, I would stand at this place and determine that we would treat the Jewish Museum Berlin as if it possessed the same depth of history as a 300-year-old castle.

Photos Ken Gorbey

LEFT: While Jim Volkert talked circulation, I drew a track through the museum. Later I would circle a few architecturally powerful 'Libeskind moments'.

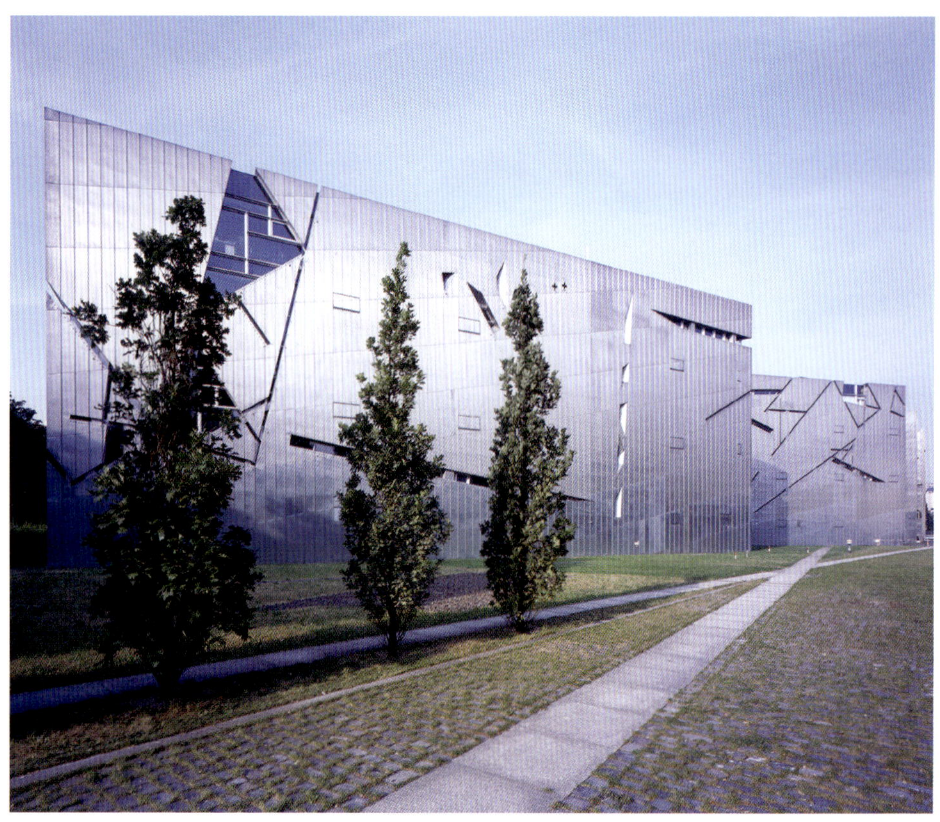

Daniel Libeskind's Jewish Museum. Berlin. In the early morning I would glimpse this building through the trees and marvel that I commanded at least a part of its destiny. It gleamed in all weathers, a building of terminal wounds.

Photo Jens Ziehe, Jewish Museum Berlin

RIGHT: Within a façade of wounded surfaces was an interior every element of which carried further the message of a culture voided out of its society. This unified whole I came to see as a Gesamtkunstwerk, a total work of art.

Photo Jens Ziehe, Jewish Museum Berlin

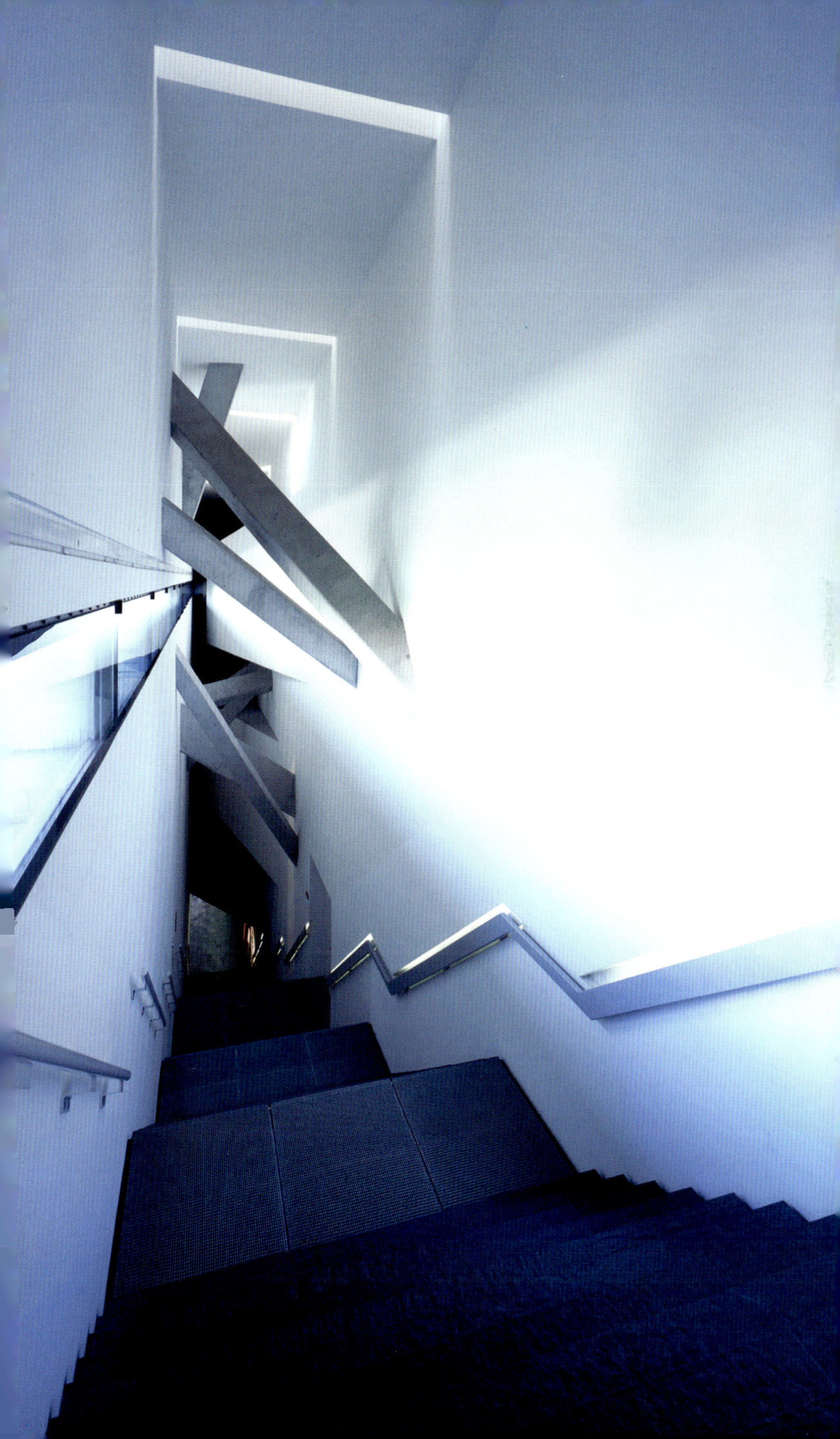

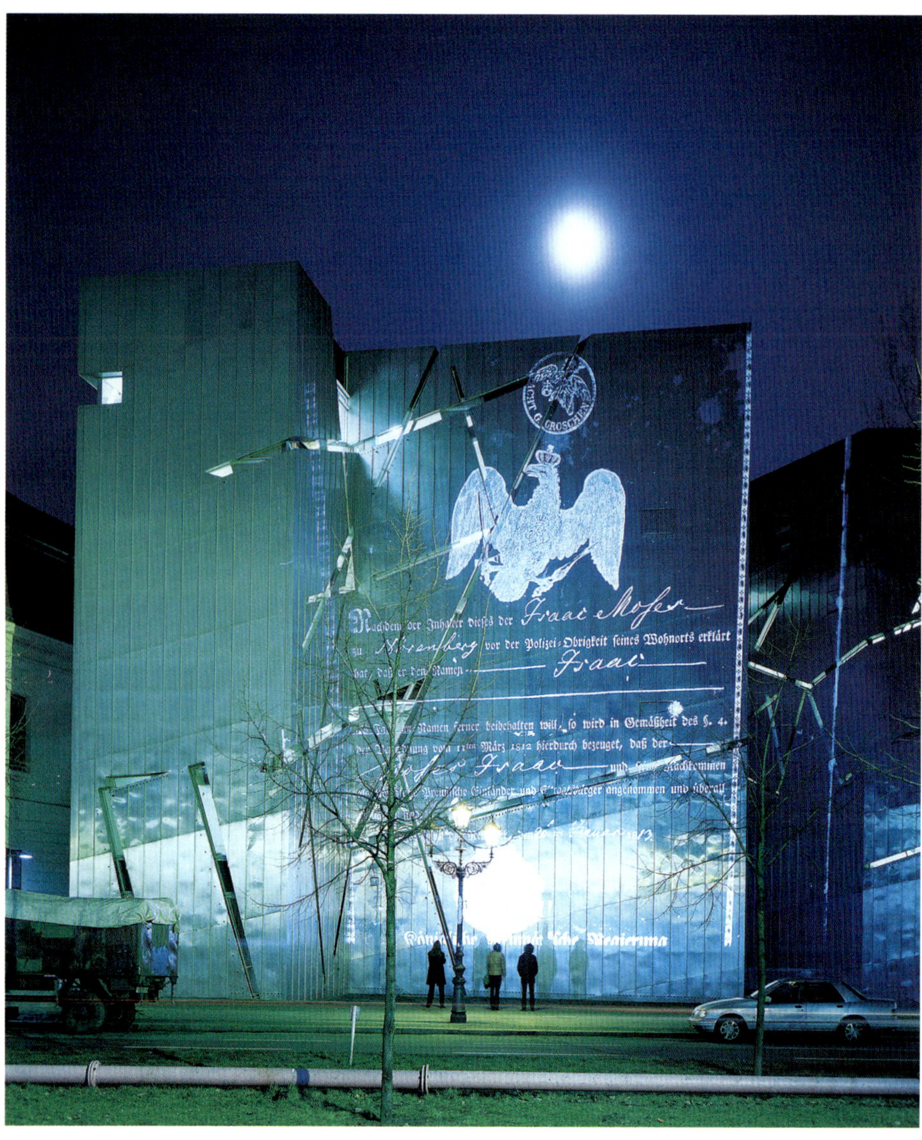

Hunched against the bitter cold I watched as light artist Jenny Holzer directed projection and photography to throw huge images across the façade of the Libeskind building. Captured with the imperial eagle is a Nazi-like truck (left) that menaced the museum for months until removed by court order.

Xenon for Berlin, 2001, © 2001 Jenny Holzer. Photo Attilio Maranzano, courtesy Sprüth Magers

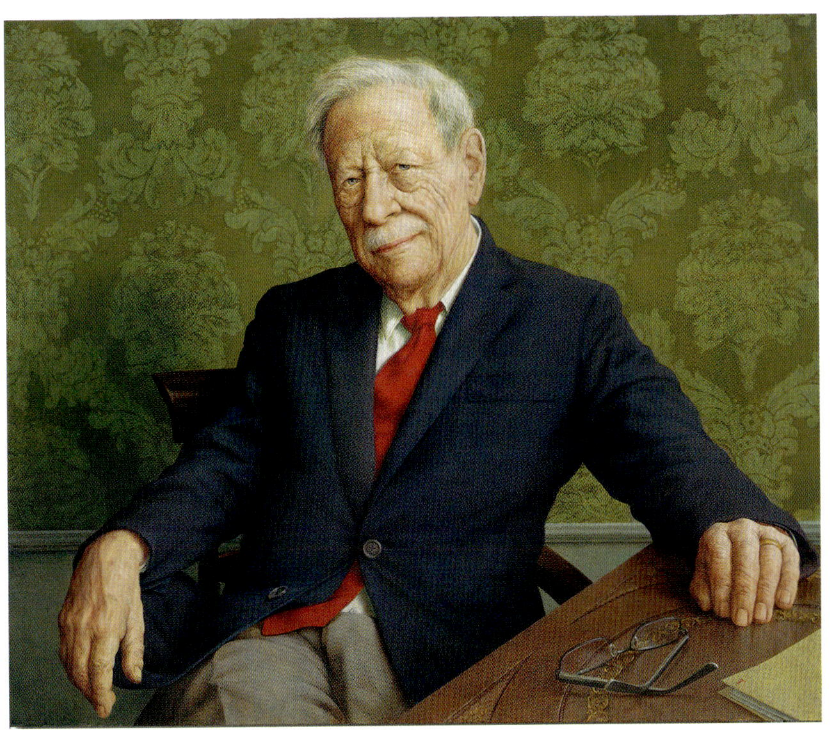

Portrait of W. Michael Blumenthal, 2016.
Michael Triegel, Mischtechnik (egg tempura on MDF), Galerie Schwind, © VG Bildkunst, Bonn

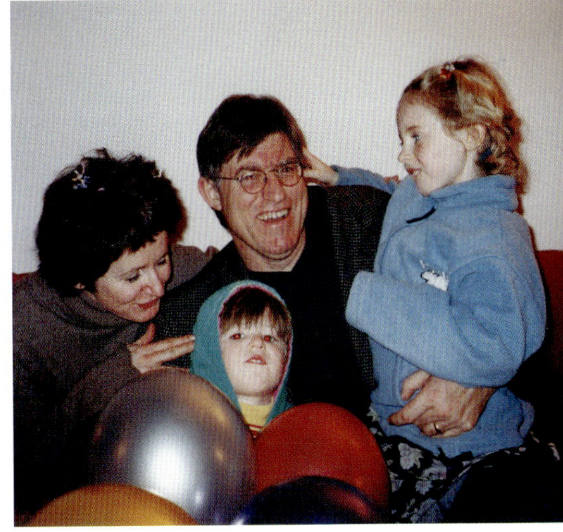

Nigel Cox (1951–2006) with Susanna and children Andrew-Jack and Katie, on the occasion of his 50th birthday, at the Foster/Gorbeys' place, Konstanzerstrasse.
Photo Ken Gorbey

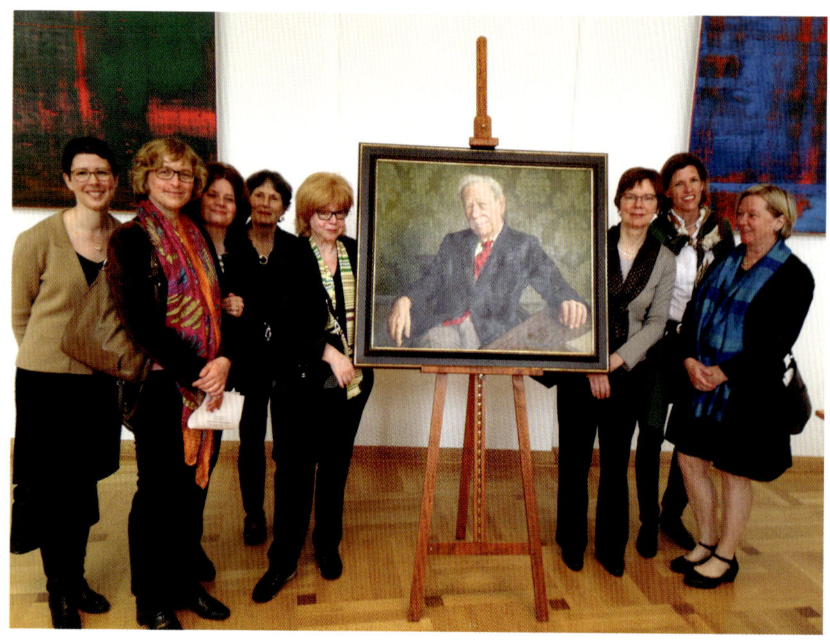

Some of the old Jewish Museum Berlin team at the 2017 unveiling of Mike's portrait at Berlin State Parliament building. From left: Johanna Brandt, Anja Butzek, Léontine Meijer-van Mensch, Susan, Cilly Kugelmann, Inka Bertz, Katharina Schmidt-Narischkin and Ulrike Sonnemann. Photo Ken Gorbey

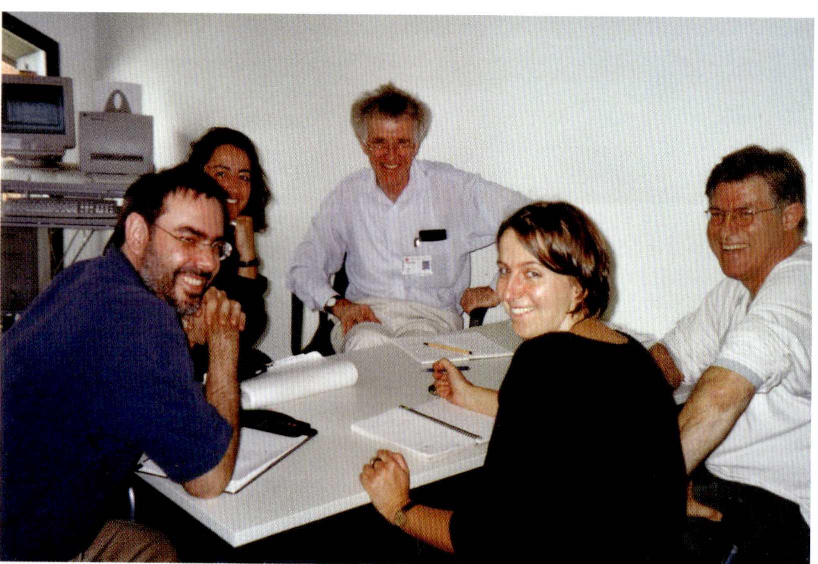

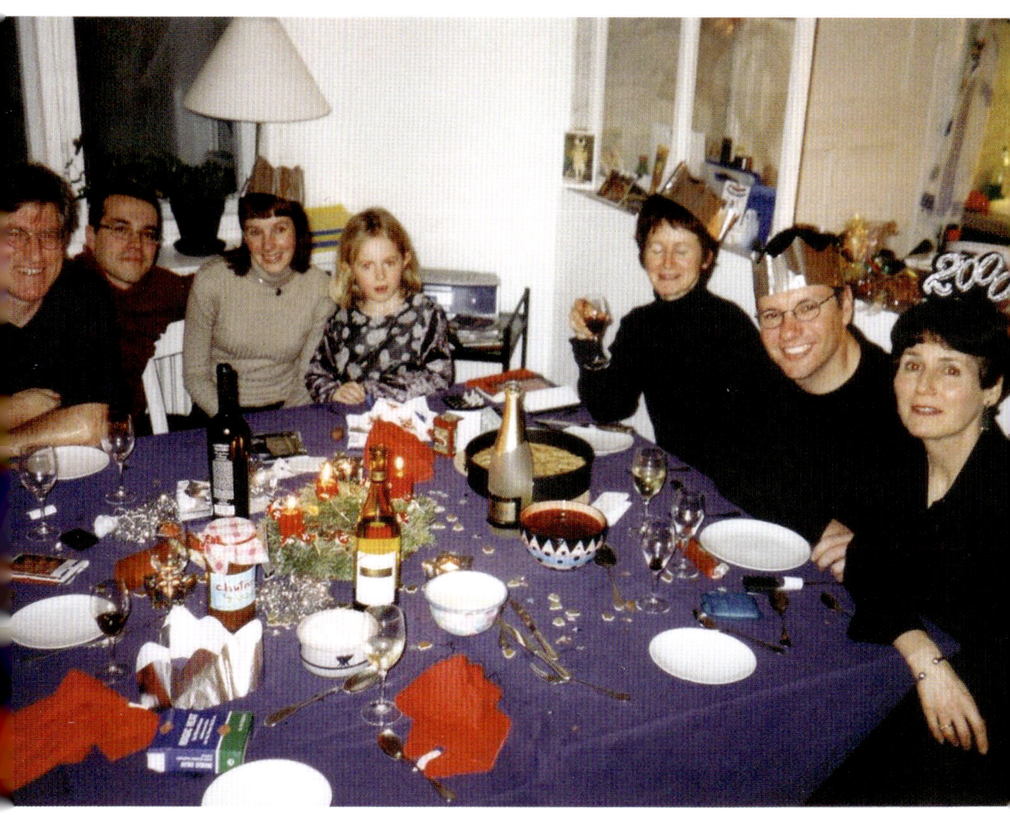

Christmas 2000. From left, Nigel Cox, Erwan Toulemonde (favourite son-in-law), Susi (daughter), Katie Cox, Susanna Andrews, Conan (son), Susan.
Photo Ken Gorbey

OPPOSITE: The last management meeting before opening, in Ken's little office. From left: Klaus Würth, Petra Winderoll, Ken, Petra Schramm, Nigel Cox. Photo Ken Gorbey

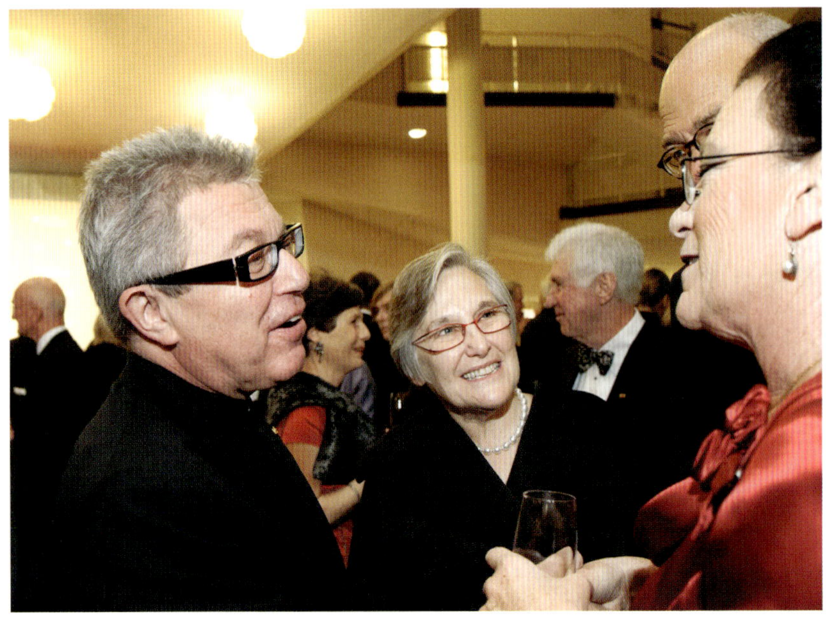

Daniel and Nina Libeskind, at the tenth anniversary of the opening of the Jewish Museum Berlin, with Susan and Ken hovering behind.
Photo Ausserhofer, Bolk, Breloer, Lopata, Wagenzik, Jewish Museum Berlin

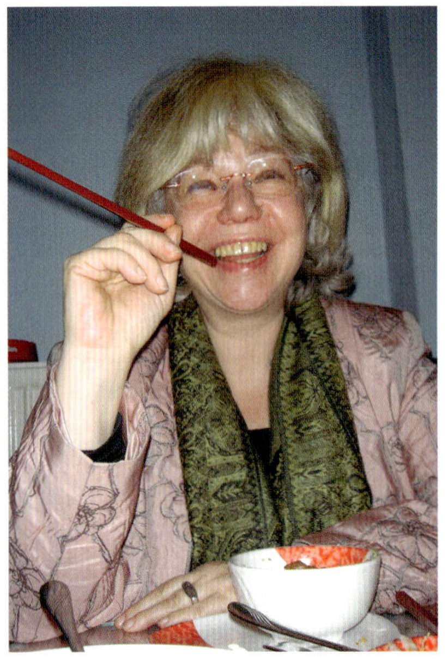

LEFT: Dense smoke clouds hung about but Cilly Kugelmann is now a smoke-free zone, brandishing a chopstick only. Photo Ken Gorbey

OPPOSITE: Inka and Ken put on happy faces in Oisteria No. 1 restaurant, the night of 9/11. We had gathered up a bunch of grieving American visitors and there were tears aplenty. The newspaper shows a collapsing tower.
Photo Ken Gorbey

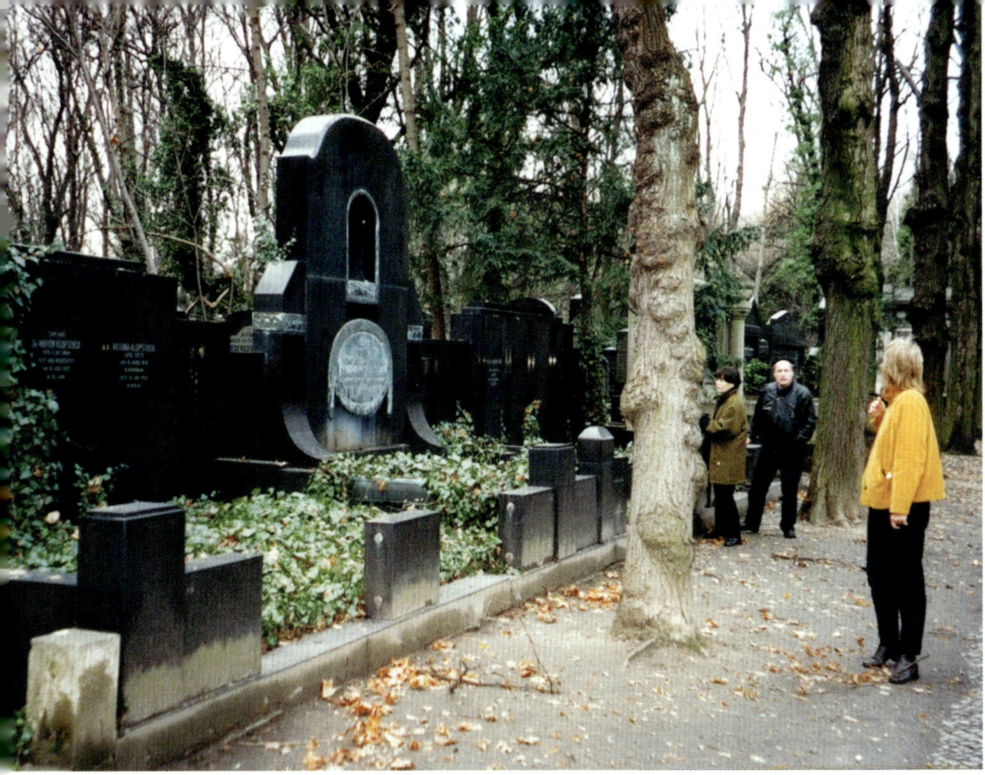

ABOVE: The 'dead cemetery' at Weissensee: Eva Söderman (foreground) and Susan and Thomas Friedrich at one of the monumental family plots no longer used after the early 1930s – Jews died elsewhere. Photo Ken Gorbey

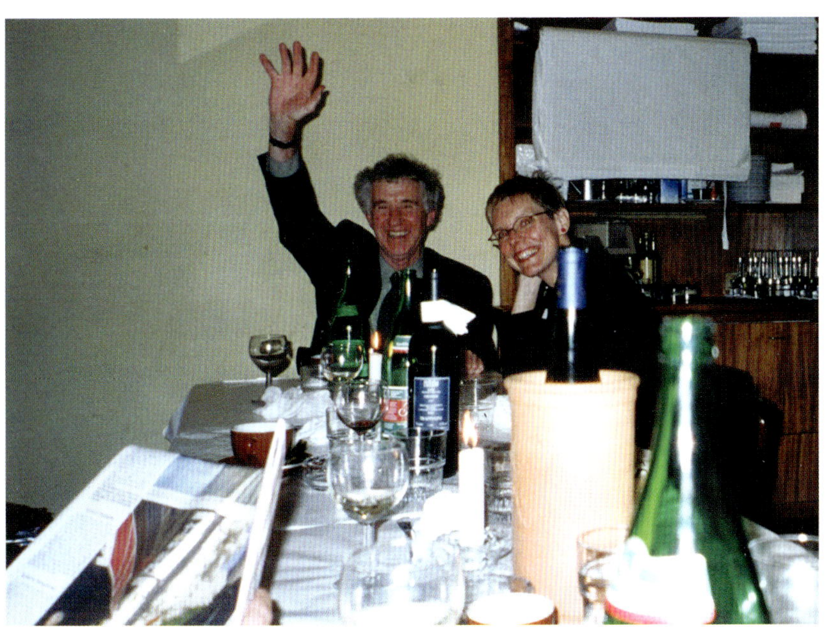

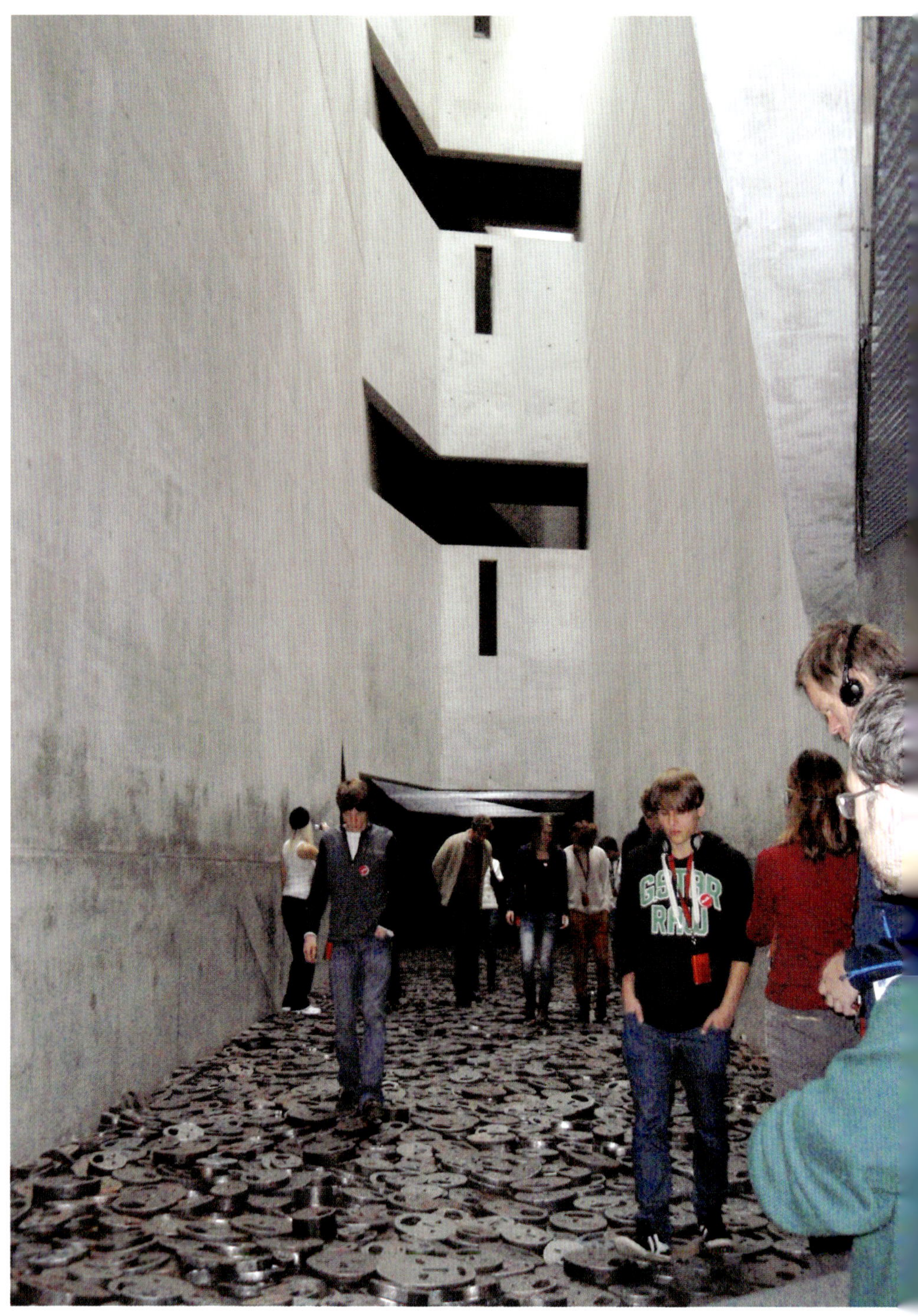

Menashe Kadishman's *Shalechet/Falling Leaves*, thousands of screaming death masks scattered over the floor of Libeskind's Main Void. Photo Ken Gorbey

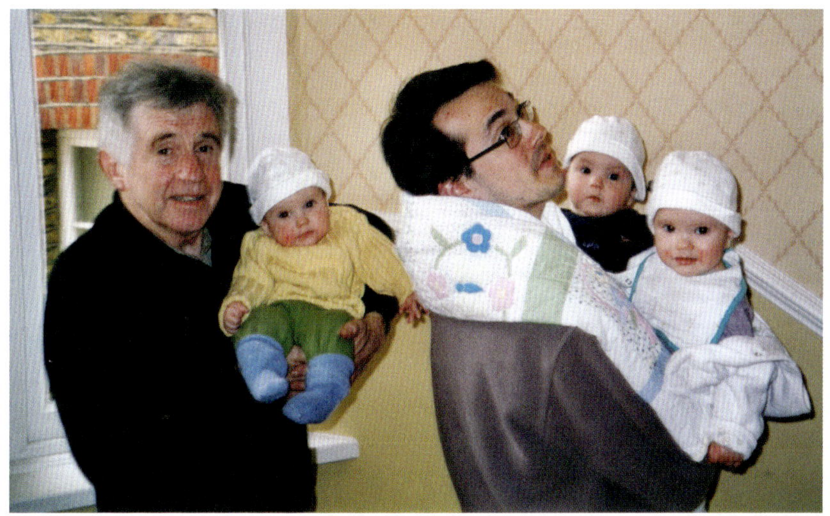

Suddenly I have three grandchildren. From left: Grandad, Lucile, Dad (Erwan), Abigail and Manon, London, 2001. Photo Susan Foster

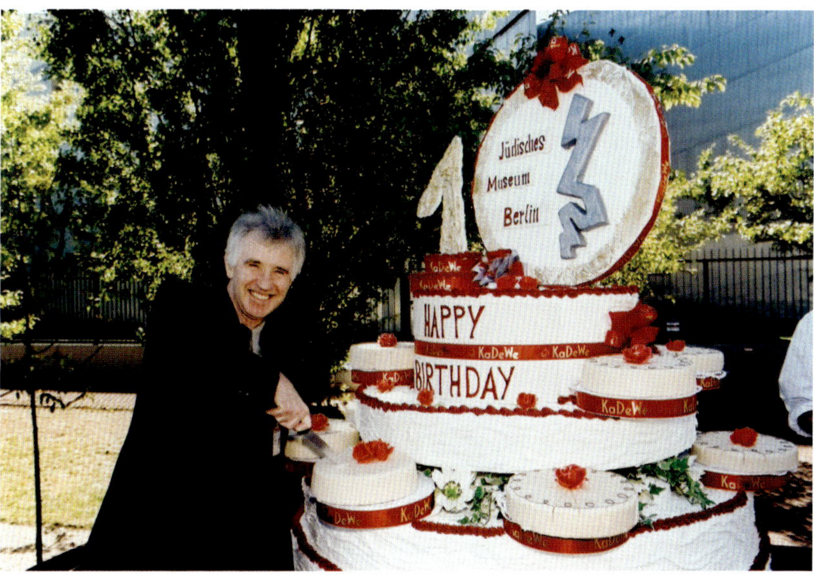

Cutting the first anniversary cake, 2001. The multi-tiered confection was supplied by department store KaDeWe. They were good to us, aware of their Jewish origins and forced Aryanisation in the Nazi years.
Photo Bildschön, Jewish Museum Berlin

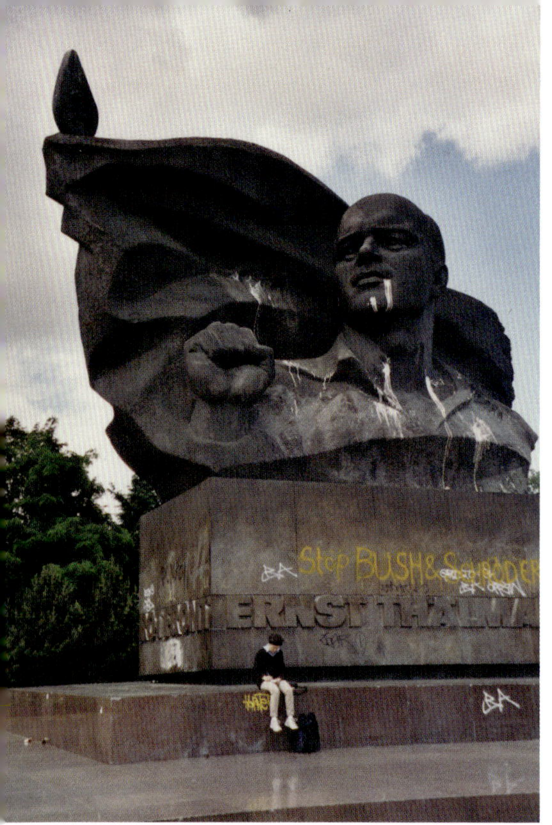

Susan dwarfed by German communist leader Ernst Thälmann, the latter too big to demolish. World leaders were in town in June 2000 so Ernst had been scrubbed down. A few weeks on he again gathered graffiti. Photo Ken Gorbey

BELOW: *1945*. The Soviet soldier standing in the centre of the mural in the Arbatskaya metro station in Moscow sparks recognition. It is the huge heroic memorial figure from Treptower Park in Berlin. To Berliners this is the 'tomb of the unknown rapist'. In a case of confused nationalism the 2003 mural honours the CCCP (USSR), even though it no longer exists. Photo Ken Gorbey

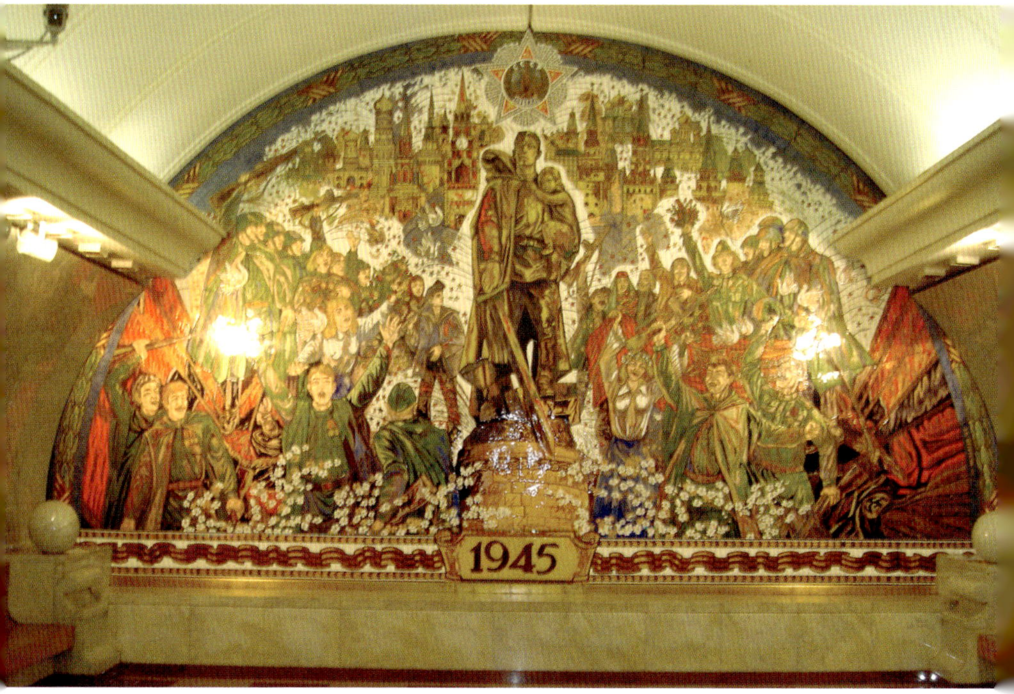

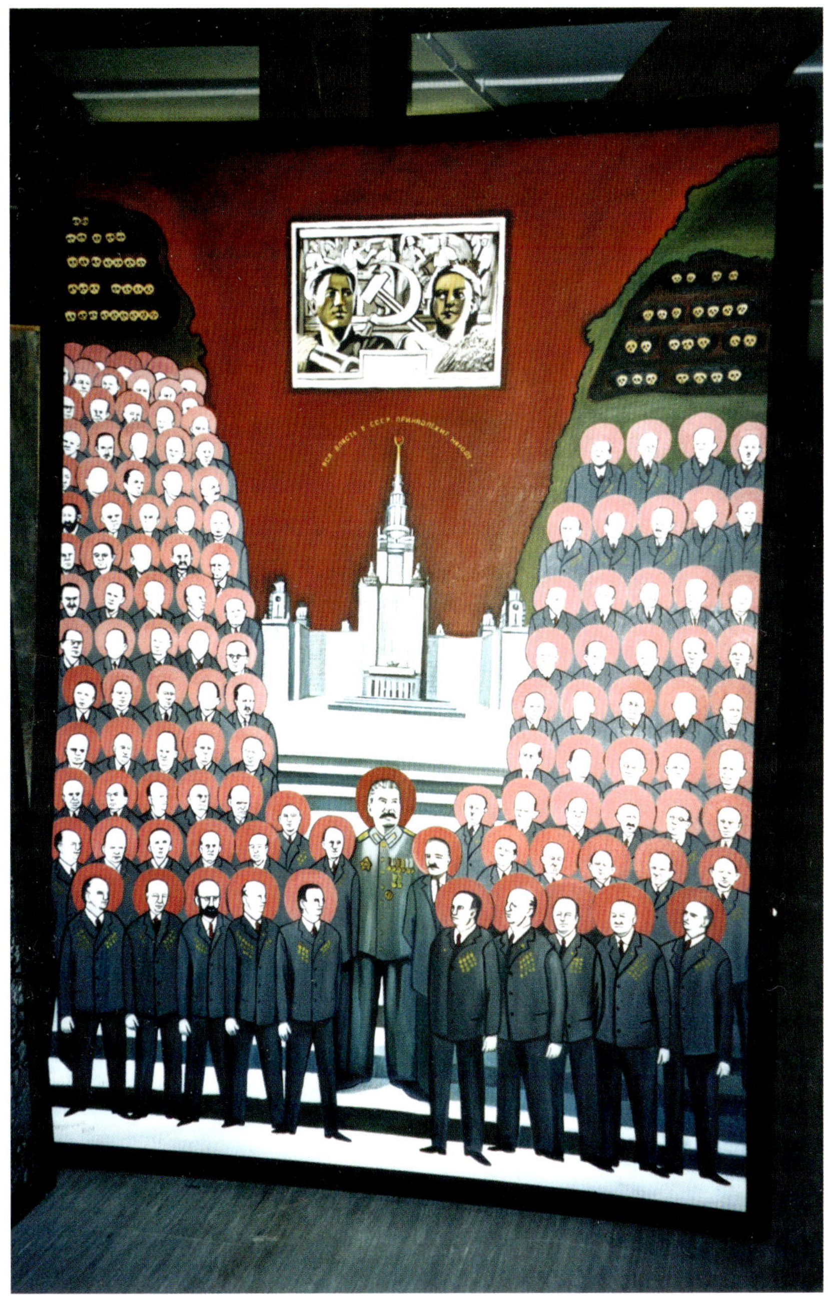

Official DDR art at Beeskow. Among the dissidence is this puzzle, showing Stalin and his pantheon of secular saints. Photo Ken Gorbey

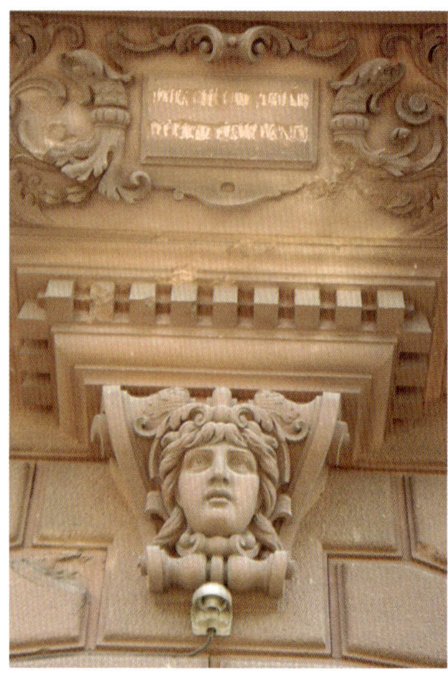

The face on the wall at 33 Vossstrasse, with its defaced plaque and lines of bullet scars, became the repository of my anger at Nazi Germany.
Photo Ken Gorbey

BELOW: The Brandenburg Gate under restoration. One calm summer evening we climbed to the top and looked out over the city of drama that is Berlin. Photo Megaposter GmbH

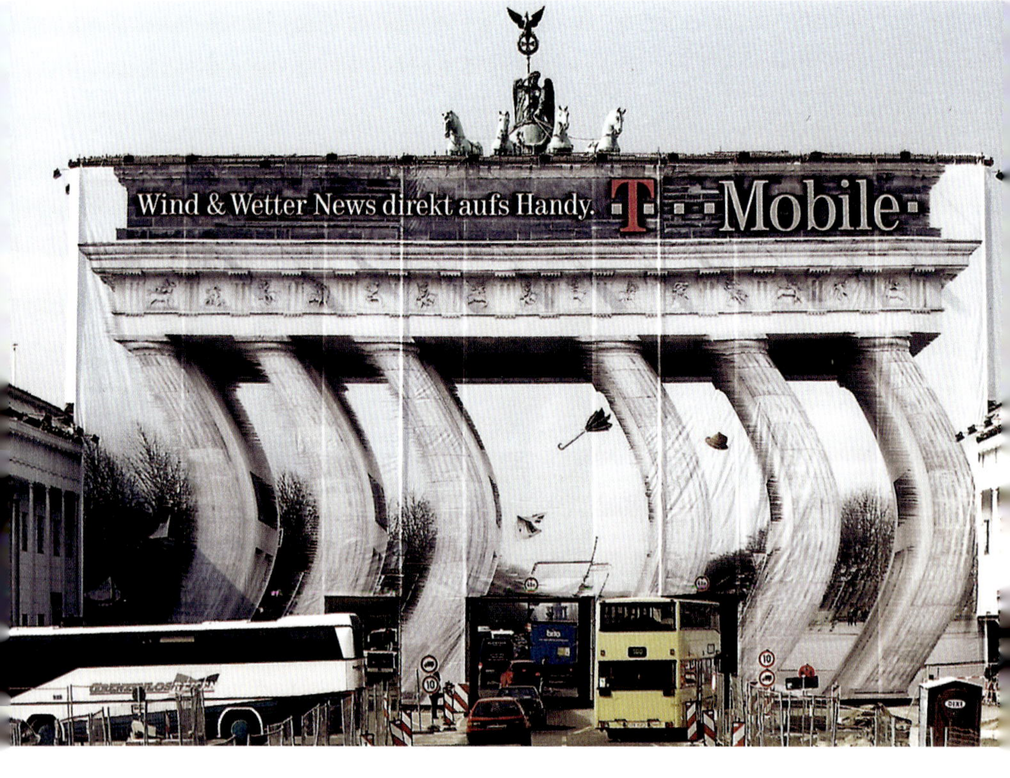

English to acknowledge my role: 'Berlin's, and my, favourite Kiwi,' he said. I was embarrassed but pleased.

As we travelled home in a splendid Mercedes, smelling of elegance, Susan said, 'I could get used to this.' At the apartment we were brought back to earth by torrents of water pouring through a bulging bedroom ceiling. The war had destroyed our building's upper floors and the hasty repairs of 50 years ago had succumbed to the night's downpour. We were not the only ones. All over Berlin that night the roofs of other war-damaged buildings gave up and let in the rain. Because tomorrow was to be the big day for donors, I slept in the front bedroom while Susan remained on guard throughout the night to monitor new leaks and empty buckets.

The next day, Monday 10 September, is something of a blank. As the hours moved into work time, the phone started ringing with requests for interviews. These I batted away as we were due at this morning's news briefing, a huge gathering in a theatre specially hired to hold the 300 or so journalists and camera crews expected. We sat lined up across the stage. Nigel later observed that we looked exhausted. I spoke to some matters, but mainly it was Mike who led.

At the approved hour, the museum was opened to the invited donors from throughout the world. These were the people who had sent back to Berlin their memories and important value-laden objects, their very German souls. There was a large contingent from the States, including groups of trustees and councillors from the Jewish Museum in New York and the National Holocaust Memorial Museum.

Nigel and I walked through together to see how they were reacting. An old Orthodox Jewish man, in traditional garb and with sidelocks, rocked and chanted to a camera before one of the exhibits. Although sophisticated, the camera was not the type used by a professional film crew. Likely this was a proud family or community recording the memories of the patriarch. It was very evident that the Jewish Museum Berlin was winning approval. From time to time we were stopped by people who wished to offer congratulations. An American couple explained that the opening of this Jewish museum had brought them back to the city of their birth for the first time since their escape before the war. Their friends, though, could not come: 'The wounds are still too raw and they are unlikely to ever return.'

Mike and Barbara hosted a reception at their apartment and later in the evening we joined the Libeskinds on a boat trip around the canals and rivers of Berlin. There was dancing; normally we would have taken part, but the effort was too great and I just wanted to sit quietly. It was some form of recovery.

*

As always, the morning of 11 September began early. I faced a full diary of media interviews, in person and by phone, which I was determined to enjoy. A meeting had been scheduled with Mike, a last run-through of arrangements for the public opening that evening. The museum would be free to any who might come and would remain open until they came no more.

It was mid-afternoon, around 9am in New York. Cilly and Peter were there, and Eva. This was a time to relax and celebrate what we had done. Then Margarete came into the room. I was sitting near Mike, facing Margarete's adjoining door, and observed her progress across the room. She was a tall woman but now seemed reduced in size. Her normal litheness had gone; her bronzed and handsome face had lost all colour and was now gravely transparent. She bent forward and whispered in Mike's ear.

He said nothing, just rose and turned on CNN. There they were. On a sunny New York morning the Twin Towers were ablaze. In that instant my first thought was a surprising one; I wondered about the safety of that nice Australian man returning to New York to his job in the financial industry, the one I polled about knowledge of museums.

At first we said very little. It was obvious what was happening, yet it took time for the full import of those images on the screen, by now including the Pentagon, to penetrate. Someone wondered aloud what would be happening at this moment in the halls of power.

'They'll be racing around not knowing what it's all about, seeking information that doesn't yet exist.' Mike spoke from experience. A visitor came in and said, 'Nuke the lot!' We knew what he meant. Even in that moment of shock I knew his response was wrong and I said so.

After perhaps 30 minutes, but what seemed like hours, Peter and I left the meeting. Peter would handle security matters. I set myself to bring those in the museum up to date. Nigel already knew. Our message was to be simple information. The Twin Towers had been hit, obviously with great loss of life. We would remain open until told otherwise. Carry on calmly and inform and comfort anyone in need. I told Josh. Might he know people there? I remember, too, meeting our lawyer, who was showing a company client through the museum. He was shocked. His firm had a New York office and he hastened back to work to see what had to be done.

I came back to find Peter with security people. From the window I could see uniformed men with guns, encircling the museum with razor wire. There was some thought that the high-profile, newly opened Jewish Museum Berlin might be the German target, if there was one. We had hosts at the main door informing the public that the museum would not open until we had assessed what had happened. An armoured car arrived and parked outside.

I went back to Mike. Now, on his own, he could let his emotions show and there were tears in his eyes. He mourned for and with his nation. He was also a very worried man. Barbara and his son Michael were on a plane back to the States at that moment. 'Here I am, irony of ironies, the refugee from the Nazis trying to get my family back to the safety of Germany.'

I felt for him, but also had a sense of terrible foreboding that the world was about to change in ways we could not yet know, that a millennium born in hope was destined to deteriorate into arrogance and inhumanity. But it cannot be all doom. There is still hope. We still live.

*

Inka came up to me in the corridor. There were some 400 American donors trapped in Berlin and we should take responsibility for them. We could not reach everyone but she had gathered up those still in the museum. To keep these grieving people occupied, we took them out for dinner. In a local restaurant we worked to keep spirits up but each had their own fears, for family and friends and for nation. The shock and grief were terrible to see. It was a night of tears.

Yet we would recover and carry on. I will always remember that *Cabaret* in the little theatre on the Kudamm and hear the company's shouted anger, but I also carry with me another *Cabaret* performance. The museum was open and the project staff had demonstrated that they were a high-performance team. It had been hard but now it was time for a Christmas party – in a Jewish museum. The high point of the evening is three of the project women, achievers each one, dressed as Kit Kat Klub girls, singing and dancing their way through a number of *Cabaret* routines. The next day I bring my *Cabaret* score to work. In it I write 'The greatest performance of *Cabaret* ever!' and they sign their names – Gelia (Eisert), Signe (Rossbach), Christina (Scholten).

CHAPTER 19

TIME TO GO

THE MEN WITH GUNS, the lines of razor wire and the armoured car stayed for some time. When I arrived each morning I would exchange a few pleasantries with these generally older members of the constabulary, their armoury of seeming equal age. They would do little to save the museum from an attack by hijacked aircraft, but their presence was comforting and they soon became part of the museum scene.

The museum opened a few days later than planned. Visitors poured in. Life went on, albeit in a world seen in a different way, the inescapable image of burning New York towers and falling, flailing people seared into our brains. The exhibition of photos of the 9/11 event came to Berlin. Past horrors had rarely been documented in such a public way. Perhaps Vietnam was the exception but here it tended to be ordinary New Yorkers in frame. I had once said, during a group discussion at Te Papa, that the image that would define the start of the new century was the Hubble telescope photo of star formation. Those immense fingers of creation deep in space talked of science offering a better perspective on our place in the universe. No more.

In a more immediate, everyday way, as authorities struggled to make air travel safe, my bags sprouted tape and stickers, the remnants of security systems hurriedly imposed, changed and employed afresh in modified form.

Part of the healing process for Susan and me was an early morning call from Erwan in London a few weeks later. Susi had been safely delivered of three little people and everything was fine. I was a grandad. Ever since Susi had announced that triplets were due we had worried, and had breathed great sighs of relief, at each step towards and then beyond 'viability'. Now they were with us. I raced about telling everyone, including a TV crew filming a programme on the museum. The producer rejigged her schedule and after a brief practice a beaming project director announced that triplet grandchildren had arrived, *Drillinge*. It is a beautiful word that remains firmly in my mind to this day. A few weeks later we proudly trundled the three baby girls about Battersea Park.

*

So it was that, despite 9/11, my life softened and changed. The museum was now part of the Berlin landscape. Each morning, some time before the appointed hour, I would see the first visitors gathering at the entrance, in pairs, threes and fours, perhaps a tour group. What would their judgement be? What would they make of our museum? Christiane and her market research started immediately questioning and we read what the critics had to say.

I would discreetly follow visitors to see how they reacted to the museum. I had done a great deal of this in the past: standing in the main concourse of the Air and Space Museum being battered by the crush of people (about seven million a year); reading the delight on the faces of visitors captivated by the swimming and drifting creatures of the sea at the Monterey Bay Aquarium; and marvelling at the busy noise that typified a normal day at London's Natural History Museum. But this museum belonged to me; it had become part of my life. Could I be the neutral observer?

The first observation was positive, a pass with distinction. Everyone said it. Our young hosts were brilliant, warm, life-affirming. In all weathers, hot or freezing, one stood at the large Kollegienhaus entry doors greeting every person with words of welcome, or at the very least eye contact and a smile. The message was clear. 'Life, not just death' was an invisible banner, and we became the friendliest museum in Germany.

The second observation was less positive. Visitors had to go through airport-level security operated by contractors, but they, and their X-ray machine, were the low point of the museum experience: officious, unpleasant, unfreundlich.

I followed the crowds through the foyer, a long hall across the back of the mellow and aged Kollegienhaus.

'Can we see your ticket, please?'

Visitors were now confronted with a starkly modern intrusion, a large vertical concrete tower that cut upward and plunged down toward a darkened bunker. The hosts standing before a large gap in this concrete silo were indicating that this was the entry to the museum proper. Certainly for some, this first encounter with unrelenting Libeskind design meant bewilderment and perhaps even anxiety. Above, a deep, infinite gloom, to be sensed more than looked into. A steel staircase of industrial quality pointed down, seemingly into part of Berlin's historical character that is underground, as in Hitler's bunker. It was a descent that played on the emotions.

Even when, at the base, the stairs turned towards light, there was no opening out into a space that invited relief, decompression and choice. Visitors would hesitate, then trustingly move forward up the long floor of the narrow corridor that is the first of the three Axes.

Exile, Holocaust and Continuity – the Axes cut across each other. Here Paul Kuttner's towel story was told and I made sure that Wellington was named as one of the cities of the world that had received Jews escaping Germany. People visited the Holocaust Tower in batches, with the heavy door clicking closed behind. The feeling is of being deep underground, a reaction heightened by a sliver of natural light at the top and the faintly heard noise of traffic and children playing in the school opposite. Nothing is required but to contemplate and absorb. A minority were deeply moved. A curator from a major Los Angeles museum broke down in the tower and then tried to explain his totally unexpected response to me and himself. Outside the Garden of Exile, with its sloping floor and leaning stele with trees planted on top, attracted similar responses, from 'That's interesting' to deep feeling.

The long main staircase, with its hovering angled beams, beckoned. On the first landing visitors would divert into the Main Void and Kadishman's *Fallen Leaves*. At the top of the main stairs the exhibition narrative began with a quiet social interaction as visitors were encouraged to write down their thoughts and hang these in the branches of a pomegranate tree. People put serious effort into choosing words.

First came the diaspora and the early Jewish settlements in Germania. The *Codex Theodosianus* was an ancient administrative record that at one level said the Jews were here early and at another granted them the privilege of being taxed more than others, an early rort to extract money from a despised minority. Sitting alongside, the Talmud with its breath-activated pages commanded greater attention. Another high point was the Glikl bas Judah Leib bag-packing game. In the section on the rise of Jewish bankers was the three minutes of scenes from the vile Nazi film *Jud Sűss* (Süss the Jew). This had been one of my most enlightening work experiences, sitting through the entire film several times, identifying the high points from an interpretive point of view. *Passage* was perhaps the most successful of all the exhibition segments: a rich and intensive examination of the emergence of the Jews as a part of German society. They excelled in so much: writing, commerce, new technologies, research, finance, medicine, film and, as Mike pointed out on occasion, crime. It was a gutsy offer.

We posed very simple but disputatious yes/no questions for people to ponder as they completed their visit. These had no right or wrong answer.

They just required thought. 'Is it okay to tell Jewish jokes?' and 'Will it ever be possible for a Jew to be chancellor of Germany?'

Aware that these could raise eyebrows, we had taken them to Mike, who in turn got the agreement of the other Mike, Naumann. The stats were telling us that people were answering in what could only be described as a politically correct manner. The majority would never think of telling such jokes, and yes, a Jew will someday be chancellor. Then, at the very last station, people were invited to send an unmoderated message to the museum, displayed on a running text board down in the foyer. Our hope was that visitors would deliberate on the best course for humanity into the future. Only once did some kids send a bad-taste gassing-the-Jews message. It was soon deleted and no one noticed.

I returned time and again to the single TV screen carrying a short excerpt from the famed Günter Gaus interview with German-Jewish philosopher Hannah Arendt. Speaking of the Holocaust and how incomprehensible and unbelievable, at least at first, were the stories filtering through to them in wartime New York, she says, 'What was decisive was the day we learnt about Auschwitz.' It was different from just having enemies. 'It was really as if an abyss had opened. Because we had the idea that amends could somehow be made for everything else, as amends can be made for just about everything at some point in politics. But not for this. *This ought not to have happened.*'

It is such a powerful statement. She spits out, 'That gang!' She addresses the German audience directly, face to face, and sends them on their way without absolution.

*

We celebrated our successes, but what did not work well? First, as predicted, in the welter of information in a long drawn-out sequence visitors became lost, both physically (where am I in the building?) and conceptually (where am I in the story?). We read it in their faces and in their enquiries of the hosts. Studies in the psychology of architecture indicated that, in buildings, a distinction could be drawn between narrow/broad, oppressive/generous and soft/hard. One scholar was prepared to say that very ordered, step-upon-step circulation 'discourages and exhausts the visitor' through 'biologically unnatural regularity of movement (working of a machine)'. Avoid the linear, was his message. But Daniel's museum was very linear: there was only one choice of direction on offer. We had made this situation worse by plying visitors with masses of hard factual information, none of it well known, in too many overloaded segments. To solve this problem, we would red-line the floor with instructions that said, in essence, 'You are here. Keep on going. You are not lost.'

But it was more than this. Each time I walked through the galleries I would mentally protest at our treatment of Daniel's architecture. Parts of his building were so strong, so sculptural, that they clashed with the narratives and collections we had jammed into every nook and cranny.

I confronted the balance of museum to architecture in my report to the board. 'Somehow our ideas have to be as dramatic as Daniel's building. We need to align the exhibitions with the Libeskind-Bau architecture and to give to this beautiful and expressive interior the freedom to breathe.'

*

People were flocking to the museum. My estimate, that we would greet 600,000 in the first year, was too low. Within the first six months 400,000 people had visited, and well over that 600,000 in the first year. This would lift to our wildest-dream figure of 750,000 annually within a few years. We had become the most visited of all Berlin museums.

Our survey results told us that a great many people came, they stayed for a long time and they were overwhelmingly satisfied with what they found. They told us such nice things: we were informative, not at all boring, stimulating, friendly, interactive, different from other museums, a place of good design; and, of course, there was that extraordinary architecture.

At the same time, we could not ignore the negatives: we were exhibiting too much; wayfinding was inadequate; we had failed to provide a clear thematic line; the experience was a long tiring journey; and we did not seem to be doing as well as we had hoped in catering for children. This last was a disappointment, and Christiane ran some tests. Yes, people acknowledged that the museum was also for children, but parents were choosing not to bring them because of the awkward questions they might ask and the problem of formulating adequate answers.

At my official farewell from Te Papa I had thrown down a challenge to my colleagues: Nigel and I planned to take the Te Papa achievement and do even better, so watch out. And we had. Despite Te Papa being roughly four times bigger than the Jewish Museum Berlin, people stayed in our museum longer and expressed greater levels of satisfaction.

*

Mike was not so interested until Christiane produced her first summary of visitor reactions. 'I want that page to go to the next board meeting!' It was the cover-sheet summary of all statistics, people voicing surprise at the impact of the experience, its openness, its lack of punitive beating about the head, and even, here and there, its moments of fun.

There is always a danger that audience research can become PR, so as well as Christiane's material I would write a paper that reviewed all intelligent critiques and append a personal take on what we had achieved and where we could do better. I entitled it 'What Can We Take from the Critics?' Some things I chose not to put in. Mike arranged for me to tour the museum with Israel Singer. 'He's a powerful man, chair of the World Jewish Congress' was all the briefing I received. Singer found nothing essential wrong apart from a lack of stated support for the state of Israel. Similar comments were coming in by mail. I would respond that our fundamental mission was about tolerance and the high cost of intolerance for a German audience; we were not a political statement about Israel's right to exist. But that I chose not to report. Israel was too hot a topic.

Instead I dwelt on two areas: what the critics were saying, and comments from professional colleagues in Germany and a number from the States and Israel.

This was serious stuff, many leagues beyond the analysis that Te Papa had, or had not, been subject to. But the criticisms echoed my early worries; we were not doing justice to the tense, ultimately genocidal, relationship between German Jews and other Germans. Israeli writer Amos Elon found 'a curious scarcity of historical tension'. Others were equally blunt. Relationship with their German neighbours and anti-Semitism were not strongly enough expressed. Our linear historical approach had not served us well; although we had attempted to capture those tensions, they were scattered across different segments. No single area in the museum carried a full discussion of intolerance, of anti-Semitic behaviour and belief, and, conversely, of tolerance.

My colleagues were all full of praise at what had been achieved, and in such a short time, but as Martin Roth summed up for them all, the place was just too full. 'Less can indeed be more,' he said. 'Greater structural and conceptual clarity can be achieved by taking material out of the exhibitions.' In response I would initiate immediate changes to rectify these problems, announcing to the board that an entire segment would be demolished and we would start again, and that we would reduce 'the intensity of the exhibits' (i.e. take things off display).

I called a further peer review, once again led by Elaine Gurian with two other powerful women directors, Sara Bloomfield of Washington's Holocaust Museum and Nina Archabal of the Minnesota Historical Society. We were also joined by Cilly's great friend and fellow smoker extraordinaire, Felicitas Jelinek of the Jewish Museum Vienna. The report, which Elaine and I wrote in a short time, included all the official directions I needed to plough ahead.

I wanted to make a point about change, and so set the senior team to work on a new concept for our barely two-month-old museum. We would restructure the exhibits in a manner better able to be understood by visitors, yet at the same time would strengthen the message. I was surprised to find that Eva, backed by Cilly, thought that the new intellectual framework we came up with would interest the media. Back in New Zealand such an internal planning development would not be news. German newspapers had a strong tradition of cultural reportage and, yes, if we were to organise a media conference they would come. It was agreed. Cilly and I would go before the press. She would lead the presentation. This seemed an ideal time to signal major changes; Cilly would be stepping into my position and I would be leaving the Jewish Museum Berlin.

*

Not long after opening, Mike had come to me with an offer: stay on with the same title, job and conditions. He made it clear that he had his desired museum and wanted me to manage it into the future. This was tempting, but Susan and I would have to think long and hard about another five years in Berlin. We had come to love the city and Germany. There was the cultural life and that growing body of friends. It was so much the centre of a world that we wanted to explore. What might take us away from this, our new home?

It was not other jobs. I had not actively sought the next challenge but a number of possibilities found their way to me. Two were on the table, both exciting developments in American cities that we would have loved to experience. One serious approach had us visiting a city very different to Berlin but in its own way equally exciting. Both projects collapsed, however, victims of a post-9/11 world. Our decision would have nothing to do with other job offers. Mainly I wanted a change. I had a feeling that there were other things to achieve and new ways of exercising my mind.

So my answer to Mike's offer had been 'No thanks'. He was surprised and for a while sought to persuade me otherwise. That done, we set a leaving date. Others found the decision incomprehensible. Three single-person delegations, people I respected, suggested that I should reconsider. Mike gave me the task of finding a replacement, someone like me. I searched among my professional contacts, but this was all play-acting since the ideal person was right under our noses, Cilly Kugelmann.

Cilly and I presented the new conceptual framework to perhaps 20 cultural commentators. It was reported and Mike was not impressed, seeing it as a challenge to the linear exhibitions he and Shaike had created. In truth it was, and we had to downplay any immediate effect beyond the changes I had taken through the board.

I retained my titles and status. The media still telephoned me to arrange interviews. I would front official occasions, and Susan and I would accept invitations and tickets and be part of the social life of Berlin. But things changed. Cilly grew into the role. My thoughts returned to the public presentation Nigel and I had given that January evening in 2000 when I had warned an embryonic staff about the reality of project work.

'After opening and your contribution is done, the museum will always be part of your experience and be embedded in your very soul. But when you return it will be as a visitor. Others will be commanding, creating, panicking at looming deadlines, doing what you once did and feeling the pride of immediate association with a great cultural institution. But you can no longer expect that feeling of inclusion and bonding that has grown in you over the months and years driving to get the museum open. The museum will no longer belong to you.'

*

Marylea from the Adlon Hotel telephoned shortly after it was announced that we were leaving, to question my sanity. How could we abandon the most exciting city in the world for a small nation in the middle of an ocean, so far removed from the central cultural reality of Europe? Finally, she accepted that we were not about to change our minds and with reference to the city tradition enshrined in that haunting Marlene Dietrich song, 'Ich hab' noch einen Koffer in Berlin' (I still have a suitcase in Berlin), she said that the hotel would hold our suitcase awaiting our return.

There was a further kind offer: she and Gianni would be putting on a farewell dinner at the Adlon for our friends. Chuffed, we began composing a list – there would be Mike, Cilly, Nigel and Susanna; Daniel and Nina Libeskind were booked in; then there were the friends who had done so much for us; perhaps the Australian military attaché and wife whom we had got to know and like.

Sometime later Marylea came back with a date. We started to discuss the invitation list. Mike – easy, on both our lists.

'We must have Danny,' said Marylea. Yes, we had already warned Daniel and Nina Libeskind.

'Yes, of course,' said Marylea, 'but how about Danny?' I was confused.

'You know, Danny! Danny Barenboim!'

She continued. 'How about Paul?' My silence indicated I was searching for this person. 'You know Paul, the English ambassador!'

'Marylea, England isn't my country!' I said, probably with some edge, which I instantly regretted. 'Paul isn't our ambassador.'

At this point I had to quickly form a new approach. I explained that Danny Barenboim had very kindly sent us tickets to the Staatsoper on occasions but we had never met; similarly Sir Paul. Perhaps the dinner should take the form of a thank you to those in the profession who had given us such support.

The evening was a huge success. On Susan's left sat Martin Roth, whom she now knew well. On her right was Herman Schäfer, who had hosted a lunch for us on a visit to his relatively new contemporary history museum, the Haus der Geschichte, in Bonn. She already had an interesting connection with this museum, having contributed several New Zealand political cartoons on the fall of the Berlin Wall.

Cilly shared Martin. Cilly, dear Cilly. She had written me a farewell note full of wondrous things, the best being that I was 'the conductor who had made an orchestra out of elephants, turtles, snakes, donkeys and birds'. The Libeskinds could not be there as a change of date had them travelling the world somewhere. Mike, Marylea, Gigi and Kallo found many connections.

Seated with Gianni, I spent a delightful couple of hours learning about a person whose whole life had been building and saving great hotels across Europe. He had also accumulated a significant personal wine cellar that, with each shift, required a truck much bigger than the last. He had now decided that the time was right to accumulate no more, and to start the serious work of drawing down on the collection. The evening was therefore marked not just by superb food from one of the world's great hotel kitchens, but also by a selection of the most exquisite wines, each of which came with a personal history recounted by Gianni. Mike rose and spoke of our unexpected collaboration and our success. Martin followed with generous tributes to my role in changing how Germans now conceived of their museums.

As the dinner came to a close, Susan and I stood at the window of the private dining room looking out across the magical cityscape of Pariser Platz to the Brandenburg Gate, grand and bathed in light. We were sad to be leaving and still uncertain about our decision.

It was late and cold when we left; there were virtually no people on the Platz. The Brandenburg Gate with the heroic Quadriga atop, Victory standing on her chariot pulled by four massive horses, had seen much and endured humiliation. She had been tweaked according to the politics of the day and sorely damaged in World War II. For much of our time in Berlin the gate was being restored and had been swathed in scaffolding, upon which were hung huge quirky images that were changed every few months. On one occasion the gate had been transformed into a vast football goal; another time the supporting pillars were corkscrewed about each other; then there were Christmas decorations; and always the sponsor's message.

Together we remembered the balmy summer's evening when, as part of an official party, we had assembled at the base of the gate. Some of the women in the group declined to wear hard hats, to avoid destroying their hairdos. Susan and I wore them, for this was a construction site. We climbed through the scaffolding to enter a small door into the interior of the gate's large hollow lintel and clambered across its uneven floor. It had accumulated the dust and debris of centuries. Toward the centre a narrow ladder led to an even smaller opening. Looking up, we saw something that will remain with us for ever. It was a clear night and we expected stars, but instead, hovering immediately above, was the underside of a huge bronze hoof of one of the Quadriga horses. We squeezed through, silent and exhilarated. To one side, dazzling, with all the brilliance of a Manhattan skyline, was Potsdamer Platz with the Sony Centre standing central; ahead the floodlit Siegessäule within the large dark embrace of the Tiergarten, yet another Victory column, this one strapped with captured cannons. To the north was the Reichstag with the new glass dome shining brightly. Beyond Unter den Linden the TV tower, pride of the defunct German Democratic Republic, and Mitte, the old quarter, in its time much damaged and much replaced. Around the horizon spread the lights of the city.

With Victory above we sipped champagne and ate our Häagen-Dazs ice cream from small tubs, looking out over Berlin, a city that in so many ways had become ours.

*

The matter of leaving Berlin did not finish with that one decision. We had moved back to New Zealand and had started a new work life, but elsewhere the matter was still alive. I was in Washington, the city more beautiful than ever for being snowbound and partly paralysed. A team of huskies raced about the National Mall. I was working once again with Jim Volkert and Elaine, at the new National Museum of the American Indian.

Susan telephoned. Mike was trying to get in touch. It seemed urgent. We arranged to link up by phone. Mike came straight to the point. He wanted me back in Berlin, same conditions, to act as his project manager and, I suspected, confidante. This was a real surprise and I was not well prepared.

'Look, Mike, I'm doing what I love and opportunities are opening up.'

'You can do that from anywhere in the world, much better in fact from Berlin. When are you going to realise that your centre of gravity is Berlin?' It was the closest thing to a shout that I had ever heard from Mike.

I pleaded that he put his trust in Cilly and Nigel. They were very capable of doing what he required. To no avail; he wanted me back.

'You're … you're …' I waited expectantly. Might it be conceptually brilliant, or a great builder of cultural institutions? 'You're a bulldozer!'

CHAPTER 20

GERMANY AND THE EAST: A PERSONAL ODYSSEY

I TOOK TO BERLIN an identity formed from experience in my island nation, mainly Western but with Māori an important influence. I had my own personal history. Family, training and life experiences formed a moral framework that had guided me through my first six decades. The rational mind had anticipated that a more complex idea of Germany as a nation, one that had confronted a Nazi past, would emerge and this would teach me something. I was prepared to learn but believed with certainty that the thing called 'me' was essentially complete, matured and in need of little change. It would see me through the time I had remaining on this planet. But Germany proved to be another powerful episode in forming character. There was nothing overly dramatic, no single bolt of enlightenment, rather a three-year intensive course in challenged awareness that I pursue to this day.

Late 2002, and we were about to take up a New Zealand life once again. It was a time of uncertainty and I needed to know how I had changed and what I wanted to achieve post-Berlin.

But a few months out of the JMB I did what I always do – I started to search for the words. The first thing I wrote was of a police convoy streaming through the darkened streets of Berlin. The second was an unexpected find, a face I discovered on a wall.

*

I searched for a playground and found a face. An authoritative history of Berlin, one of the first I had picked up in Wellington, had told me that I could reach the playground off Vossstrasse. Most of my second trip, November 1999, had been overcast gloom but there came a day of clear, blue sky when I ventured onto the U-Bahn. My professional excuse was that I wished to visit the InfoBox, a bright red temporary information centre that stood on stilts among the cranes and rising buildings of the Potsdamer Platz development. The real draw was that playground.

Vossstrasse was not far away but, given construction activity, the search was challenging. Finally, I stood looking across the street. What I took to be the playground was an elevated fenced zone, comfortably embraced by a better class of East German apartment building. At one time, these were reserved for communist apparatchiks, senior and reliable servants of the state who could be trusted with glimpses into the capitalist world lying beyond the Anti-Fascist Protection Rampart, aka the Berlin Wall. It had stood at the end of the street. Perhaps those same servants, stripped of their status with no wall to oversee, lived there still. But unlike the school opposite the Jewish Museum Berlin, my supposed playground generated none of the noise of children at play. On this, my first visit to Vossstrasse, the silence seemed appropriate, for my research had indicated – I was actually 100 metres or so out – that this marked the site of Hitler's bunker.

I had images in my mind of the building that had loomed opposite. Albert Speer had used all his skill to create for his Führer the Reichskanzlei, the Reich Chancellery. Its fundamental purpose was to trigger fear: everyone who might enter would be cowed and feel the promise of impending savagery. I could encompass all this; I had my academic hat on and the scene was not emotionally taxing. That is, until I turned 180 degrees to find myself staring war in the face.

Across from the supposed playground a deserted survivor building stood on its own. It looked nineteenth-century and I decreed it to be Prussian without even knowing if there was such an architectural style. Central within the red stone decorated façade was a face.

Female, but also strangely androgynous, framed by flowing coiled hair and supported on heraldic whorls, she was handsome rather than pretty, eyes sunk deep, heavy and intense. It was the archetypal Teutonic visage loaded with nationalistic myths to give simplistic cohesion to the emerging power of Bismarck's unified Germany. This one, though, unlike so many others, had no military helmet.

Her face was untouched although the surrounding façade was scarred. The most obvious damage was to a plaque that sat above, positioned to announce something of importance, a name most likely, perhaps a worthy quote. I had no way of telling for at some time a worker had been dispatched to climb up and chisel out the two-line inscription.

There was more; the building was wounded. A single cannon shell had exploded out an impact crater. Then an angled line of cruelly logical bullet wounds traced diagonally across the space between plaque and face, perhaps from some deadly confrontation, bursts of fire as Russian soldiers closed in on the chancellery early in May 1945. They would have fought through this street on their way to the ultimate prize, the Reichstag, now little more than a kilometre away. Or perhaps the battle was done and some victorious soldier laughed as he brought his automatic weapon to bear on those staring eyes. Perhaps a recent recruit from a far-flung Soviet or a hardened campaigner who had survived the battles of the Eastern Front. Perhaps he was drunk.

The building had clearly been a superior residence, part of prospering, newly confident Berlin. It was well adorned, though not as demonstrative as some. The face observed life through decades of change. Brown shirts prowled her street and the party imposed its will. The Führer's chancellery rose opposite. Then the Nazi regime ended in calamitous street-fighting. After the gunfire died and the acrid smoke of war cleared came Stunde Null, zero hour – a pause between destruction and defeat and Germans starting life again. But not at 33 Vossstrasse. The building became frozen in time as part of the dead Berlin Wall precinct.

My first visit to Vossstrasse was just a few days after my encounter with the flame-spalled archway in Lindenstrasse. Part of me had to accept that the fascination of Berlin as Nazi capital and battleground was strong. I would return several times to the face, but there was far more to my expeditions than just a search for Adolf Hitler.

At its simplest level, place is physical, a room, a building, a street, a landscape of valleys and hills, a seascape; but at a personal and communal level, place is a charged, seldom neutral, entity. We read the different territories of our life according to what is in our mind at the time of first and subsequent encounters. We can never quite capture in words the feelings we experience roaming, savouring the air, reading the land, the sea, the sky. They form something beyond the rational. It was almost with disappointment that I later, quite by accident, stumbled over a map in a bookshop and learnt that the building with the face had been a government-department headquarters in World War II with bunkers and tunnels beneath. I much preferred the ignorance I took with me on that first encounter.

I needed that face on the wall at Vossstrasse, as part of a tablet on which I might scribe and confront ambiguity of being in a Germany in which the crimes of the Nazis would be ever present, but where I made warm friendships with people who were part of the new and moral Germany. The face on the wall would exemplify 'old Germany', and I would load onto her my anger at the unfathomable and the dark.

It was an inescapable fact that many of the older German generations were guilty. They were young adults and children at the time of Germany's defeat in World War I, or were born in the following decades and became Nazi functionaries. In their everyday lives, they faced a brittle economic reality and were encased in a recent history of militarism. Their nation had lost a war and had suffered the wrath of the victors. This was fertile ground for an instability that brought forth a leadership group of cruel and vicious inclination who gave direction and personal power to the mob they soon owned. Criminals became model citizens enabled to do the regime's dirty work beyond the law.

The leaders who might have countered this toxic tide of ill will, the churches and liberal political institutions, were in disarray and seemingly unable to translate moral judgements into cooperative ethical action. Ordinary people were left to make their choices without strong voices being raised to define what was truly ethical.

Some collaborators were activists, some careerists, who willingly joined the regime. Many would fight to the bitter end. Some were propelled into the ranks of the perpetrators, say as soldiers or policemen on the Eastern Front. Others were passive, finding safety in indifference and inaction. As individuals they might not have employed the rifle or the gas canister, but as administrators they took pride in ensuring that the machinery of state ran smoothly. At war's end they would deny personal knowledge of events unfolding on killing fields far away. Subsequent research has delved into this denial and says: Not likely. You had that knowledge. The sins belong within you.

All, including those few who resisted, would suffer as the war turned against them. Many died. Whatever, as perpetrators they would place the burden of the Holocaust and the slaughter of the Slavs upon their children, their children's children, and beyond. Now those children write tentative family histories that try to separate the myth from reality.

The number of people slaughtered and gassed is impossible to comprehend. I endeavoured to make some sense of the statistics by comparing them with my home nation. At the outbreak of war, New Zealand was a small nation of around 1.6 million souls. The six million or so Jews killed was roughly 3¾ times our entire population. My new awareness of the Slavs to the east told of terrible suffering among those people who happened to be on the road to Moscow, Leningrad and Stalingrad, and of the millions of Russian prisoners of war starved to death. Vasily Grossman, a Russian Jew, has written graphically of the Holocaust in which he lost his mother and of the Great Patriotic War. Russia's losses? Say, around 17 times the New Zealand population destroyed in the space of four years.

These statistics fail us in that they obscure the individual cruelty. Scholarly texts, with their neutral language and detached perspective, tend to hold reality at arm's length. Novels are tougher, for fiction allows portrayals of raw face-to-face violence and of humans without humanity. In the knowledge of their inhumanity, the German war generations fell silent, but this silence was challenged. Leaders, in West Germany at least, boldly said that the nation must acknowledge this great sin and begin the long task of winning back the right to membership of the principled, ethical nations. In 1955 Günter Grass embeds deep within *Dog Years* his judgement on that generation, delivered as machine-gun bursts of condemnation. The children born into peace turn 10 years old and find a new craze, Wunderbrillen, glasses through which they see their war-implicated fathers with great clarity:

> Episodes which are kept from the younger generation for one reason or another are made palpably clear … The scenes that recur over and over again in the twin spheres of the father-recognition glasses are acts of violence performed tolerated instigated eleven twelve thirteen years ago: murders, often by the hundreds. Aiding and abetting. Smoking cigarettes and looking on while. Certified decorated applauded murderers. Murder motives become leitmotives. With murderers at one table, in the same bed, boat, officers' club. Toasts, emergency directives. Record entries. Blowing on rubber stamps. Sometimes mere signatures and wastebaskets. Many roads lead to. Silence as well as words can. Every father has at least one to hide. Many lie buried curtained siloed, as if they had never happened …

He went on. Auschwitz 'belongs to us, is branded into our history'. On two occasions I heard Michael Naumann say something very similar: 'The Holocaust is a pillar of our democracy. Should we lose memory of the Holocaust our democracy will be under threat.'

The protesting students of 1968 would not countenance that knowing forgetfulness. Part of their nation's conscience must be defined by Auschwitz, Holocaust and Nazi. They searched and found that former followers of the Führer quietly occupied high places in postwar administrations and that their grandparents may well have seen ragged columns of concentration camp prisoners being driven down their streets ahead of the Soviet army's advance. The young people shouted their anger.

Now I, the Kiwi from far away, was a small part of the generational dispute among Germans. It seemed as if every week a new study appeared as the sins of the older generations were scrutinised by scholars. I read all I could, a crash course in atrocity. One staffer told me that he was quite prepared to accept one scholar's argument, that all Germans were Hitler's willing executioners, hardwired to commit genocide. I argued against this; it was just too simplistic, indeed erroneous. It had been pointed out that if it was just the Germans we had to worry about, the task of preventing genocide in the world would be so much simpler. According to this proposition, only the Germans were tainted and the rest of the world was automatically pure and innocent. But what, I asked, of all the other genocides of history?

I told myself that I could handle this knowledge of the Holocaust, and generally I did. It helped to be detached by birth and geography. But then there were the images, taken by soldiers who carried small cameras with them into Poland and Russia to send photos home to parents, wives and girlfriends, and by officials recording for the sake of history. They were almost pornographic in their intensity and number, much more invasive than the words of scholarly texts.

A group of Jews cower. They are digging their own graves. The soldier stands over them. He raises his rifle to shoot a standing woman, who instinctively turns away to protect the baby in her arms. We know what happens next. Detachment is no longer possible. Such proof of terrible deeds blights the nation's past and its present. It hangs in the air. It plays with my mind. It is a debilitating presence that skews the intellect and affects my ability to get things done. I will myself to force it aside.

Onto the face looking out over Vossstrasse I could load the failure of the German leadership and citizenry in the first half of the twentieth century. The face made it easier for me to know that Susan and I did not live among Nazis and militarists, but rather people of conscience who have built a principled nation of great moral strength and continue to work through situations that require thought and the exercise of goodwill. Four million resident Turks, once guest workers, are now German citizens. What a wonderful start.

*

Despite such positive developments, many German citizens, particularly those of the old East, rely for direction on false and outmoded myths pedalled by extreme nationalist leaders in the face of the recent influx of Syrian refugees.

Susan and I discovered this at first hand some years after leaving Berlin when we arranged a field trip to the pretty medieval Hanseatic League town of Stralsund, now a UNESCO World Heritage site. Our train north to the Baltic coast rambled through a rich agricultural landscape. Crowding in on the track were the ruins of early railway buildings; standing behind were forlorn DDR structures; then further back occasional concentrations of large modern silos, evidence, apparently, of a newly prosperous Germany of the east. We discovered and looked out for fleeting glimpses of the work of a graffiti artist of some quality, who obviously 'owned' the older surfaces. Our hotel sat right on the shore and had its own flock of patrolling swans.

Our objective was to see, at the German Oceanographic Museum, the new Ozeaneum, an aquarium housed within a striking modern metal tent. It was very well done and the crowds of happy, involved visitors were evidence that cultural institutions could really have a positive impact on the economic circumstances of a place.

So why did the people of Stralsund, and the old East Germany, vote in such numbers for the right-wing nationalist and anti-immigration party, AfD, Alternative für Deutschland? Under the old DDR regime Stralsund had a thriving shipping industry. A museum in the town speaks of the area's obvious pride in the ships it launched. But then the guaranteed market that was the USSR collapsed and the ships the world needed were being built elsewhere. The industry could not compete and faded to nothing. Outside the impressive St Marienkirche was a Soviet memorial, but the words on the plaque had been stripped off. The political forces accompanying reunification had changed history and the local people had had little say. We lose our economic base and the skills we have developed count for nothing. Raised on the falsehood that we were the brave resisters who confronted and defeated the Nazis, we can now tell only stories of failure. We are threatened and vulnerable to any politician who blames the 'other' – no longer the Jews, but the migrants.

Yet the people we came across in that pretty town were helpful. Okay, the evening meal took an age to arrive at our table but in their everyday dealings they were pleasant folk, not at all unlike our friends back in Berlin. But they had suffered the consequences of their history and turned to the AfD for leadership. Not that these extremists have the answer. It is like Brexit, a lashing out, even if in doing so they scare no one more than themselves.

*

Toward the end of our time in Germany, in 2002, the long day when we visited Eisenhüttenstadt was drawing on and we found a pub on the banks of the Oder. I ate horse for the first time, loudly lamenting my duplicity at consuming one of the extended family of my trusty old steed Judy from Maungatautari days. She was with me that evening, memory of a sublime moment of exhilarating freedom as I galloped her around a copse of trees in the home paddock, bareback, my little seven-year-old legs clasped into her side. The summer evening darkened, the lights went on and the mosquitoes came out.

The Oder was an ordinary stretch of water, not that wide, part of a vast, frequently swampy terrain that extends deep into Russia and beyond to the cold of Siberia. Tens of thousands of years ago modern humans came into Europe, displacing poor old Neanderthalensis, probably others, and pushed out onto these plains freed from ice sheets. Tribes made this territory their own. Warlords from east and west disturbed the lives of the people. States emerged with their own forms of fractious peace but always there was the threat of plunder, devastation and famine, the mark of misrule and invaders.

The last disturbance had been within living memory. That bank across from us was Poland, which provided not just Lebensraum, space for Hitler's vision of the German Volk state, but also a site to carry out mass killing. Across the river lay the terrain of the Holocaust.

According to Hitler's doctrine, peoples were ranked by a strange anti-science ordering device called blood and this placed the Jews at the bottom of the racial heap. The cause of all the ills of the world, they were good only to be exterminated. His was not just a vision for Germany and the conquered nations; he had grander, more terrible, plans. The Wannsee Conference, held on 20 January 1942, in a pleasant villa that still stands on the outskirts of Berlin, was a meeting of administrative functionaries gathered to plan the realisation of 'the Final Solution of the Jewish question in Europe'. The meeting did not initiate the Holocaust – that was already well under way – but required functionaries to make the transportation and the killing more efficient. There were undoubtedly other similar meetings, but oversight, an accidental survival, means that we do have a record of this conference –just a few sheets of paper. The intent was clear: to kill all the Jews of Europe, an estimated 11 million people. Included were the territories yet to be conquered: England, Sweden, Ireland, Spain … The 'large majority' would be 'eliminated by natural causes', and those who survived would be 'dealt with appropriately', that is exterminated. Most were 'dealt with appropriately'. Einsatzgruppen,

SS death squads, ably assisted by the army and local Jew-haters, had already begun their work with bullets and blunt instruments. This was deemed to be inefficient, and special industrial-scale killing centres were being planned, at places with names that resonate still – Belzec, Chelmno, Majdenek, Sobibor, Treblinka and Auschwitz.

Other peoples were ranked according to impurity of blood. The Roma and Sita, and homosexuals, were not to be tolerated as human and were doomed. The Slavs were little better: good only as a slave people. When encountered in the field of battle they could be slaughtered with impunity.

'Thirty-five million Russians died in the Great Patriotic War!' a client later told me. He was biased, the champion of a President Putin-endorsed and oligarch-funded project, but by then I was well-enough informed to know that there was some statistical support for his contention, though the more generally used figure was around 27 million Soviet citizens and soldiers dead over four years of extreme savagery.

When Hitler's armies crossed into Soviet territory in 1941 they found an ineffective army whose leadership had been greatly reduced by Stalin's purges and decision-making mired in ideological posturing. The German army raced toward Moscow at breakneck speed, overrunning vast areas of territory. Perhaps 2.9 million Soviet soldiers were captured immediately and starved to death. The Soviet Union was fighting for survival, but it would prevail.

In 1977 a conference took me to Leningrad and Moscow. It was the height of the Brezhnev era and what I saw confirmed that this was a country dictatorial to its very core and, as a result, dangerous. The citizenry seemed absent; almost no one used the vast streets. A man, dead drunk, was carried by two friends. The life of a whole region was closed down for many hours just so a fleet of buses could have sole unencumbered access to the motorway system to deliver delegates to and from the ancient cities of Vladimir and Suzdal without incident. We stopped at a local shopping centre. The bookshop had hundreds of copies of a limited range of titles. I bought a roll at the bakery, about all that was on offer. It was spirited back to New Zealand to sit on my work desk for some years, fresh as the day it was baked. Finally, it oozed a dense alien growth and was buried in haste. As special guests of the state we got to the head of the queue that stretched out of sight to view Lenin in his tomb. An accompanying conservation expert, pointing out the high levels of lighting above the cadaver, confirmed the story told many, many times. 'He has to be at least 90 percent, more likely 100 percent, wax.'

One day word was about that Nikolai Podgorny had been removed from some important post. An arranged meeting with 'artists skilled in depicting Lenin' was cancelled. That evening a delegate was able to indicate to us that Podgorny had already been airbrushed out of the group photo, though the label still included his name.

I railed at being always allocated strictly policed seating with the Dutch. Any change could not be countenanced. 'You come from Zeeland! Yes?'

I was exposed to one, just one, example of capitalism at work when a blowsy woman at the door of the hotel asked, 'You want me?' Was she also a state functionary?

But the Great Patriotic War was another, more serious, thing. The museums of Leningrad and Moscow were full of it, and despite the heavy propaganda, the metres of red bunting and the standard factory busts of Lenin and Marx (Stalin was by now long gone), I saw a different history. The honoured battles were not the ones of my youth. They were Moscow, Leningrad, Stalingrad, Kursk, Bagration and Berlin. With time, through a widening array of films and TV programmes and in the general reading of histories and great novels, I came to know more of these as the decisive conflicts of World War II. The great military figure of the war was Georgy Zhukov. Few know his name in the west.

The devious, perhaps even stupid, dictatorship at the time of the 1977 conference confirmed in me a somewhat arrogant and naïve belief that the people of this nation were my enemy. I regret this view. Fortunately, it had changed by the time I sat with friends over a meal of horsemeat on the banks of the Oder. One of my guides in this greater understanding was, once again, Primo Levi, through *The Truce*. After all the texts of killing and misery, I was encouraged to find a Holocaust survivor talking about a world of hope and life after Auschwitz. Early one cold morning, as Levi and a fellow prisoner are taking another dead body outside, the camp is discovered by Russian soldiers: 'four men, armed but not against us: four messengers of peace, with rough and boyish faces beneath their heavy fur hats. They did not greet us, nor did they smile; they seemed oppressed not only by compassion but by a confused restraint, which sealed their lips and bound their eyes to the funereal scene.'

Levi here begins a narrative of recovery, a march back into a living world. But the journey could only be east, into the Ukraine and away from his native Italy. For that way, towards home, was a war zone, hundreds of kilometres deep, full of confusion, distress and lethal potential. Levi joined locals damaged by four years of war, and the roaming hordes of the displaced. He describes people who got up to all sorts of tricks but, driven together by the task of survival and healing, displayed wondrous, chaotic humanity. *The Truce* is a tribute to all people recovering from war and to the Russian army. These were not Cold War warriors. Rather Levi portrays them as saviours who were doing their best to organise, house and feed people traumatised by killing. After all those thousands of other pages and images of distress, it was for me an affirmation of life.

I was, therefore, in a quite different frame of mind when I visited Russia again in 2007. I could see it as a country ravished by centuries of privation, revolution, genocide, starvation, corruption on an epic scale, and purges that destroyed any thoughts of an emerging class confident in leadership and innovation. Stalin might be dead but his brutal and twisted spirit lived on. Corrupt oligarchs of extreme and criminally acquired wealth exercised all political and economic power. They controlled the message, a crude nationalism that denied any form of dialogue.

Yet an intelligent and educated populace was struggling with the nature of their history. How many families could say they did not include 'an enemy of the people', a grandparent who survived, or did not survive, incarceration in one of the thousands of gulag camps scattered across the nation? The memoirs existed for all to read. Yet, as a nation it was still a work in progress where citizens of the new Russia must exercise some care. They knew that those who governed them were corrupt and controlled what people got to hear. My interpreter told me how she would vote for the status quo in the forthcoming elections. It was not a matter of choosing the promise of a plan for a better future. 'No,' she went on, 'to do otherwise would be to invite another gang of powerful scoundrels to steal yet more wealth from the people.'

This conversation took place overlooking a motorway. The silence of 1977 was long gone; the broad and deserted streets I had seen then were now choked with multiple lanes of cars, each seemingly making its own choices according to its own rules. I walked faster than the traffic. Here a convoy of large, shiny black wagons with darkened windows, and a security detail, had been halted in the democracy of a traffic jam. Their doors were flung wide to reveal the dubious fashion sense of bored women held back from the shops they hankered after. But they did not try to claim the vacant length of streetside parking, guarded by a burly man who was obviously well armed. He stood outside a fabulous restaurant, perhaps one of the vanity projects of an oligarch. There I was dined sumptuously but always aware that not one car had attempted to pull into those vacant parks.

An irrational madness was in the air. I now knew enough to argue strongly that a Russian museum of tolerance could be all the more effective if it had the Great Patriotic War at its centre. That was a time in recent history when the Soviets at least tried to openly embrace and honour the diversity of its peoples in order to bring them together in defence of the motherland.

'Let's deal with real people, like [writer] Vasily Grossman,' I said, addressing the first meeting called to bring together the overarching exhibition concept for the museum, 'and not cardboard cut-outs made for propaganda purposes.'

The problem was that the Stalin inheritance of that war as nationalistic glory and willing sacrifice still held sway. The official stories and presentations were all too heroic and glorious. The recently complete tiled mural in the Arbatskaya metro station was a monument to historical confusion, yet also to resilient self-belief. The USSR (CCCP in Russian), that broad federation of states clustered about Moscow and Russia, was dead 12 years when the mural was unveiled, but above all the floating star inscription said 'CCCP'. The diverse peoples of the CCCP hailed the national hero. No longer Stalin, but I knew the new hero well – it was the huge Soviet soldier from Treptower Park in Berlin, complete with rescued child. The title of the mural was '1945'.

The official Russian war museum was marked by a monumental pillar of a height that suggested it was intended to top some other competing obelisk. At the top floated spirit figures, while within stood a large bronze soldier with standard raised fist. The gallery-sized battle-scene dioramas seemed strangely tame, bloodless, places where the sacrifice was willing and clean.

Yet the Great Patriotic War was, and remains, a matter of tremendous pride to the people of Russia. They believe they won the war against the Nazis and suffered terribly in so doing. They complain that those in the West do not give them their due. In the name of common humanity, I could not help but agree.

The Russia I saw this second time would fray at its edges even further the following year as the economic crisis bit, exposing the smoke and mirrors of an oil-based command, and criminal, economy at work. History and culture seemed not to have prepared the people to experiment and take hold of their own future. That will take many generations. In confusion, and at the behest of a state-run media, people will cling to the false promise of crude nationalism as the future. Russian leadership has much to answer for but surely there are ways in which we can empathise with and support ordinary Russians, their lives and their predicament.

*

Living in the Germany of West and East, and visiting and working in Russia, I met people I could relate to as fellow human beings. They were moral people. For the most part, they exercised the ordinary virtues in their dealings with me and others and all at least hoped for the support of those agencies of community and government that grew, maintained, ordered, protected and nurtured their lives. But history, particularly the consequences of World War II, the Great Patriotic War, had shaped their sense of self in ways quite different to that of a Kiwi from the far side of the world. The individual might want to move on but every dispute among nations, newspaper article, anniversary, political manoeuvre and proposed memorial would summon divisive reactions and all too often bitterness.

Some elements of that history I had learnt and with that came better understanding: of the citizens in former East Germany, for decades decreed to be the blameless resistors who had stood with their Soviet allies against Hitler; of Russians who could claim with justification that they had defeated fascism; of the people of Western, and now reunified, Germany who still carried the guilt of World War II and the Holocaust; the sadness of Brexit – damn it, we won the war and yet the Germans get all the goodies.

I thought back to my taxi driver in Chattanooga, still haunted by a civil war fought 140 years earlier. She defined herself as being of the South and foreign to fellow countrymen in the North. She was still angry.

These complexities I would take back to New Zealand as I began a new career.

CHAPTER 21

A NEW VIEW OF NEW ZEALAND

BY THE TIME I WAS ATTENDING SCHOOL in the 1940s and 1950s our ally Russia had become a demonised enemy, a threatening force lurking behind an Iron Curtain. I was a Cold War child. Russian history did not figure in our curriculum and seldom appeared in family conversation, though my grandfather was an old socialist with interesting books full of upright communist workers confronting the looming threat of Fascism. My friends and I went to movies that featured Dunkirk, El Alamein and D-Day. The Battle of Britain was a favourite, represented in film after film. I remember still *Angels One Five*. Yet I was never a follower of war. Perhaps it was my small stature that had me shy away from conflict. I joined the military band to get out of cadet training, at the time still part of the New Zealand secondary school curriculum. With time and a career in museums, war became for me a local moral issue, that of a colonial government using armed conflict to satisfy new settlers' greed for Māori land.

But I now know that war, and the memory of war, has done much to shape my nation and New Zealanders' view of themselves. It is hard to deny the shock when I found that some of the poems in *Just Us* featured war and Hitler, and that one of the vessels looming out of the clouds was a battleship. It could not be otherwise given that the book was published in 1944.

Yet such memories are not confined to me as a child born in the war years and able to remember the uncle returning from service in the British navy, the oft-heard stories of war time chaos and adventure (one hilarious instance involving the Home Guard), and the returned servicemen's request and news programme on radio. In the run-up to the centennial of New Zealand's involvement in World War I, I was employed to consider how an extension to our national war memorial in the capital might be interpreted. This was an important project; the whole of New Zealand seemed to be preparing itself to be involved. Consultations with Returned and Services Association members and other worthies were called for, but I also had to ensure that wider perspectives were included. There was a good amount of agreement. The war memorial was more than sacred ground. It was also a place that expressed national identity and social development. It would take account of 'ally and adversary', both historical and contemporary – Australia, the Pacific Islands, Britain, the United States, China, the United Nations, Canada, Germany and Japan.

But there was a problem. Several contributors to the debate, while having no problem whatsoever about the involvement of the old enemy Germany, were terribly unsure about Japan. 'Still too raw,' said one. The Pacific war had parallels to the conflict in Europe: it was strongly driven by racial stereotypes and the brutalities that come with such engagement. We have yet to come to terms with that cruel fact.

*

I had read about the 500 or so policemen charged with killing Jews in Poland during World War II. Many had been recruited before 1939, when policing was a vocation, an honourable job. Now, in the midst of war, they had another duty to attend to. A small number, perhaps 10 to 20 percent, resisted and found various ways to avoid killing fellow humans. But the majority, while appalled at their task, followed the willing shooters into the carnage. The author, Christopher Browning, reviewing the motives of these ordinary men, concluded that peer groups can exert a terrible pressure on our behaviour and even how we characterise what is moral. No group of people anywhere in the world is immune from the pressure to become killers. Aleksandr Solzhenitsyn drew on his gulag experiences to state in the simplest terms that 'all the evil of the twentieth century is possible everywhere on earth'.

This message presented an intellectual and moral struggle for me and for Susan. Browning challenged any comfortable thought that 'we' might in some way be better than 'them' by asking us all to consider whether 'we' could become shooters under particular circumstances. His work has been criticised, but his conclusion is compelling, especially when placed alongside other studies of appalling things done in time of war based on hatred of the 'other'. There are so many examples, including the cruelty of colonial systems imposed throughout the world by European powers.

I had tried to acknowledge this at that Kristallnacht commemoration on the cold streets of Ahlen, but always I had the comforting thought that my generation had been somehow more moral. Certainly, our episodes of hateful colonialising crime were now at some remove, and wasn't the terrible massacre of worshippers in two Christchurch mosques in March 2019 perpetrated by 'an outsider'? Could I really apply Browning's thesis to test New Zealanders' status as bearers of a greater virtue?

In 1939 New Zealand went to war. Perhaps it was less jingoistic than the beginnings of World War I, for the horrors of that conflict were still fresh in many people's minds. We may have hoped that the peace would be longer, that deadly conflict was not the natural state of human existence, but we were prepared, yet again, to be part of a European war. Prime Minister Michael Savage expressed our resolve, explaining that we had no particular hatred of the German people. Why, he even quite liked their songs, poetry and music. But it was a given that we would side automatically with Britain. 'Where she goes, we go; where she stands, we stand,' he famously said as we plunged into war.

What if circumstances had been different? What if, back in 1936, there had been no abdication crisis in the Windsor family and the British Empire, of which New Zealand was a stalwart part, had ended up with a Nazi-sympathising king? What if those who believed in appeasement had prevailed? What if the war – and Hitler's whole plan and economy was about war – that darkened Europe had been an Aryan and Anglo-Saxon bloc facing the political and racial threat from the East? Would our cultural links have surmounted all as we slavishly stood with Britain?

I suspect the answer would have been 'yes', and we would have found ourselves in an alliance, albeit uneasy, with Hitler and the Nazi regime, heading for a confrontation with the USSR over Poland and Ukraine. Loyalty to all things British would have created the strong pull necessary to make an ally of the recent enemy Germany. But was there enough anti-Semitic belief for the racial war against the Jews to resonate with New Zealanders? The Jewish community was small, but anti-Semitism had travelled intact to New Zealand with mainly British settlers. One of the most senior civil servants overseeing immigration in a New Zealand government department at that time was an ardent anti-Semite. There were others. Could New Zealanders have ended up on that Eastern Front doing the dirty work of racial purification?

Counterfactual history – what might have happened – can be dangerous in that it can allow an alteration of history to suit a particular cause. But as a mind experiment, playing with beliefs and attitudes deeply embedded in our thinking, it had value for me. I went to Berlin with a smug view of New

Zealanders' inherent decency as a people. The museum, Berlin, Germany and Russia forced me to re-examine those assumptions. I am less inclined to be dogmatic. I see chinks in our moral armour. We did not need to build a wall to keep out the 'other' because it already existed in the surrounding oceans, and we have used this barrier to very good effect to greatly limit the arrival of those we deemed to be undesirable. I have always thought of New Zealand as a robust democracy and a just, law-abiding and safe place. But after a deep immersion in the history of a recent war and the Holocaust, I am more open to the idea that, given the right situation, any people may be capable of joining a cruel cause that takes their nation step by step toward evil, either through ignorance and indifference, or through hysteria, manipulation and wilful distortion of belief.

It rests with each of us to maintain and strengthen our nations and communities as stable, open entities to achieve good, and to at least greatly limit evil. This may require individual citizens to demand honesty and vision of our leaders and, where necessary, to become leaders themselves. So often the shouted promise of conflict and ultimate victory is presented as the best way to solve the ills of the world: attack, subdue, even eradicate. But, as history shows, it is talking and negotiating that has achieved long periods of peaceable accord. We need to keep talking, to learn from one other, to honour and respect our fellow human beings, to negotiate and to forge common positions that will always be based on acceptance of other points of view.

With a changed view of myself and of the future of New Zealand and the world, I made decisions about the work I was best qualified to do. Not everything would be about museums.

*

Back in Wellington throughout 2003 a local tax official was busy trying to unpick our German affairs and find something nasty. It took time to resolve but soon his early letters threatening severe penalties became muted apologies and admissions that we were fiscally clean. Of greater interest was seeking activities that would keep the earnings flowing and make life interesting.

One of my first major pieces of work was a tourism strategy for the cultural institutions of Northland. I stood on a pavement looking across the street at a public lavatory. Each time a car went past I noted interest in the toilet, photos taken. Did they park and come back for a better look, even a cup of coffee? This was not any toilet but a highly decorated temple to bodily function by

Friedensreich Hundertwasser, seemingly the principal attraction the small town of Kawakawa had to offer the visitor. Not far away the locals wanted a museum to pull in tourists. Instead our recommendation (I was by then working with a tourism company) was a night-time tour of the huge kauri trees of the Waipoua Forest. It worked – the sponsoring hotel's occupancy rates shot up and their season expanded thanks to word of mouth and media interest.

There was museum work on offer, especially overseas: Te Papa had status among those seeking new ways of defining and operating their museums. This took me to new and exotic parts of the world. It was so pleasing to see and hear of the impact of Te Papa. Okay, we were not the first but we had learnt much from the early activists and had unashamedly copied their best ideas. We were known to be in the vanguard of those trying the maximise the impact and worth of older institutions, and establish new ones. There are, perhaps, as many as 70,000 museums in this world. Many of them, far too many, are old and sad. But some shine out as beacons of change.

The Imperial War Museum in London is a great museum of social conscience. It was established and named immediately after World War I. In some respects, its early purpose was to recover imperial prestige lost in the senseless slaughter of that war, placing a premium on the glory, and the toys, of war. Once famously described as 'the biggest boy's bedroom in London', it is now a study of the frequently stupid causes and sorry consequences of conflict. As is to be expected, the exhibits are very English. Today there is a small section devoted to the Great Patriotic War, hardly proportional to the scale of the destruction wrought, nor to the crucial import of the Soviet contribution to Hitler's defeat, but it is a start.

At the Science Museum of Minnesota I saw how the service skills and interpretive techniques of the leisure industry could be applied to museums. The Monterey Bay Aquarium was a place to learn about educational potential and volunteer guide management, though the impact really came from the spectacle and majesty, laced with not a little humour and artistry, of the undersea world. I sent a staff group to the Canadian Museum of Civilisation and would have loved to visit the Tunnels of Moose Jaw, a smaller museum reinvented as immersive theatre and transforming the economy of its small home town. Then there was Disney Imagineering.

I know that Te Papa influenced the National Museum of the American Indian. The director, Rick West, visited us and I worked for them. This was a museum that made a commitment not unlike Te Papa, to ethnic peoples having more than just a role as the represented, their own voice at the centre of the nation's capital. Others would follow suit, such as the Musée du Quai Branly in Paris. Another important group of museums were those devoted to twentieth-, and then twenty-first-, century atrocities. The best known of these was the National Holocaust Memorial Museum, and it was followed by others, notably the National September 11 Memorial & Museum in New York, and POLIN Museum of the History of Polish Jews on the site of the destroyed Warsaw ghetto.

These and other museums have reassessed the very foundations on which they are based. They share power; they delve into new and uncomfortable areas that challenge fondly held views of national and personal self. The scholar may speak the best current truth, the politicians talk of current realities, but the newly encompassed communities and cultures also have a voice and they are sharing responsibility for what is said and how. This opens us to frequently uncomfortable criticisms and discussions, but generally it is all for the good.

This is dangerous ground and it is easy to draw back into the comfort of conservative attitudes. A few years back, I plucked up courage and gave my first paper on Te Papa to a Victoria University conference in Wellington. Perhaps I feared the response, since Te Papa had many detractors in academic circles. As part of my preparation I asked six Kiwi colleagues, whom I have always thought had great influence on New Zealand museums, to comment on what was important. A broad list came back: visionary leadership and inspiring role models; greatly strengthened iwi and community relationships; international professionals, movements, sources and models; the idea of the 'vibrant visitor attraction'; the world boom in dance music and electronica (including a Dylan song). But one consistent response was that, in respect of Te Papa, 'a strong backlash is the predominant legacy'. That came from Cheryll Sotheran. We could not help but agree. The consensus was that, within the museum profession, Te Papa was honoured more overseas than within its own nation.

*

It hurt a little but, in many respects, it did not matter. Take the example of Geelong, where my brief was to enliven the town centre. The local art gallery director was sure that, given my background, I would recommend an increase in gallery space so that more artworks could be displayed. Perhaps the city needed a museum. But as I came to know this town, famous for its Australian Rules football team, I found it was also known for a wonderfully humorous series of sculptures by Jan Mitchell which portrayed different pieces of Geelong life and history. The professional woman meets a client down at the wharf, the local brass band plays, the leader of the surf lifesaving team has a black eye from a dust-up in the pub the night before. Visitors came to Geelong to see these pieces. This was museum in another guise: as 'ubiquitous and dispersed agent', as one of the profession's leading theorists has painted our future. What I thought Geelong needed was a proper central public library. The idea took hold, and sometimes money does follow the best ideas. It was built at a cost of $45 million (Australian).

In Australia comes the opportunity to turn a pretty town back toward its famous river after years of high floodbank separation. I work with a team of planners on a waterfront development of theatre, museum and commercial zone. A small hapū confronts the problem of restoring and maintaining a nationally important marae. Around a table, police, educationalists, social services people and the local museum seek to strengthen the social well-being of a city. Experimentation, exploring new horizons – this was cultural project as adventure and I relished every moment.

In the midst of this work the Jewish Museum Berlin announces it will demolish those exhibitions I slaved to get in place. It will start again with a new vision of a Germany that has changed. The Turks, Germany's biggest minority at 4 million strong, are no longer Gastarbeiter or guest workers. They are now second- and third-generation German citizens. Then there are the Syrian refugees, about 1.2 million in the last two years, and the efforts and money going into preparing them for life in a new country and integration into German culture are bearing fruit. Memories of World War II are fading among the young. The Jewish community in Germany, now around 120,000, is small but carries a message relevant to the emerging multicultural nation. The Jewish Museum Berlin will tell this new story. I am so pleased. Wherever I can I shower praise and messages of encouragement upon my former staff. Such courage.

New Zealand has also changed. A quarter of a century ago Te Papa's intellectual structure was created in fractious times but the Treaty of Waitangi settlement negotiations have made our nation into something quite different. The time is right to recast Te Papa. Our Place is firmly established in our minds as a single idea. Why not abandon the current exhibition territories, which have outlived their purpose, and use Our Place, coupled with the idea of standing together on and within this island nation, tūrangawaewae, as the basis for the new? The Jewish Museum Berlin can do it – why not us?

*

Te Papa is below our Wellington hillside house – 10 minutes by car or 30 minutes by bus, with the excitement of a too-wide, too-long vehicle squeezing between parked cars on narrow roads. I visit Te Papa frequently. It works, still. Peter Tapsell would be well pleased. It is for all New Zealanders; it tells a wide range of our stories; its expansive vision of our society says that the negotiation of biculturalism is part of this place. People stream through the door. It is a great place to take friends, New Zealand's principal visitor attraction. Had Te Papa been modelled on the traditions of the old museum and gallery this would not have been so. It would have been a national disappointment.

Instead born users, our grand-nieces, seven-year-old Susie and younger Amelia, love it.

'I love stairs!' says Susie, as she races ahead. Parents are using the museum as adults do, studying and reading labels, but the girls are searching for moments that command their interest. They find these in abundance.

'Come and see.' Susie drags on Susan's arm. 'It grunts.' Sure enough, when we have made our way into the bowels of a forest a wild pig (stuffed) grunts at our approach.

Outside, in the fossil pit, Amelia joins other children excavating the mosasaur. Water is a big attraction. They polish the greenstone boulder with an application of grit. We rest while Susie finds a new friend to play with inside the whale's heart. She tries the earthquake-measuring device and then joins with other kids in a coordinated jump that really makes an impact. Involuntary shrieks in the earthquake house. Then it is time for lunch. Visit the shop. We are involved in fun and adventure and socialisation, for these small children know that this place is for them. There is no fear or hesitancy. No one holds them back. There are no obstacles placed in the way of enquiring minds, and by their actions, their personal performance, they bring the museum alive. And they take away with them impressions and images that may help to form their young lives in a moral society. I go back to those discussions Nigel and I had in a plane high above Asia. We searched for a word to gather in all we tried to achieve in our museums. Was that word character or posture, personality or voice?

A lot has happened in the intervening years. Some of it relates to toxic nationalism, Trump and Brexit, and is very sad. I object when an English woman justifies her vote to withdraw from the exercise in tolerance and peace that is the new Europe by expressing disgust at the Polish language that dominates an aisle of her local supermarket.

'Is that all?' I shout at the TV screen.

Then writer Pankaj Mishra raises an awkward thought. Have we, the bearers of enlightenment morality and upholders of the liberal democracy, been unable to accommodate, have even dismissed, our fellow citizens to the point where they feel humiliated and held in contempt by an arrogant and manipulative bunch of exploiters who hold power? Mishra suggests that these citizens are 'threatened [by] the vanity projects of an intellectual elite' and that their support of Trump and Brexit arises from a deep-seated feeling that they are missing out, or even worse, are deemed unworthy of inclusion. Are museums one of those vanity projects? Are we who work in them guilty of being unable to consider the feelings and beliefs of others when they conflict with our liberal own?

Now we are accused further, as some museums become the willing bearers of narrow and regressive nationalism, the type that debars people from belonging, the type that builds hatred. A museum claims the higher purpose of human rights when in fact it is an instrument of authoritarian politics, a museum of war in which one side is pure white and the other black. That museum can incorporate nothing of Primo Levi's grey zone.

It is hard to sheet home this accusation to Te Papa or to the Jewish Museum Berlin. I see young New Zealanders Susie and Amelia using a museum as their own emotional and intellectual place and it is good. I see the Jewish Museum Berlin reinventing itself as part of a deeply moral new Germany.

A word comes to me. The word is soul – these two museums assemble stories and place them in a complex theatre where rituals of the visitors' own making can be fashioned and performed. Both belong to and are of their people. They are reasoned but not autocratic, nor do they dismiss. Their culture is one of openness and welcome and hope. These two great museums are a force in the service of morality.

Soul. Why, Nigel, did we not think of that?

ACKNOWLEDGEMENTS

IT'S 27 APRIL 2017. I'm sitting with my former boss Mike Blumenthal in his office in the Jewish Museum Berlin. Susan is with me. Mike congratulates me on my memoir.

‘I didn't realise you could write.’ He had only seen the project director at work. ‘But why is your focus only on your time in Berlin? Your story has to include Te Papa.’

Although he had never visited, he had come to regard Te Papa as the benchmark for his museum, its market research materials becoming, in part at least, the measure of the JMB's success. He had not been disappointed. But, for Mike, my Berlin story was but a partial record, missing the insights that had come with growing up Kiwi, struggling with bringing multiple points of view to a cultural institution, and then immersed in Te Papa. This experience had come to inform so much of the thinking behind Mike's museum in German.

‘Here's your title,’ he said. ‘“Te Papa to Berlin”.’

There was good reason for me to limit writing to my years in Berlin. Although the Te Papa project had allowed me to bring together the knowledge and experience gained in the cultural and museum industry, it had been a harsh management environment. Incidents seared into memory could still cause my stomach to churn.

‘I just don't want to revisit the pain.’

Mike then offered advice that was to serve me well in the coming months. Recalling his approach when he was writing about his sometimes difficult relationship with President Jimmy Carter, he said, ‘I wrote out a ledger of the man's achievements and set this alongside the negatives. I was as honest as I could be.’

Susan, who knew more than anyone how testing Te Papa had been, quipped, ‘Maybe you can go into therapy for three months.’

On return to Wellington I began an exploration of the goals shared by these two projects on different sides of the world and of the dedicated teams I was privileged to work with.

Mike and Susan deserve special recognition. Mike Blumenthal was a talented and inspiring boss. He is a truly civilised person, respectful of others and their points of view but still able to deal appropriately with people who would stand in the way of his main project in life, reaching for a better world. Conversations with Mike were always a stimulating examination of history and the state of the contemporary world. As my first reader, Susan, who brings laughter to my life, corrected and shaped and challenged my evolving manuscript, and occasionally questioned my memories of events.

One of the great joys of my task in Berlin was to be inspired by architect Daniel Libeskind and to find how a building, his Jewish Museum Berlin, could shape my thinking. I came to value Daniel and Nina Libeskind both as friends and as mentors who tutored me in a realm of architecture that I did not know existed.

Elaine Heumann Gurian insisted that I be part of the October 1999 review, thereby instigating the Berlin adventure. Our friendship goes back many decades. I am constantly enriched by our discussions, shared (and disputed) points of view and the challenges we offer each other. Elaine's studied and always to-the-point comments have greatly assisted the writing of this book.

Similarly, museological and academic super-achiever, Professor Barbara Kirshenblatt-Gimblett of New York, took time to encourage me to drive for full understanding. One cold and windy Wellington day I returned to my university days as she questioned how I had structured the manuscript. 'You're not doing an exhibition, Ken. This is a book.'

Similarly, former Te Papa colleague and human resources guru Peter Farrell was an exacting but never harsh critic of my text, particularly as it negotiated Te Papa relationships, some quite dark.

Professor Conal McCarthy of Victoria University of Wellington brought to bear his knowledge of the modern museum world while Jock Phillips and Léontine Meijer-van Mensch read drafts and offered useful suggestions, deletions and additions. I am indebted to Cliff Whiting's sons, Dean, Gary and Paul, who have assisted with reviews of my interpretation of their father's many contributions to New Zealand arts and identity. Over some decades I have valued the support and good humour of museological raconteur Bill Tramposch.

Looking back, I realise how blessed I was by the encouragement and assistance of extraordinary leaders. Te Arikinui of Tainui, Dame Te Atairangikaahu, and her people offered me an introduction to Māori culture that I value and will always carry with me. Mike Minogue and Stuart Lenz in Hamilton, Sir Peter Tapsell in Wellington and former German federal minister of culture Michael Naumann, all moral human beings, taught me how to flourish in the face of challenge.

My thanks go to two wonderful mentors in things to do with mātauranga Māori, Apirana Mahuika and Cliff Whiting.

Cilly Kugelmann and Nigel Cox were a great deal more than colleagues; they were fellow adventurers and friends. Both were bursting with ideas. Cilly had a depth of knowledge that opened my thinking in a new world of knowledge, not just in German-Jewish history, but also that territory, physical and intellectual, that lies east of Berlin. Nigel was both a words man and leader of people. He and I were the 'two Kiwis' who taught radical thinking and the power of structured discussion to the JMB team. Joined by Cilly we were a formidable team.

Martin Roth guided me into the German museum world. Similarly, my thanks go to Klaus and Petra of design firm Würth & Winderoll of Munich for getting those exhibitions open on time and within budget.

Marylea and Gianni van Daalen at the Adlon Hotel offered support and friendship.

My career, and life, have been blessed through association with talented people in the cultural industry. In my first museum post, at Waikato, Campbell Smith, Rose Young, Kees Sprengers, Bruce Young, Chris Currie and others were part of a young crew that experimented with ideas of the moral community.

Then, in Wellington, Cliff Whiting, Graeme Shadwell, Raewyn Smith-Kapa, Neil Anderson and Sean Sweeney did so much to make my Te Papa sojourn safe and profitable.

Others of the old Te Papa project have offered support and insights, some without knowing they were doing so: Desmond Brice, Jocelyn Cranefield, Raewyn Cumming, Janet Davidson, Peter Farrell, John Field, Arapata Hakiwai, Jenny Harper, Sue Harrop, Chris Hay, Geoff Hicks, Geoff Knox, Rosemary Laurenson, Karen Mason, Conal McCarthy, Diana Minchall, Ian Mills, Mac Moran, Stuart Park, Robin Parkinson, Alison Preston, Carolyn Roberts, Bronwyn Simes, Michelle Tayler, Tim Walker, Paul Thompson, Ian Wedde.

My Berlin colleagues are a fine bunch of people who faced, and rose to, the seemingly unachievable – opening the museum: particularly the Kit Kat Klub girls from Christmas 2001, Gelia Eisert, Signe Rossbach and Christina Scholten, and Oliver Bätz, Vera Bendt, Inka Bertz, Christiane Birkert, Anja

Butzek, Joshua Derman, Bülent Durmus, Michal Friedlander, Thomas Friedrich, Rainer Kappe, Stephanie Kluth, Waltraud Kratzenberg, Maren Krüger, Leonore Maier, Gisela Märtz, Léontine Meijer-van Mensch, Marion Meyer, Yvonne Niehaus, Horst Olbricht, Margarete Sabeck, Peter Sauerbaum, Petra Schramm, Eva Söderman, Antje Spielhagen, Doreen Tesche, and the kind men of the Wache (the security force) who were always willing to try out a bit of English on me in response to my stumbling German. Special thanks go to director Peter Schäfer (recently resigned), archivist Aubrey Pomerance, Mathias Groß, and that Berlin-based citizen of the wider world, Boris Moshkovits.

Friends and acquaintances taught us about the new Germany: Alona and Sepp Baiz; Herbert and Ulrike Beck; Olaf Brosig and Maria Lampiris; Sonja and Joachim Elm; Margaret and Reinhard Eschenhagen; Karl-Heinz and Gertrud Jaspers; Elisabeth Klotz; Gudrun, Juliane and Josefine Lenz; Barbara and Peter Matthias; Michael Naumann and Maria Warburg; Carla and Jean Jacques Nuss; Anne Sparenberg; Ingrid and Richard Stehle; Christa Unzner; Frances and Boris Warneck; Robyn and Berndt Wiesener; and Wiebke and Knut Heuer of Munich.

I also greatly appreciate the different perspectives of, and positions taken by, the many hundreds of scholars, writers and creative artists who have allowed me to form some better understanding of the world. They range from religious philosophy as explored by the likes of Karen Armstrong to Professor Edward O. Wilson searching for new dimensions in the world of science. But I do need to give special acknowledgment to the writings of Primo Levi; the novels of Günter Grass and Vasily Grossman; the searching artistic expression of Anselm Kiefer; and let us not forget Woody Allen.

The good people at Victoria University of Wellington – Professors Brigitte Bönisch-Brednich, Richard Hill and Harry Ricketts – offered always relevant insights and guidance. Professor, and near neighbour, Rolf Brednich, of Georg August-Universität Göttingen, brought his deep knowledge of the world of folklore to the face on the wall at 33 Vossstrasse.

Birgit Maurer-Porat, at the Jewish Museum Berlin, and David Riley and Anita Schrafft at Te Papa went beyond the normal call of duty to search out photographs that fitted my already written captions, while Jocelyn Chalmers assisted by pointing out, and delving into, productive image repositories.

I owe a great debt of gratitude to Rachel Scott and Vanessa Manhire of Otago University Press / Te Whare Tā o Te Wānanga o Ōtākou. This is not just for having faith in my memoir but also for the great care they exercised to ease me through the steep learning curve that has been taking *Te Papa to Berlin* from pages of words to a completed project, a book. This was new territory for me, a place of worries and many questions, but also answers arising from Rachel and Vanessa's deep understanding of the art of publishing.

The studied interventions and kindly stated suggestions of editor Anna Rogers greatly enhanced the flow of the story line and simplified the entanglements of my sometimes over-complicated language.

This memoir would not have been possible without my life companion, Susan Foster. Susan put her study of political cartoons on hold so that she, too, could be thrown into the heart of a city that stands at the centre of humankind's definition of the meaning of the twentieth century. We were surrounded by people expert in the actions of the perpetrator so that in every discussion, every piece of personal research, we confronted horrendous inhumanity, indifference and death. This could have been damaging but we had each other, so could transform our circumstances into life-asserting hope.

Susan came back from Berlin to pick up her writings on political cartoons and begin to record her personal memories of her time in Germany. She inspired me to start on this memoir.

It is to Susan that I dedicate this book, with much love.

QUOTED MATERIALS

Just Us by John Brent, illustrated by Stopford [Stop] G. Wrathall, (p. 15) published by Morning Post Printing House, Rotorua, 1944 (copy held at the National Library of New Zealand).

Edward O. Wilson invited the arts and humanities to colonise the sciences (p. 56) in *The Meaning of Human Existence,* Liveright Publishing, New York, 2014, p. 12.

The quote about the Einstein/Haber theatre (pp. 145–46) is taken from Fritz Stern's essay 'Together and Apart: Fritz Haber and Albert Einstein' in his *Einstein's German World,* Princeton University Press, 1999, pp. 59–164.

Professor Pare Keiha has allowed me to use his words, spoken and email, on collections without life (p. 189).

The 'wonder glasses' paragraph (p. 213) is from Günter Grass, *Dog Years*, Harcourt, Brace & World, New York, 1965, pp. 455–56. For the German original see *Hundejahre,* Steidl Verlag, Göttingen, 1993 (first edition published 1963).

Levi's quote on the liberation of Auschwitz (p. 218) is from Primo Levi, *The Truce: A Survivor's Journey Home from Auschwitz*, Bodley Head, London, 1965, p. 12.

Extensive use is made of Christopher Browning's conclusions in *Ordinary Men: Reserve Police Battalion 101 and the Final Solution in Poland*, HarperCollins, New York, 1992 (especially on p. 224).

Pankaj Mishra's 'vanity projects' quote (p. 231) is taken from his article in the *Guardian*, 'Welcome to the Age of Anger', 8 December 2016. His larger thesis is found in his *Age of Anger: A history of the present*, Allen Lane, an imprint of Penguin Books, London, 2017.

INDEX

Bold denotes illustrations.
A1, **A2**, **B1**, **B2** etc denote picture sections page numbers.